Politics In Music

POLITICS IN MUSIC
Music and Political Transformation from Beethoven to Hip-Hop

Courtney Brown

Atlanta
FARSIGHT PRESS

FARSIGHT PRESS
First published by Farsight Press, a member of Farsight, Inc.

10 9 8 7 6 5 4 3 2 1

Publisher's Cataloging-in-Publication Data
(Provided by Quality Books, Inc.)

    Brown, Courtney, 1952-
      Politics in music : music and political
    transformation from Beethoven to hip-hop / Courtney
    Brown. – 1st ed.
      p. cm.
    Includes bibliographical references and index.
    ISBN-13: 978-0-9766762-3-2
    ISBN-10: 0-9766762-3-0

    1. Music–Political aspects. 2. Political science.
  I. Title.

ML3916.B76 2007   780'.032
                  QBI07-600211

This book is printed on acid-free paper.

Dedicated to

Aziz MacPherson Brown

Contents

Preface

This book is an outgrowth of a course that I have taught at Emory University for a number of years. The course is titled, "Politics in Music," and the idea of the course is to introduce undergraduates to the political content of music (mostly Western) as it has been expressed since the time of Beethoven up to the present. This requires a broad survey approach to the subject. To teach this course, I typically have the students read from a variety of books that cover more specialized areas relating to political music. This is fun for me to do since there are many such books, and I assign different books most terms, thereby keeping the course interesting to myself as well as to the students. The authors of some of these books sometimes offer their own theoretical perspectives that are useful to those students who want a more in-depth approach to the subject. But it has always been disconcerting that my lectures seemed to find no connection with a book that "fits" the general orientation of the course more closely. What I needed was a book that identified and summarized where political content can be located in a broad spectrum of music.

Interestingly, a university press editor contacted me after looking through my course syllabus and other materials that I offer on my web site (www.courtneybrown.com). The editor suspected that a book could be written from the course material, and he told me that he had done his own investigations prior to contacting me to confirm to himself that there was no broad-spectrum book in the extant literature that covered the subject in the manner that I address it in my course. He encouraged me to write such a book, and said that it might be a nice contribution to his press's list. With that hopeful idea in mind, I began writing this book. Eventually, the editor decided to leave his position at the university press, and I was faced with the question of whether or not to complete this book. I finally decided that (minimally) the existence of the book would make teaching my course easier since

I could include material in the book that I did not have time to present in my lectures. I also considered that a more general readership that extended beyond the university environment may enjoy the book as well. So I pushed onward.

This is my first book that relies almost totally on secondary sources. That is, this book is in large part a summary and synthesis of what many others have written about the political content of music. While I have certainly added my own interpretive arguments to the mix, I have avoided writing this book from a rigid theoretical perspective. Rather, I have approached this subject with more of a journalistic orientation, encouraging readers to add their own interpretations along the way. Again, my main purpose here is primarily to describe where politics can be found in music, not to promote a particular ideological or academic/theoretical point of view.

For those readers who want to do additional reading in the subject, I might suggest starting with the references that are listed at the end of some of the chapters. Here I identify important sources from which I drew much of the information for the chapter in question. These sources often offer theoretical focuses that some readers may find useful or interesting. These sources also tend to be rich with additional information, and they offer other references that readers may want to pursue. The exceptions to this are chapters 4 and 6. Chapter 4 focuses on nationalist and patriotic music, whereas chapter 6 deals with movement and non-movement related political music. The primary sources used for these two chapters are too varied to include in a short list at the end of the chapters. For these chapters, I suggest following the various references that are included in the text itself and listed in the larger reference section at the end of the book. Some readers will also enjoy conducting their own literature searches to find other in-depth sources for the subjects of these chapters.

Finally, let me mention a bit about chapter 3. In this chapter, I offer a controversial interpretive connection between the music of Richard Wagner and Bob Marley. It seems likely that some readers will find my enthusiastic comparative pairing of Wagner and Marley intriguing and lots of fun. Perhaps some will even find the argument compelling. Nonetheless, I am also certain that some readers will find the comparison insufficiently defended, or even preposterous. Comparing an iconic operatic genius with a "people power" Reggae star is not normally done, at least in academic circles. Nonetheless, I am raising ideas in this chapter, not trying to sell them. I like to make the Wagner and Marley comparison in part because I think there is something to the idea, but also because it may help some readers think "out-of-the-box." To draw from my own teaching experiences, I sometimes fear that students too often seek to find the "right" answers rather than their own answers. Combining ideas from highly divergent schools of thought can sometimes provide an opportunity for original thinking. This is how I view the Wagner and Marley comparison. I hope readers find the comparison between Wagner and Marley compelling. But if some readers do not find the argument compelling, I hope they at least find the ideas sufficiently provocative such that they serve as a basis for subsequent political argumentation with friends and colleagues. Arguing, after all, is much of what politics is all about! Thus, in the spirit of inciting a healthy and intellectually stimulating good spat, I offer the Wagner and Marley comparison with serious enthusiasm.

CHAPTER 1

Music as a Conveyor of Political Messages

Music is filled with political content. One only has to be a casual listener of any number of musical genres to observe this. For example, hip-hop music is historically rooted in the expression of social and political protest as voiced by urban African-American youth. Similarly, the protest music related to the Vietnam War and the Civil Rights movement in America during the 1960s and 1970s was profoundly political, and country music is widely laced with overtly patriotic overtones and politically explicit content. But music has also been a venue for profound political expression for centuries, with contributions coming from composers as diverse as Beethoven, Wagner, Verdi, Mussorgski, Sibelius, Copeland, and many others.

The potential for music to directly influence the political evolution of society has long been recognized by some thinkers, and even Plato warned that "the modes of music are never disturbed without unsettling of the most fundamental political and social conventions" (Republic, Book IV: 424). Indeed, the need for social scientists to understand the interaction of politics and music is especially cogent given the potential long-term impact this phenomenon is likely to have on current and subsequent generations of young adults. Ignoring this would of course put contemporary social scientists in the same position as Marshall D. Beuick subsequently found himself in when he prophesied in 1927 that the content of radio broadcasting was not likely to ever penetrate the national consciousness, that the attraction of radio would be a passing fad, and "the sophisticated city dweller will tire of the novelty" (Beuick 1927, 622).

Many of the extant social and political investigations of music have been conducted by social scientists and musicologists who focus on musically-mediated approaches to social theory. For example, Cerulo (1984) demonstrates that music creation responds to the events of society, and societies that experience dramatic change or trauma tend to develop music with message content that reflects these circumstances. Elsewhere, Cerulo (1989) examines how degrees of social and political control by elites correspond with the choice of musical styles in the creation of national anthems. Blau (1988) finds that listening to popular music is related to feelings of social dislocation and alienation, while listening to music with elite appeal (such as classical orchestral music) corresponds with low levels of alienation. Peterson and DiMaggio (1975) argue that evolving musical styles can reveal emerging classes within cultures that are defined more in terms of consumption patterns than by socioeconomic criteria. And Ballantine (1991) examines the social role of Black Jazz in the growth of radicalized political consciousness in South Africa. An excellent (although early) survey of research examining the political relevance of music as a force of change can be found in an examination of musical preferences of college students by Fox and Williams (1974). Scott (1997) and Bokina (1997) have published research that extends the idea of linking musical analysis to the examination of social and political thought. Here Scott (1997) explores the connectivity between the musical writings and political philosophy of Rousseau, while Bokina (1997) offers political interpretations of a variety of operas.

It is most likely that political and sociological musicology will continue to mature as an area of research as social scientists become increasingly aware of the developing interactive dependency between the evolution of our society and the music that it generates. Also, the productive interaction between political science, sociology, and psychology in the study of music seems inevitable as music continues to be recognized as a cardinal element of political and social change, and indeed one can see Peter Martin's attempt to create a sociology of music prescient in this respect (Martin, 1995). Leppert and McClary (1987) also attempt to extend such a discussion of music in much the same way in their interesting collection of essays on music and its social and political groundings.

What is new about the contemporary relevance of music as a conveyor of political ideas is not that music is being used at all in this regard. Rather, what is new is the magnitude of this phenomenon combined with technological advances in the distribution and accessability of music, minimally affecting hundreds of millions of mostly young adults across nearly all cultures in the world today. It is not difficult to witness music's potential as a political force. For example, it is arguably a common experience for many to observe passengers in cars who are singing (or rapping) along with a song containing politically potent lyrics that is being played on a radio or from a tape, CD, or iPod, and one can assume that this activity is repeated in countless other settings as well. To do this, of course, the lyrics must be memorized by such listeners. Forcing a comparison with a more traditional source of political information, I have yet to meet an individual who has memorized the words of any recent speech made by a presidential candidate over the past few elections.

Here we see a continuation and possible acceleration of the diminishing role of political parties as socializing agents and informational pipelines which guide both the formation of attitudes as well as the influence of political behavior for members of mass society. (See Wattenberg 1984, and for a contrasting perspective, see Hetherington 2001.) This well-documented process of party decline began in earnest with the rise of network television, and continues with the emergence of the Internet and other alternative sources of political information. Indeed, and crucially among the younger generation, music is now a primary player in this increasingly diverse competition for the attention of the masses with respect to the dissemination of political ideas, and the increasing importance of political music is not at all limited to the most recent ascendancy of rebellious hip-hop.

Representational vs. Associational Music

There are two primary approaches by which music can convey political content. The first is "representational," and this is by far the most direct method of linking music with a political perspective. Representational political music presents a clearly defined political point of view that corresponds with the composer's intent with respect to the music. This is normally the consequence of the composer placing explicit political content into a piece of music. Obviously this can be done through the lyrics in a song, and a national anthem is one example that fits into this category. Normally, representational political music addresses politics that are contemporary with the composer, but this is not an absolute requirement. It is possible for music to convey an explicit political message that is entirely relevant to a time period that resides in the future relative to the life of the composer. For example, a composer may write a song about the destruction of the Earth's environment and the political corruption that is ultimately responsible for that destruction. This is an explicit political message that would directly address the precise issue regardless of time period, and so this song would remain an example of representational political music long after the death of the composer. But again, it is far more common for representational political music to be identified as such in relation to the politics that are contemporary with the life of the composer, and future representations of that same political message tend to be more the exception than the rule.

"Associational political music" is somewhat of a mirror image of its representational counterpart. Associational political music is the result of activities by individuals who are normally not involved in the original composition of the music. Typically, associational political music is created when someone or some group makes a connection between a particular piece of music (or in some instances, the entire collected work of a composer) and a political message or ideology. This individual or group makes this connection as a means of using the music to support a political agenda. A classic example of a composer's work being exploited to support a political campaign long after the death of the composer was the 20th century portrayal of Beethoven's music by Germany's Nazi Party as intentionally supportive of a fascist world view (see chapter 2), an occurrence that would have surprised no one more thoroughly than Beethoven himself.

When political music is associated with purposes or meanings that are not intended by the original composer, it is typical for this to happen after the composer's death. It is obvious that the composer cannot protest the use of the music in this manner, and other defenders of the composer's original intentions can be more easily drowned out by the general noise of political campaigns. Also, in many situations it can be unclear as to what a composer actually intended with a particular piece of music, and the defense of a political association with that music may not be entirely demonstrable without resorting to after-the-fact interpretations of the composer's own political perspective.

But it is also possible (although less frequently) for associational political music to appear in venues that are contemporary with a composer's own political setting, such as when a musical composition written for a particular purpose nonetheless seems to tie in well with a related or similar situation or setting. In such a situation it can sometimes be quite clear that the association between the music and the new setting does not strongly violate the original explicit meaning of the music, yet the connection is not so clear as to warrant calling it "representational." A good example of such music would be an anti-war composition that was composed in response to, say, the involvement of the United States in the Vietnam War, but which might find itself revived in connection with a future conflict between the United States and another country, or perhaps a conflict involving two entirely different nations. Indeed, sometimes the composers themselves attempt to connect their old protest songs with new conflicts, a phenomenon that has occurred recently with respect to the invasion of Iraq by the United States military in 2003 (see especially "Decades Later, 60's Icons Still

Live by Their Message," by James Barron, *The New York Times*, Sunday, 30 March 2003, p. B15[N]).

Orientation

Politically laced music is present in every culture on the planet, and it is impossible for any one book to address satisfactorily the great diversity of such music. For this reason, the current volume focuses primarily on political music originating from Western society, from the classical period to the present. This also is a large body of music to include in any single volume, and one could easily argue that no book could cover every element of even this more limited collection of material. Indeed, one need look no further than Ben Arnold's extensively organized and heavily annotated discussion and listing of war-related music to understand how challenging it is to be truly comprehensive in any single volume dealing with musical interpretations of significant social and political events (see especially Arnold 1993, pp. xiii-xiv). But since one of the primary purposes of writing this book is to identify both the clear existence as well as some of the dominant strands of political music within Western society over an extended time period, heuristic choices regarding particular musical genres, composers, and musical pieces become a desired and necessary element of the discussions included in these pages. Thus, this volume is not a collection of essays defining the absolute scope of extant political music, nor is this volume a comprehensive listing of political music within any one society or genre. Rather, it is a tracing of some of the most important political themes that have resonated in much of the music of Western society for over two-hundred years.

Crucially, this book is not about music as music. Rather, this volume is a discussion of politics as it has been—and continues to be—expressed musically. This may require some flexibility from the reader with respect to traditional approaches to music categorization and history. For example, from a musical perspective, it would be natural to object to comparisons between the music of Richard Wagner and that of Bob Marley, or perhaps to discussions of nationalist and patriotic music that extend from the Romantic period all the way up to contemporary examples in the pop and rock genres. But the politics in music is quite different from the music itself. In the above examples, I obviously cannot compare the *music* of Wagner with that of Marley. But in these pages I do examine their political ideas relating to revolution and other matters that they expressed musically. Similarly, and again for example, I cannot compare Modest Mussorgsky's music with that of Bruce Springsteen, but I can and do point out similarities in the manner with which both composers have expressed their nationalist political ideas in their music.

In the chapters that follow, these discussions are arranged according to general themes. Many of these themes may also appear to have a rough chronological ordering as well, and this is certainly a consequence of the way in which history self-organizes itself to inspire new waves of political music. But chronology is not the dominating element here, as can clearly be seen in an early chapter on political manifesto music that combines discussions of Bob Marley and Wagner's "Ring" operas.

Among all classical composers, none have had their musical works more often and profoundly exploited for political purposes than Ludwig van Beethoven. The next chapter focuses on the way much of Beethoven's music has been laced with political meaning from the time of the composer's life up to the present. This chapter also offers an early opportunity to demonstrate the concepts of representational and associational political music, since both ideas are appropriate in various contexts to a discussion of Beethoven. Since identifying the way in which music is connected with politics is a required component of any analysis of political music, the clarity of the dual usage of Beethoven's music in this regard provides an ideal opportunity to offer a base-line application of the representational and associational ideas that assists with the discussions that follow in later chapters.

Chapter 3 introduces the idea of "political manifesto music." This type of music is so blatantly political that it is hard to miss at least the overt elements of its political content. But there are nuances to such music, and indeed for the general category. Political manifesto music has the added element of offering a more coherent set of political ideas than is often the case with political music more generally, and so it usefully expands early-on the discussions in this volume that address the range of purposeful uses of music as a political tool. This chapter juxtaposes two very different musical personalities, Bob Marley and Richard Wagner. Readers may find it intriguing that two such diverse composers can be analyzed in the context of one chapter, and it is here that the definition and purpose of political manifesto music becomes so crucial to that treatment.

When nations emerge through war or merely the codification of cultural boundaries, the new citizens seek various means of political expression. Nationalist political music (or simply, nationalist music) plays an important role in this regard. In chapter 4, nationalist music is both defined and identified through the works of various composers who mostly appeared in the late-Romantic Era (late 1800s) which immediately followed the Classical Period. However, there are nationalist composers that are very active today, and their works span a variety of musical genres, including contemporary pop. The discussions in chapter 4 differentiate nationalist compositions from those that are more clearly patriotic. The distinction is important since the purpose of nationalist music is quite different from that of patriotic music.

The 20th century was a period of tremendous growth for political music that had a working class or labor orientation. Chapter 5 focuses on this brand of music by following the development of labor music primarily in the United States. The discussion begins with an introduction to the highly controversial figure, Joe Hill, and it includes an outline of his involvement with a number of labor luminaries of his day. The discussion then extends through the century up to the modern period, addressing examples of such music from sources as diverse as Woody Guthrie and The Rolling Stones.

When many people think of political music in general, they

probably thing of protest music emerging from the Vietnam War period. This indeed is much of the focus of chapter 6. While it is obvious that protest music can emerge from a political movement as potent as the anti-war movement of that troubled period, this type of music can also occur without the presence of a major movement. Chapter 6 addresses the general topic of protest music as it may appear in both movement and non-movement situations. This is probably one of the most powerful genres of political music, and without doubt its importance to the transformation of society becomes clearer during intermittent times of national stress.

Hip-hop is a very contemporary genre of politically rich music, and it is the focus of chapter 7. Born of the inner-city ghetto, the style and content of hip-hop is transforming the political and musical landscapes in new and provocative ways. Lyrics—spoken poetically with driving rhythms—have assumed a significance that rivals that of the strongest examples coming from the genre of protest music. Watching this relatively new hip-hop genre continue to develop is one of the most interesting elements in the general evolution of political music today. There are both subtle and sublime elements in this genre, and I attempt to outline the most important political characteristics of this type of music in that chapter.

Never has there been a more pregnant opportunity than now for people to turn their attention to an investigation of how music conveys political ideas in our society. Following more traditional paths of research, social scientists have long examined how the flow of political information to individuals and groups affects the development of political attitudes and behaviors in our society. The focus of such research usually has one of three orientations: (1) psychological influences (e.g., Campbell, Converse, Miller, and Stokes 1960), (2) theories of rational decision-making on the individual level (e.g., Downs 1957), and (3) the influences of social and political contexts (such as those identified in group-defined milieu) on mediating the acceptance or rejection of political information (e.g., Berelson, Lazarsfeld, and McPhee 1954; Huckfeldt and Sprague 1988). Nearly all of these approaches focus on political information as it is presented to individuals through orthodox informational conduits, such as through political parties, nightly news broadcasts, interactions with campaign workers, candidate advertisements, and so on. However, a huge amount of political information is now transmitted to contemporary society—particularly younger elements of society—through nontraditional sources, and it serves us well to examine these other contributions to our informational mix more closely.

Music is one of the most important of these increasingly pervasive new sources of political content. It is perhaps because of the explosive rise of music as a venue of political expression that it has become so timely to take a retrospective and generalized look at the phenomenon. If politics is the blood that feeds our societies with the energy to evolve, then music is an essential ingredient to political transformation. We listen to music not only to be entertained. We listen to music to understand ourselves both individually and collectively. Yet it is precisely because music is so entertaining that it carries such great potency as a venue for political expression. It conveys more than the written or spoken word. Through rhythm and tone, music becomes a powerful link between the emotionally rich ideas of a political thinker and the listeners. We are both political and musical creatures. This is, indeed, one of the things that makes it so fun to be human, and this is also why it is so crucial to understand the potential of music as a mediating factor in the political transformation of society.

CHAPTER 2

Classical Music as a Political Voice: The Case of Beethoven

The Classical Period for music ran approximately from 1750 to 1820, and it followed musical periods known as the Middle Ages, the Renaissance, and the Baroque Age. It is called the "Classical Period" because its music dropped much of what musicians sometimes call "ornamentation," and instead emphasized a more straightforward approach to composition that composers of that time considered reminiscent of the style of art in Classical Greece. Politics in Europe and America were in turmoil during this period, as was evidenced by the widespread manifestation of revolutions or revolutionary movements. The European musical center during this time was Vienna, and the three great composers of the Viennese musical school are Franz Joseph Hayden, Wolfgang Amadeus Mozart, and Ludwig van Beethoven. The influence of the Viennese school was so profound on the musical world that one of the major impetuses for the genesis of the Romantic Era which followed the Classical Period was to allow for new composition to emerge that reflected a more diverse collection of national and cultural settings.

From a political perspective, the most important musical figure of the Classical Period is Beethoven. Beethoven can be placed at the end of this period, and he is sometimes considered the last of the great classical composers. Indeed, he can be seen as a connecting link between the Classical Period and the Romantic Era. Yet the interaction between Beethoven's music and politics was not limited to the events of his lifetime. Indeed, Beethoven's music has had a notable impact on the politics of Europe (although, most importantly, Germany) from the time of the original performance of many of his works all the way through the 20th century. A detailed chronology of the long-term interaction between Beethoven's music and German politics is offered by David B. Dennis (1996). As with the approach by Dennis, I categorize Beethoven's political influence on German politics according to five major periods: (1) during Beethoven's life, (2) the Second Reich, (3) the Weimar Republic, (4) the Third Reich, and (5) post-World War II Germany.

But there is another reason for beginning this volume with a discussion of Beethoven. In general—and certainly in terms of its major manifestation—the use of music to convey political meaning that is addressed directly toward the masses really begins with the Classical Period. Previously, most music was composed to be played in the courts of the aristocracy and nobility, as well as in the churches. In these venues, the social and political elite paid for the music to be composed and performed, and their primary interest was to be entertained or inspired within strictly limited settings. An exception to this, of course, would be early war-related music, especially that which was played on the battlefield to inspire the troops during a battle (see Arnold 1993). Within the court and church settings, composers obviously sought employment, and they composed music that would satisfy the interests of the sponsoring elite. But the idea of putting a significant range of political content into musical form had to wait until music was being performed in settings that were attended by more ordinary people. This required venues that sold tickets, and the sale of these tickets paid for the costs of composition and performance. Thus, Beethoven's musical genius intersected with an opportunity in the historical development of music—theaters. Beethoven fully exploited the potential of this new venue by composing music that could appeal directly to the political sensibilities of the masses, or at least the masses who were sufficiently well off to be able to buy tickets to a concert. (For a discussion of the political significance of another classical composer, see, for example, Bokina's discussion of Mozart's *Don Giovani* [Bokina, 1997, chapter 2], and also see *Cosi? Sexual Politics in Mozart's Operas* by Charles Ford

[1991].) Beethoven wrote lots of nonpolitical music as well, of course, from masses to sonatas, and just about everything in between. Yet even many of these pieces have been used by others to convey political messages. Thus our interest in Beethoven is two-fold. First we are interested in Beethoven's own political thoughts that he represented musically. But second, we are also interested in the political thoughts of others who wished to associate their own ideas with Beethoven and his music long after his death.

Beethoven's Music and His Contemporary Political Environment

Beethoven never expressed a single and unambiguously coherent political philosophy or ideological viewpoint. Indeed, it is a bit of a wonder how Beethoven's music later became so deeply politicized given his seemingly erratic political ideas as spread out over his entire creative life. Nonetheless, it is possible to discern what one might call a "Beethovian political perspective" by observing the influence that others have had on his life and career, as well as by taking note of some of the dedications for his works, the tone of a few blatantly patriotic pieces, the symbolism in his one opera, and the use of Frederick Schiller's poem in his Ninth Symphony. It is through these markers (some very strong), that the case can be made that Beethoven consciously created representational political music.

Beethoven's early life seems to have influenced much of his later political philosophy. He was born in 1770 and lived in Bonn until 1792. From 1784-1801, Bonn was ruled by Maximilian Franz, the brother of emperor Joseph II of Hapsburg. Both Maximilian and Joseph II ruled with a similar philosophy, a philosophy Dennis has characterized as relatively enlightened despotism (Dennis 1996, p. 24). The society around Beethoven prospered during Franz's rule, and Beethoven seemed profoundly influenced by this early political environment that "worked." Beethoven witnessed first-hand how a single gifted leader enabled a society to develop productively, and it seems that Beethoven inwardly searched (or hoped) for the return of such a leader for remainder of his life (especially, see Solomon 1977, pp- 38-9; also Cooper 1985, pp. 88-9).

During this early period, Beethoven learned about the ideas of Kant, Voltaire, Rousseau, as well as the radical thinker Eulogius Schneider (Dennis 1996, p. 25). Some of Beethoven's musical mentors were also members of the Order of the *Illuminati*, a secretive anticlerical organization. Thus, even though Beethoven himself may have been relatively apolitical at this early stage, he nonetheless knew of political intellectuals, and he was aware of at least the basic content of their thoughts. It is this exposure that seems to have set the stage for the subsequent period in his life in which he seemed to respond to the revolutionary happenings of France and elsewhere. This second period in his life lasted approximately from 1792 to 1804, beginning when Beethoven moved to Vienna to continue his music studies. This period overlapped with the 1789-99 span of the French Revolution, and seems to have ended when Napoleon made himself Emperor in 1804.

While in Vienna, Beethoven first mentioned that he wanted to put Frederich Schiller's poem "Ode to Freedom" to music (Solomon 1977, p. 39; Dennis 1996, p. 26). Beethoven also dedicated his Symphony No. 3 (*Eroica*, composed in 1803) to Napoleon Bonaparte, who at the time seemed to resemble the sought-after redeemer despot. This dedication is one of the clearest indications that Beethoven was attracted to the early Napoleonic republican principles. However, when Napoleon became Emperor, Beethoven changed the dedication of this symphony to Prince Franz Joseph von Lobkowitz (see Solomon 1968; also Solomon 1977, pp. 132-42). Also during this period, Beethoven worked on his opera *Fidelio* (originally entitled *Leonore*). In this opera, a nobleman is unjustly imprisoned by a political opponent. The nobleman is eventually rescued by a king who seems to want to end tyranny and promote justice, which again returns us to the idea of society being preferably ruled by a redeeming despot.

It seems clear that in Beethoven's mind during this period there is a conflict. On one hand he is being influenced by the republican fervor for revolution that is contemporary with his life, but on the other hand he still remembers the ideal of an enlightened rule by a gifted individual. Indeed, it is not until the end of his life that he seems to finally accept that this latter solution is not practical or likely, as is evidenced in his Symphony No. 9. Further evidence of this conflict within Beethoven is his composition of some songs during this period that supported notably non-republican Germanic politics. Some of these songs were used to support Austrian military fights with Napoleon (Solomon 1977, p. 87; also Dennis 1996, p. 28).

Beethoven's third period in his political evolution was from 1804 to 1815. At this point Beethoven was clearly distancing himself from the French ideas which he entertained previously. While Beethoven was finishing his opera *Fidelio* (at that time, *Leonore*), Napoleon was fighting to capture Vienna. Beethoven's hearing was beginning to decline seriously, and he had to protect it as best he could during the shelling of Vienna by hiding in his brother's basement while holding pillows over his ears (Dennis 1996, p. 29). In 1813, two years before Waterloo, he wrote "Wellington's Victory" (the so-called "Battle Symphony," op. 91) in support of the victory over the French in the Battle of Victoria. This work is militaristic in tone, even containing copious battlefield sounds. Beethoven also wrote a number of other musical pieces (e.g., "The Glorious Moment," op.136; "Chorus to the United Princes," op. WoO 95; and "It is Achieved," WoO 97) during this period that patriotically (from a Germanic perspective) celebrated the French defeats (Dennis 1996, pp. 29-30). This, of course, culminated with Napoleon's final collapse in the Battle of Waterloo in 1815. This was Beethoven's most conservative period in which he celebrated the restoration of the prior establishment.

The French defeat at Waterloo ended a period of war and conflict that lasted for 23 years, spanning the French Revolutionary Wars (beginning in 1792) and the Napoleonic Wars (from 1803).

This also initiated a period of very repressive post-Napoleonic European politics. Beginning in 1816 and ending with his death in 1827, Beethoven returns to more progressive political leanings. The Ninth Symphony (composed between 1822 and 1824) is a product of this final period in Beethoven's political evolution. Here Beethoven finally puts music to Schiller's hymn in the famous choral to the Ninth Symphony. The revolutionary potency of this work is such that when it was first performed in 1824 in Vienna at the *Kärntnertor* Theater (also known as the Imperial Court Theater), the audience was so struck by it that they gave it five standing ovations, ultimately silenced by the police commissioner who aggressively ordered quiet.

As a piece of music supporting revolutionary political ideals (at least as it was perceived by many at the time), the Ninth Symphony is Beethoven's most forceful example of representational political music. The words of the 4th movement are clearly suggestive of revolutionary intent, vigorously encouraging the masses to take their destiny into their own hands, their actions guided—and perhaps endorsed—by divine providence. At the time of its first performance, it was clear to at least some of Beethoven's contemporaries that the piece indeed hit its political mark, such that it would likely have been censored entirely by the authorities in advance of its performance had they known the type of emotional response it could elicit from an audience (Knight 1973, p. 168; Dennis 1996, p. 30-1). Also, both Solomon (1977, p. 256) and Dennis (1996, p. 31) point out that Beethoven and his colleagues would have been arrested had not the authorities not felt certain that he was insane, and had his reputation not been so great.

The Re-invention of Beethoven During the Second Reich

The evolution of Beethoven's music into associational political music began in earnest with the approach and creation of the Second Reich. Reviewing a bit of history, the Napoleonic Wars in the early 1800s are the formal markers of the end of the

Holy Roman Empire, and they forced the many ethnically German principalities to form a loose union. In 1860, the Congress of Vienna created the Deutsher Bund, which included 38 states led by Austria. Otto von Bismarck began his more serious involvement with German politics in the 1860s. Two ethnically German states, Schleswig and Holstein, were controlled by Denmark, which planned to annex them formally. To prevent this, Prussia and Austria invaded these states, with Prussia taking Schleswig and Austria taking Holstein. Then in 1866, Prussia won a seven-week war with Austria and annexed the country.

While this was going on, Napoleon III encouraged the war since he wanted to weaken both Prussia and Austria before France expanded eastward. With the encouragement of Bismarck, Prince Leopold (who was a relative of the Prussian leader Wilhelm I) tried to become King of Spain. France objected to this, and warned Germany not to meddle with Spanish politics again. Wilhelm I politely refused to foreswear any future involvement in support of Leopold, and the French ambassador sent this message in a telegram (famously known as the "Elm telegram") to Napoleon III. Bismarck intercepted the telegram and edited it, changing it to seem as if Wilhelm I rudely dismissed Napoleon's request. The telegram trick worked, Napoleon III was outraged, and France declared war on Prussia, with France seen as the aggressor.

Briefly summarizing the next 45 years, France lost the war, and Paris was captured in 1871. Wilhelm I became the Emperor of Germany, and the Second Reich began. Bismarck was then appointed as the Chancellor of Germany, and over the next 20 years Germany grew to become a major industrial and military power. When Wilhelm I died in 1888, he was succeeded by Frederick III, who himself died three months later. Then Wilhelm II succeeded Frederick III, and Bismarck's period of influence ended when he was forced to resign. Finally, in 1914, World War I began, and this concluded the first period in which Beethoven's music was transformed to have associational political meaning.

The person who most notably worked to associate Beethoven's music with explicit political meaning during the period of the Second Reich was Richard Wagner. Wagner himself was a hugely political persona (as I discuss in greater detail in the next chapter). Wagner used his own speeches and writings to make these connections between Beethoven and Wagner's own political agenda. Since Beethoven was no longer alive to defend himself and his music, Wagner had considerable latitude in re-defining Beethoven with a new image. While Wagner had to compete with others during his time who also wanted to portray Beethoven in their own ways, Wagner's enormous presence in Germanic culture—combined with his own considerable energy—allowed him to be the most decisive instrument in the drive to re-shape Beethoven politically. Wagner also had his own supporters (such as the conductor Hans von Bülow, and the editor Hans von Wolzogen) who promoted the Wagnerian interpretation of Beethoven.

Basically, Wagner was a revolutionary, and he saw Beethoven in revolutionary terms. Wagner portrayed Beethoven as a revolutionary and nationalizing Germanic hero (Dennis 1996, p. 39). While there is little direct evidence that Bismarck himself interpreted Beethoven's music politically, it was clear that Bismarck and his associates found Beethoven to be a useful accompaniment to their overall political agenda, and Wagner's promotion of an explicit Beethoven "Germanic hero" myth was a useful backdrop to their other nationalizing efforts. Numerous governmental activities helped to accent this growing myth, including the designation of Beethoven's house of birth as a national landmark (Dennis 1996, pp. 38-9). Stories were also promoted that linked Bismarck with the belief that Beethoven's music inspired heroic military deeds on the part of German soldiers. Indeed, a virtual cottage industry arose that attempted to make various associations between Bismarck and Beethoven. Dates, of course, were always of consequence, and efforts were made to link assorted Beethoven anniversaries and other notable dates with nationalist events, such as when Beethoven's 100th birthday was connected with Germany's defeat of France, and when concerts were performed on dates that supported Bismarck's own career. Some of these concerts were accompanied with speeches in which the connections between Beethoven and an explicit political agenda were made clear.

After Bismarck's departure from the German political scene, Beethoven's music continued to be used for political ends. Some racist groups found new energy in arguing that Beethoven was an example of the natural dominance of the Nordic race (Dennis 1996, pp. 55-6). Other groups across the entire political spectrum had Beethoven's music played at their political functions as a way of insinuating a connection between their own political viewpoints and those of the composer. From both the right and left ideological wings, Beethoven was used to support attacks on the Wilhelmine status quo, and thus there was a lively competition with regard to the "true" political interpretation of the composer.

World War I brought with it a considerable growth industry in terms of re-defining Beethoven as a war-invigorating engine. Selective play of various Beethoven marches, together with a general over-play of Beethoven's music at both political and war-related functions helped propel the composer into the front ranks of the German war machine. Beethoven's own dislike for the French during the violent Napoleonic period also helped solidify the propaganda point of German superiority over the western peoples. In general, during the war there was an intense patriotic fever combined one-sided political, cultural, and militarized interpretations of Beethoven's music. Contrary views were typically suppressed, or at best, raised meekly. It was not until the war ended that German society was freed from the imposition of this one-sided political positioning of Beethoven's music. And the war's end, of course, did not bring back a "true" understanding of Beethoven's musically mediated ideas. Rather, it opened a new box of re-interpretive possibilities as the composer was re-deployed in a new national setting with new actors needing new musical and political associations.

Beethoven and the Weimar Republic

The Weimar Republic was created as a result of Germany losing World War I. When the war ended, Germany was not demolished physically, as it was at the end of World War II. The country itself remained almost intact (a 10% reduction in territory and population), and foreign troops never occupied the country. The population of the Weimar Republic felt betrayed by the Treaty of Versailles, which was considerably different (and much harsher) than the original 14 points that Germany agreed to when it asked Woodrow Wilson to arrange an armistice in October 1918. Thus, the political groups that were active during the Weimar Republic faced an intense collection of issues that connected current problems to past events, and the ideologies of these groups tended to reflect these intensities, sometimes calmly, but all too often with a shocking level of extremism. This potential for extremism within both the right and left wings of German politics remained a force to be reckoned with all the way up to the beginning of the Nazi era in 1933.

The Weimar Republic was a full-fledged democracy (see Brown 1982, 1987). The full political spectrum was represented by both new and old political parties from 1919 to 1933. Large numbers of people started voting for the first time in Weimar, and change was the general order of the day. There were eight elections during the Weimar years. The dates of these elections are 6 June 1920, 15 April 1924, 11 July 1924, 20 May 1928, 14 September 1930, 31 July 1932, 11 November 1932, and 5 March 1933. The close spacing between some of the elections reflects some of the more difficult moments of electoral struggle that was common during the life of the Republic.

In general, nearly all social groups found representation among at least one of the political parties. The workers tended to support the Social Democratic Party (SPD) or the Communist Party. The bourgeoisie (the middle class, often tradespeople) typically voted for three newly formed parties, including the German Democratic Party (DDP) and the German People's Party

(DVP). Catholics largely endorsed the Catholic Center Party, while conservatives supported the German National People's Party (DNVP). The Protestant peasants and disaffected bourgeoisie (including some Catholics) offered great support to the Nazi Party (NSDAP—See Brown 1982 and 1987.) All of these parties used music during their political campaigns as a way of attracting voters to their rallies and other events. Beethoven was often the favorite composer for these politically-related performances. Nearly all people in Germany had a deep affection for the music of Beethoven. His music represented something cultural that connected them to a heritage that extended well-beyond the temporal and geographic boundaries of the Weimar Republic. Interestingly, of all the political parties that were active during the Weimar years, the Nazi Party was least able to exploit music for political gain due to logistical and other practical reasons, a relative inadequacy that was eliminated completely after the Nazis took power in 1933.

The basic strategy used by all political parties during the Weimar years was to attempt to develop and maintain an association between Beethoven's music and their own political themes. Since there were so many groups trying to do this, there was a fierce debate regarding Beethoven's "real" political leanings. This resulted in various versions of a "Beethoven myth," a point described in detail by Dennis (1996, chapter 3). Few of these myths had any strong historical grounding in fact with regard to Beethoven's actual political views. But all pointed to aspects of Beethoven's life and music that seemed to "prove" their case.

There were two primary goals involved in a political party's attempt to create a Beethoven myth. The first was to create a sense in the voters' minds that particular pieces of Beethoven's music offered evidence that Beethoven himself (a representative of the "true" German culture) supported at least the general idea of their partisan agenda. The second was to supplement this musical linkage with stories (both written and verbal) that supported the idea that Beethoven was a kindred spirit in ideological and cultural terms. Since the Weimar Republic was a newly invented outcome of the Treaty of Versailles, voters in general did not have a longstanding exposure to the voting process, or for the idea of repeatedly supporting one particular political party over time. This addresses the idea of partisan institutionalization, which essentially references a pattern of habitual support for each voter's most preferred party. In the absence of a history of voting, partisan institutionalization was minimal during the Weimar years, and it became all the more important for all of the political parties to create and maintain culturally-dependent linkages between the newly mobilized voters and the parties.

After creating a Beethoven myth, political organizers would play certain musical pieces at political events in order to create a politically correct ambience with the audience. When speeches were made, ideological and political guidance would then be emotionally anchored by the music in the minds of those listening. Dennis has pointed out that this process worked in a fashion similar to that performed by chorales in churches with regard to religious purposes (Dennis 1996, pp. 97-8) .

In general, Weimar leftists tended to emphasize Beethoven's support for a republican agenda, as evidenced by his removal of the original dedication to Napoleon of the *Eroica* Symphony. The Catholic Center Party organizers argued that it was Beethoven's inner Christian faith that enabled him to write such beautiful music (especially church music) under physical hardship (i.e., his deafness). And the conservatives organizing for the DNVP were able to argue that Beethoven was a counterrevolutionary and nationalist hero, as evidenced by his support for the Germanic resistance of Napoleon's eastward invasion, and by the fact that Beethoven obtained employment from the established aristocracy. In essence, all groups could find some evidence in Beethoven's complex life to support their own interpretations of the composer and his music.

The extreme right-wing groups (such as the Nazis) tended to emphasize the counterrevolutionary interpretation of Beethoven, and they also significantly modified physical descriptions of Beethoven to correspond with their favored view of Nordic

German racial purity. Some conservative theorists argued when pressed that if Beethoven did have "mixed blood," he fought to conquer it in order to produce his pure Nordic music. This struggle acted to raise Beethoven beyond his limitations to the status of a Nordic hero. Indeed, this struggle paralleled the perceived need for German culture to dominate other world cultures. In particular, the Nazis emphasized that Beethoven hated the French, he supported authoritarianism, he disliked the social disorder characteristic of revolutions, and his music was vigorous and thus symbolic of the vigor of the Nazi movement (see Dennis 1996, p. 133). However, due to the fact that the Nazis did not make a large impact on German politics until late in the Weimar period, they were not able to fully compete with the other political parties in the creation of their own fleshed-out Beethoven myth. Of course, this all changed after the Nazis took power. Thereupon they were able to marshal the resources of the state to fully exploit Beethoven's potential in creating potent associational political music.

Beethoven and the Nazi Peril

German music during the Nazi period was largely perceived and thus re-configured as a vehicle for propaganda delivery. For example, a huge emphasis was placed on the composition and performance of political songs as a propaganda tool (Baher 1963, p. 244). Also, a significant portion of the music of Beethoven, Bruckner, and Wagner were deeply incorporated into the Nazi propaganda perspective as a means of "demonstrating" the superiority of the Aryan race (Arnold 1993, p. 188-9). Beethoven was a central focus of their efforts to establish political music that would effectively enhance their overall agenda, and he presented the Nazis with a few personal difficulties which they needed to "smooth over."

Once the Nazis controlled power in Germany, their propagandists worked to "purify" the image of Beethoven. For example, they fabricated a new relationship between Beethoven and his father, a mean drunkard whom Beethoven hated (Dennis 1996, pp. 146-7). Indeed, the Nazis created a new heroic father for Beethoven. This was of particular importance since the image of a powerful guiding father-leader was so important to the Nazi political agenda. The propagandists also managed to boost the image of Beethoven's mother (a persona whose image did not require as much tinkering). She was portrayed as a near perfect parent and care-giver. (In addition to Dennis 1996, see also Schröder 1986.)

The Nazis took seriously the job of refining the use of the available propaganda machinery to further their cause. The enhancement of a Nazi version of the Beethoven myth was central to this, and they used radio, newsreels, and especially live concerts at political events to accomplish this task. In general, the Nazis promoted the idea that Beethoven believed in National Socialist ideals. They particularly fostered the idea that Beethoven supported the concept of a wise and powerful leader (in Nazi terms, a Führer). The Nazis also argued that Beethoven was himself a "world conqueror" through his music, and thus he would have been supportive of Germany's efforts to dominate the world politically as well.

Crucial to this effort was the attempt to link Beethoven to Hitler himself. For example, connections were made to identify Hitler with the heroic-savior character Fidelio in Beethoven's sole opera. In this instance, care was taken to ensure that Hitler was not compared with Pizarro, the cruel jailor who tried to kill Florestan. Joseph Goebbels, the Nazi propagandist, was particularly active in establishing these propaganda connections. Goebbels was also active in utilizing other specific Beethoven musical pieces (such as using the Edmont overture to precede key speeches, as well as various approaches to exploiting the Third, Fifth, and Seventh symphonies) to create particular mental connections with the Nazi agenda. German musicologists were also "encouraged" to support the campaign to connect Beethoven with the Nazi agenda, which many did with significant enthusiasm. (Again, see Dennis 1996, chapter 4 for a detailed documentation of these items.)

It is useful to note that the Nazi effort to utilize Beethoven in their propaganda effort addressed a diverse variety of venues. For example, children were systematically indoctrinated to the Nazi-Beethoven myth through both concerts and teachings, essentially establishing Beethoven as a Nazi role model (Valentin 1938, also, Dennis 1996, pp. 154-6). Similarly, elements that could detract from this effort were either eliminated or restricted, such as when Jewish organizations were prohibited from playing Beethoven's music.

Post World War II and the Fall of the Berlin Wall

When Germany was divided at the end of World War II, each half of Germany was able to experience Beethoven's music in separate ways. For West Germany, the Nazi experience followed by the freedoms associated with democracy led to a deep rejection of the Nazi-derived Beethoven myth (Dennis 1996, p. 176). This led to a near whole-scale abandonment of the attempt to use Beethoven for political purposes. Serious discussions of Beethoven's works remained more dominantly within the realm of technical and psychoanalytic arguments (Dennis 1996, p. 191).

East Germany followed a different path entirely, however. While rejecting the Nazi's Beethoven myth that connected the middle class to a fascist ideology, the German Democratic Republic was nonetheless able to utilize the basic principles of myth-making to shape the appreciation of Beethoven's music into a leftist and revolutionary mold (Rackwitz 1970, also Dennis 1996, pp. 177-8). As leftist ideologues had done in the past, Beethoven was re-positioned as a left-wing revolutionary, and his music was portrayed as supportive of communist ideals.

West Germans in general responded to this new utilization of a Beethoven myth by the East Germans with considerable distaste, which only amplified the West German desire to keep discussions of Beethoven on more technical or musicological levels, as well as to engage in psychological examinations of the composer with respect to his actual and true biographical past. Indeed, West

German scholarship delved deeply into the problems Beethoven had with his interpersonal relationships, his sexuality, and even the management of his financial and personal affairs.

Yet perhaps the most potent use of Beethoven and his music as symbolic of German culture and politics arrived with the end of communism in the East. When East and West Germany essentially collapsed into one nation in late 1989, the Jewish conductor, Daniel Barenboim, led the Berlin Philharmonic Orchestra on the 12th of November in a performance of Beethoven's Seventh Symphony as well as a performance of his First Piano Concerto. This event was eclipsed in its meaningfulness only by the performance of Beethoven's Ninth Symphony in dual performances in both East and West Berlin led by Leonard Bernstein on 23 December 1989. Beethoven and his music now held unambiguous political meaning—freedom and liberation. This meaning was no doubt amplified by Bernstein's idea to insert the word "freedom" wherever the word "joy" occurred in the ending chorus (i.e., thus changing the "Ode to Joy" to the "Ode to Freedom").

We have probably not seen the end of the politicization of Beethoven and his music. Indeed, that this should continue is a consequence not of Beethoven or his music, but rather a result of the nature of humans to express their political ideas musically. A "political Beethoven" may simply be one manifestation of the ever-present politics in music in a world in which the general phenomenon is now ubiquitous.

Primary Sources for Further Reading

Brown, Courtney. 1982 (June). "The Nazi Vote: A National Ecological Study," *American Political Science Review*, 76(2): 285-302.

Brown, Courtney. 1987(February). "Mobilization and Party Competition within a Volatile Electorate," *American Sociological Review*, 52(1): 59-72.

Dennis, David B. 1996. *Beethoven in German Politics, 1870-1989*. New Haven, Conn.: Yale University Press.

CHAPTER 3

Political Manifesto Music: The Cases of Bob Marley and Richard Wagner

"Political manifesto music" is one of the most pronounced forms of political expression through music. It is more than merely music with political content, or, more delicately, musically-mediated political thought. Rather, political manifesto music requires the identification of a coherent conceptual focus amidst a generally complex collection of related political ideas, all of which have to be recognizably located within a significant body of music. Thus, a song cannot be considered an example of political manifesto music simply because it has political content. Rather, the artist has to have a coherent set of political views, and the artist needs to address at least the bulk of the complexity inherent in these views in a material part of his or her music.

Minimally, a political manifesto is a statement of political opinion or policy. This implicitly requires that creators of political manifesto music use their music to express a perspective on politics, society, or even the human condition. But political manifestos are typically intended to be catalytic documents that help to create political change by virtue of the affect that they have on their readers or listeners. Thus political manifesto music may also play the activist role whereby it serves as an agent that triggers significant change in our political world.

To understand political manifesto music as a potent force in society, it is sometimes useful to compare both contemporary and historical examples of musical works that have conveyed content-rich political messages. Perhaps nowhere do we find more brawny examples of music's involvement with politics than with the musically-mediated political thought of Bob Marley and the "Ring" operas of Richard Wagner. Both Marley and Wagner had unambiguously coherent and well-developed political views, and both used music to convey their complex political ideas. This chapter discusses both of these composers, and I also present some comparisons between the political ideas which they have musically expressed to connect heuristically some of their most significant works to the more general idea of political manifesto music. Moreover, it is the transcendent nature of some of these ideas that suggests their continued relevancy to our modern and politically-troubled world.

Bob Marley, the Reggae musician who became popular in the 1970s and who remains a politically relevant musical personage today—well beyond his death in 1981, is vitally important to the contemporary development of political music, and recognition of this can be found among many sources. For example, *Time Magazine* named one of his recordings (*Exodus*) as the "Album of the 20th century," while the BBC labeled one of his songs ("One Love") as the "Song of the Century." "Purists" might at first retreat from the idea of comparing a classical composer of Wagner's stature to any contemporary popular artist, especially a popular artist who does not utilize the classical style of music. But focusing on musical styles threatens to miss some of the interesting similarities between Marley's and Wagner's perspectives of the political world and, indeed, the human condition. If the political philosophies of Marley and Wagner are to continue to be seen as valuable contributions to our own understanding of politics in this 21st Century world, one should not let variations in musical styles act as a screening variable that prevents us from perceiving how two important musical personas see many aspects of human life and its political organization in a sometimes strikingly similar fashion. There are, of course, great differences between the two composers, and I do not suggest that the comparison be taken too far. The primary idea here is to make a case for political manifesto music, not to force a comparison beyond its limits. Marley and Wagner are seen here simply as examples of composers who have created such music.

It is not essential that the current analysis be comparative, and I only take the idea of comparing Marley with Wagner up to a heuristically useful point. But music in general is "fun," and it is also usually fun to make comparisons between artists, especially when the artists are musically very different. Since I do make some explicit comparisons between Marley and Wagner in this chapter, it is helpful at the outset to explain why I extend the discussion in this way rather than simply limiting my explanation of political manifesto music to two separate treatments of the two composers. Much has been written about individual composers and performers, and there is no shortage of written work offering interpretations of Marley's or Wagner's music individually. But commentaries that are strictly limited to aspects of individual artists limit the scope of the analyses to themes that do not transcend the unique characteristics of the individuals concerned. Transcending artist individuality (without avoiding it altogether, of course) is often helped by making some comparative comments relating to themes of social and political theory as presented by those artists. If we want to understand how music can present a generalized political perspective, we can note some of the common social and political ideas conveyed in the music without downgrading the generality of these ideas to idiosyncracies of isolated artists.

Among all the chapters in this volume, none are so clearly positioned to elicit heated argument among readers as this one, and it is not my desire to attempt to resolve fully the controversies that will inevitably be raised here. Political music is supposed to be controversial, and political manifesto music is arguably the most controversial type of political music since the political ideas presented in the music have the opportunity to be more fully fleshed out. But the most serious issue, of course, is whether or not a comparison between some of the political ideas of Marley and Wagner is possible in the first place. By the end of this chapter it will become obvious to all readers that I think such a comparison can be made, and that such a comparison is at least heuristically useful to the broader purpose of describing some of the complexities that are inherent in the ideas of both artists considered separately. That is, I find that I gain some added understanding of Marley when I look at his musically expressed ideas from the perspective of Wagner, and visa versa.   In particular, I find that Marley and Wagner have their greatest point of connection with regard to how they each see love as an engine of revolutionary change, and toward the end of this chapter I discuss at some length the merits of this idea.

Nonetheless, it is certainly not necessary for readers to agree with this or other comparative ideas that I offer later in this chapter between the political views of Marley and Wagner.   The comparisons are made with a serious sense of musical enthusiasm driven by a desire to understand each composer in as broad a sense a possible, and it is in my general nature to encourage this type of engagement in discussions of musically mediated political ideas. But some readers may want to focus on the two artists as separate examples of composers of political manifesto music, and no harm is done here if the comparative ideas are downplayed.   Indeed, the purpose of this chapter is not to force the comparison (however useful it may or may not be from a heuristic perspective), but rather to describe how some artists can embed complex and generally coherent political perspectives into music.   The possibility of approaching the material presented in this chapter via multiple interpretive paths is made easier since I treat the two composers separately before making comparisons, leaving the reader with the individual decision of how to appraise the subsequent comparative ideas.

Before proceeding further, it is useful to qualify what the current analysis is not.   This is not a definitive and comprehensive treatment of the political views of either Bob Marley or Richard Wagner as defined individually.   It would not be possible to do this within the page limits of a single essay, or perhaps even an entire volume.   Thus, some readers may wonder why I have not addressed favored aspects of either of these artist's life, music, or political views.   For example, I have made no attempt here to offer a contextual, Jamaican, or even Third World interpretation to the origins of Marley's political thought.   Similarly, I have avoided a discussion of Wagner's more notable eccentricities, such as his concerns about vegetarianism or antivivisectionism, and I make no mention of his quarrels with Frederich Nietzsche (see especially, Magee, 2000, chapter 17). As interesting as these things are, much has been written about them elsewhere, and they remain peripheral to my main argument. Here I dwell on the case for political manifesto music, and by necessity I must restrict these pages to a discussion of the political ideas of Marley and Wagner that most clearly support this case.

I begin this discussion with a focus on the germane aspects of Bob Marley's political thought as it appears in his music, allowing the focus to encompass his integration of politics with his deeply spiritual view of life. I then introduce Wagner and his "Ring" operas. From there I move to a discussion of some crucial similarities between Marley's and Wagner's views of politics, love, the state of Nature, and the consequences of these ideas on the issue of revolution.

Robert Nesta Marley

Less has been written about Bob Marley than Richard Wagner. However, Timothy White's book, *Catch a Fire: The Life of Bob Marley*, is by far the most extensive, definitive, and updated work describing Marley's life, his musical accomplishments, and his Rastafarian beliefs (White 2000). (See also on the web, http://www.bobmarley.com, accessed December 2002.) Bob Marley, the Jamaican-born singer and songwriter, together with his band, The Wailers, composed and performed some of the most political songs of the last century. His preferred style of music was Reggae, which is a musical form that evolved from Ska, which itself has roots in the rhythm and blues sounds of New Orleans and elsewhere. Marley forced two primary evolutionary leaps onto Reggae. The first was to incorporate new musical forms and sounds, including rock and electric ideas, very much the same way Waylon Jennings and Willie Nelson transformed country music through the development of the "outlaw" sound. But the second was to tie Reggae irrevocably to a politicized view of Rastafarian spirituality.

Marley often utilized political allegory and symbolism, and examples of such exist in abundance (e.g., the meaning of the "Small Axe," White 2000, pp. 23-4). But he also used his lyrics to convey explicit political messages. These messages were in essence political speeches aimed largely at the poor, under-represented, and often illiterate masses. His audience utilized him the same way contemporary readers utilize op-ed pieces in, say, *The New York Times*. Marley interpreted the world for these people, people who suffered and who desperately wanted someone to explain to them why they were suffering. As with all op-ed pieces, there was a slant or spin to Marley's words, and his spin was to view the world in both Rastafarian and political terms. It was not inevitable that these two ideas, one spiritual and the other secular, would bond so closely. Indeed, it was Marley's unique energy and charisma that made this happen, and he ended up being the world's leading proponent of this potent fusion of ideas, virtually an ambassador to the world for political Rastafarianism.

In the Amharic language of Ethiopia, "Ras" means "prince." The Ethiopian Emperor Haile Selassie I was named "Ras Tafari" before his coronation. Thus, Rastafarianism is a religion named after Prince Tafari. The religion has its origins with a speech by Marcus Garvey in Madison Square Garden in New York City in which it is claimed (with some dispute) that he stated that blacks of African descent should "Look to Africa for the crowning of a Black King. He shall be the Redeemer." The splendor of the coronation of Ras Tafari was such that many black residents of Jamaica's poor saw this as the fulfillment of prophesy, and a religion was born. Rastafarianism began to spread quickly in Jamaica in the 1930s, no doubt driven by the same desperation that held the attention of other parts of the world during the years of the Great Depression.

The beliefs and practices of Rastafarianism are important to understand since they are the underpinning of Marley's political views, and some readers may find that these views sequentially lead to the heart of the intellectual correspondence between Marley and Wagner. Among Rastafarians there is, of course, the strong tie to Ethiopia, which is viewed as a holy land by Rastafarians. The religion views itself as a correction to Judaism and Christianity which are seen as having been corrupted by what one might loosely call modern society, or what Rastafarians would call the "Babylon system," which I discuss below. Three Rastafarian practices are important to introduce at this point: (1) the use of marijuana, (2) vegetarianism and other dietary matters, and (3) dreadlocks. None of these things can be understood adequately without first delineating the Rastafarian perspective of the Babylon system.

For Rastafarians, the suffering that exists in the world is due to the Babylon system. The term "Babylon" refers to much more than simply modern civilization. It references the idea of confusion and the inability to communicate, or even to know one's self. Babylon is the product of a false sense of existence that is defined by the market-based valuation of human life combined with behavioral rules and social order that are contrary to Nature. The Babylon system is maintained by continually enforcing this rule-based, illusory and distorted concept of reality on a large body of oppressed masses. Indeed, there is a great deal of similarity between the idea of the Babylon system and the Sanskrit concept of *"maya"* (roughly, illusion) as it has been expressed by pundits of Vedic philosophy. Babylon addresses a way of thinking that acts to bond people to a way of life, and to suffering. It keeps people working, slave-like, in an economic and social system of exploitation by eliminating their ability to see themselves for whom they actually are, free beings created by God (or "Jah" for "Jehovah"). Of course, this idea of an enslaving false consciousness among the masses is not new, and Marx and others, using different intellectual designs, have addressed the issue in the context of evolving industrial societies. But the Rastafarian perspective of the Babylon system seems to find greater correspondence with the Sanskrit idea of *maya* than with many other manifestations of the idea of false consciousness.

Bob Marley's primary mission with regard to his music and

lyrics, is to help people break free of the Babylon system of thought. In a sense, until people are free from this intellectual and spiritual confinement, they are asleep, or perhaps not fully sentient and self-aware. They need to awaken to free themselves. While the role of a messiah, prophet, or teacher is to help the people wake from their Babylonian mentality, it is nonetheless the responsibility of the people to rebel and finally free themselves from this imprisonment once they are awake.

It is here that Marley's Rastafarian understanding of the state of Nature becomes so important, and, indeed, this is a potential point of contact between Marley and Wagnerian thought as expressed within the "Ring" operas. Within Rastafarianism, people are born innocent of the rules of society, those very rules that organize all of our human world. In this innocent state, people are naturally in spiritual alignment with Jah, living in harmony with Nature and at peace with themselves. But the rules of society invade the way people think of themselves, leaving them in the end without a clear knowledge of who they really are, without understanding their true value as beings, and without any sense of their connection to Jah. The spiritual goal of Rastafarianism is to return people to that innocent state of Nature so that they can love not only Jah, but themselves as well.

It is from the perspective of the Rastafarian understanding of the state of Nature and the mental condition one has to have in order to be in tune with Nature that one needs to view the use of marijuana (alternately called "herb" or "ganja"). Rastafarians believe that most people need help to free their mentality from the intellectual and spiritual bondage of the Babylonian system. Marijuana is used to help transcend Babylon's control of the personality, and its use should be understood only in terms of this limited context. Although Rastafarians have often been dismissed in Western society as endorsing a "drug culture," this is not an appropriate portrayal of this group or their belief system. Indeed, Rastafarians have strict dietary rules that prohibit the use of all other intoxicants, including all alcohol and tobacco products. Rastafarians also have other dietary prohibitions, including the avoidance of all meat (with an emphasis on pork), various forms of marine life, snails, and even salt (White 2000, p. 12). This dietary orientation is similar to some aspects of Kosher and Islamic diets, although much more restrictive than either. The basic idea is that one's food should be as "pure" as possible, which supports the notion that one's diet should encourage a bonding with Nature.

It is perhaps helpful to view the Rastafarian use and concept of marijuana in the context of methods employed by other religions to allow people to transcend the barriers of the physical world. For example, Islam has its own approaches to mystical spirituality, and Sufism is one such tradition. Within Sufism are orders such as the Whirling Dervishes, Howling Dervishes, Shaven Dervishes, Silent Dervishes, and others. The common bond between these orders is the belief that it is possible to do things (mostly in trance-like states) that enable a person to bypass the conscious mind in order to have true spiritual experiences. Catholics count rosary beads in order to escape the limitations of conscious-mind thinking and to focus on the spiritual realm, while contemplative traditions (Buddhism, Hinduism, etc.) variously use postures, repetitive words (mantras), concentration, and/or breathing techniques to accomplish much the same thing. The general idea among all of these approaches is that ordinary consciousness confines one's inner vision, and that something out of the ordinary is needed to transcend this barrier. What is different for Rastafarianism with respect to these other spiritual approaches is not the belief that the conscious mind is often incapable of seeing a greater spiritual reality without help, but rather that the type of help that is most useful is a psychoactive plant. The Rastafarian choice to use marijuana for spiritual growth is certainly more of a consequence of the wretched poverty of the agriculturally-based Jamaican masses than of any conscious effort to exploit marijuana as a recreational drug.

Dreadlocks are yet another important component of this Rastafarian quest to re-unite with Nature. The term "dreadlocks" was originally used by believers to mock those who looked aghast at the Rastafarian appearance (since they were looking in "dread" at what they saw). But the idea of not cutting or combing one's hair is tied to the idea that the mental and spiritual control of the Babylon system over the lives of the masses is re-enforced by repetitive grooming practices that require people to look a certain acceptable way. Again, conformity to rules that are antithetical to the state of Nature is the primary issue. But there is more. By allowing one's hair to grow naturally into twining ropy dreadlocks, one is constantly reminding oneself of one's true nature. When a Rastafarian looks into a mirror, he sees a being that is out of conformity with the Babylon system, and this helps to re-affirm to the Rastafarian believer his true identity as a creature of Nature and a child of Jah.

Bob Marley often wrote and organized his music in a fashion that encourages the analysis of its political content. He tends to compartmentalize the music within his albums, with each song addressing a distinct aspect of his political and/or spiritual philosophy. Sometimes there is very little repetitive overlap between the subjects of the various songs on one album. Indeed, it is often best to examine his albums as unified works that portray a complex point of view that can only be understood by listening to all of the songs as one mix.

For example, one of Marley's most significant political albums is *Survival*, released in the Summer of 1979. For heuristic reasons, I use it as a primary focus for the analyses presented here. *Survival* contains ten songs, all of which tend to focus on one component of Marley's belief system.

Some examples of Marley's organizing style across songs are helpful in the current context. With Marley's first song in the *Survival* album, "So Much Trouble In the World," he acknowledges the difficulties that exist in the world by outlining both their depth and scope. The troubles are not just among the downtrodden masses, but across all social levels. Marley inserts a note of pregnancy in this song, suggesting that revolutionary change may come quickly and unexpectedly in the current setting, and that people should be on the lookout for this potential. His second song, "Zimbabwe," acts as an example of how the oppressive system is maintained. This song was written specifically to support the consolidation efforts of the new nation following its struggle to emerge from the wreckage of Rhodesia. The message also addresses the need to avoid internal conflicts among the two primary groups of Zimbabwe freedom fighters (one led by Joshua Nkomo and the other by Robert Mugabe). There is an explicit reference to the plan of white Zimbabweans to continue to control black Africans by encouraging division and discord between Nkomo and Mugabe supporters. It is worth noting that this is a good example of Marley as a political opinion writer who seeks to explain contemporary politics to his listeners.

Marley's next song on the *Survival* album, "Top Rankin," acts to generalize the theme of the more targeted perspective of "Zimbabwe." A recurrent idea in Marley's thought is the need for the oppressed to avoid division among themselves. In "Top Rankin," Marley returns to the point that the social elites are trying to encourage discord among the oppressed as a way of controlling them. He declares that those elites are frightened that the masses may unite and pose a real threat to the established order. Following "Top Rankin," the next song contains an explanation of the Babylon system, including how it works through the educational and religious institutions of society. As the remainder of the album continues, each song sequentially adds an extra layer of social theory that in total is aimed at offering Marley's oppressed masses a more or less complete world view that identifies the roots of oppression, offers examples of such, explains how the oppressive and corrupt system works, and outlines the means to liberation through a return to a "natural" state that is immune to control and manipulation by social and political elites. Indeed, this album taken as a single coherent treatment of political ideas can be seen as an example of a musically-mediated political manifesto.

We can now turn our attention to Richard Wagner to describe how some of his music can be viewed in a similar "political manifesto" context. Following my introduction of relevant aspects of Wagner's thought and his "Ring" operas, I extend the discussion to compare some elements of Marley's ideas to those of Wagner. Again, the comparative ideas are done with a spirit of musical enthusiasm that I find inherent to the field of political musicology generally, and my hope is that some readers find these comparisons intellectually engaging.

A Prelude to Wagner

One cannot discuss the politics of Wagner's music without at least mentioning the politics of Wagner (see also Bokina 1997, pp. 86-90). A great deal has been written and said about Wagner's horrifically antisemitic views (for example, see Katz 1986, Magee 2000, pp. 343-80; and Berger 1998, pp. 365-70) , and it is unfortunate that his antisemitism has occasionally hindered consideration of some of Wagner's other political ideas. Some commentators simply stop their discussion of Wagner's political views with the observation that he was one of Hitler's most favored composers. While this was also true of Beethoven (Dennis 1996, chapter 4), it is largely due to Wagner's explicit antisemitism that the charge of a Hitler association sticks with greater force. The fact that Wagner died in 1883 does not save him from this condemnation because of the transcending historical significance of the Holocaust. Similarly, he is not saved by the fact that his personal politics were those of a leftist anarchist/revolutionary and not those of a proto-fascist. The magnitude of the tragedy of the Holocaust simply crushes any attempt to separate Wagner's antisemitic views from the eventual manifestation of antisemitism that led to the torture and death of millions. One can understand why even playing Wagner's music is still so controversial in Israel today, despite professionally courageous efforts to separate Wagner's music from his antisemitic beliefs by a variety of conductors and performers, such as Daniel Barenboim, the Jewish conductor who has conducted some Wagner pieces with a German orchestra under daring conditions in Jerusalem [see "Playing a Bit of Wagner Sets Off an Uproar in Israel," by Joel Greenberg, *The New York Times*, 9 July 2001, p. A9(N)].

Wagner nonetheless presents a profound collection of political ideas in musical form that remain material to us. Indeed, it is as if there are two Wagners: (1) the personal and vile Wagner, and (2) the musical Wagner. Reconciling the two Wagners has long been a subject of debate. But there can be no doubt that the musical Wagner was a genius, and his ability to interweave potent political allegory into his music finds rare equal in the operatic world even today. The "Ring" operas are perhaps the best example of this, and it is to these works that we now turn.

The Essential Plot and Allegory of the "Ring" Operas

The plots of Wagner's "Ring" operas have been summarized and interpreted numerous times elsewhere, including the now dated but still valuable treatment by George Bernard Shaw (1966[1898]) in which Shaw outlines much of the political content of the works with respect to Wagner's own anarchist beliefs as well as the events and conditions of his day. Another helpful and detailed discussion of the plots of these operas can be found in Volume I of Ernest Newman's examination of the stories of Wagner's operas (Newman 1930, pp. 158-285). Yet a brief treatment of the plot and its allegory is needed here as a baseline from which interpretations and comparisons can then be made with respect to the more general topic of political manifesto music.

The "Ring" (formally, *Der Ring des Nibelungen*, or "The Ring of the Nibelung") is a collection of four operas that are intended to be performed sequentially during a nearly week-long performance (including breaks). To call the collection of four operas simply the "Ring" is a commonly accepted shortcut reference, and this convenience is used here throughout. The four "Ring" operas are: (1) *Das Rheingold*, (2) *Die Walküre*, (3) *Siegfried*, and (4) *Götterdämmerung*. All four "Ring" operas follow a single plot, and for the purpose of this essay, it is not necessary to discuss the political meanings of the four operas separately since the plot elements, the allegory, and the symbols are continuous throughout.

The "Ring" opens with a scene of three beautiful water

nymphs who both attract and tease a lustful dwarf named Alberich. The nymphs reside in a blissful and naive state of Nature. They have a serious job: to guard some magic gold in a rock that can be forged into a ring of world-dominating power. Part of their naivete is to assume that no one can use the gold since only someone who abandons love could forge such a ring. Alberich promptly swears to abandon love forever and steals the gold. He then makes the ring of power and uses it to enslave his fellow dwarfs in mines from which he amasses even more gold.

In this setting, the nymphs represent those who live in a perfect and unperturbed state of Nature. They have not encountered beings with motives that would violate the harmony that is normal for that state of Nature—especially the abandonment of love, and thus are naive when they then encounter Alberich. Alberich represents the type of being who gains and maintains power by force, in the sense of a totalitarian leader. There is no attempt on Alberich's part to civilize his rule over his fellow dwarfs, and there is no ambiguity that he serves only his own selfish interests.

The "Ring" then introduces a variety of gods, the king of whom is Wotan. As with Alberich, Wotan also rules his own realm. But Wotan tries to govern by developing a civilized code of behavior that includes the practice of making formal written agreements (contracts). These contracts are between agreeing parties, and they represent documents such as constitutions and laws. For Wotan, contracts are written on his large staff, which is a masculine representation of the threat of force which may be used to ensure compliance with the contracts, thereby maintaining social order. One can think of the staff as an allegorical representation of the police and military in a modern polity ruled by law.

Central to the theme of the "Ring" operas, Wotan's essential nature is not much different from that of Alberich, despite Wotan's use of the organizational trappings of modern civilization (rules of behavior applicable to all). While Alberich takes what he wants by force, Wotan uses legal trickery to get the same results. For

Wotan, contracts are not used for creating a society with a generalized code of justice, but rather for forcing the masses through legalistic means to act as he wants them to act. Wotan simply twists the interpretation of contractual obligations such that he can achieve whatever he wants in the end. In his more potent moments, he relies on Loge, a trickster god of fire (one can loosely read in this, a lawyer who has a tendency to lie), who is a specialist in finding loopholes in contracts. This idea is introduced early by having two giants build a castle (Valhalla) which is to be the official residence of Wotan and the other gods. The fortress represents a capital city from which a society is ruled. Wotan avoids paying for the fortress in the manner agreed to in the contract which is written on his staff, but in doing so he is forced to steal the ring of power from Alberich and give it to the giants.

Wotan and his trickster companion, Loge, travel to the underworld to steal the ring of power from Alberich. By the time they get there, Alberich has also obtained (through "research and development" done by his brother, Mime) a helmet that allows the wearer to become invisible as well as to change shapes. He uses this both for defense and to spy on those whom he oppresses. As Shaw has noted, the helmet represents the "High Hats" of society. "It makes a man invisible as a shareholder, and changes him into various shapes, such as a pious Christian, a subscriber to hospitals, a benefactor of the poor, a model husband and father, a shrewd, practical independent Englishman, and what not, when he is really a pitiful parasite on the commonwealth, consuming a great deal, and producing nothing, feeling nothing, knowing nothing, believing nothing, and doing nothing except what all the rest do, and that only because he is afraid not to do it, or a least pretend to do it" (Shaw 1966, p. 19). The use of the helmet also finds correspondence with efforts at intelligence gathering for the purpose of controlling others, and this would be comparable to the use of spying to both maintain order within a society as well as to protect a regime from foreign aggression. Modern-day comparisons would include everything from the centralized maintenance of credit and tax histories for all members of society to governmental surveillance of persons considered to be risks to the community.

Wotan and his companion trick Alberich and steal the ring of power, the magic helmet, and Alberich's stock of gold. Wotan eventually gives all of this to the giants, thereby escaping from his earlier contractual obligation with them. One giant kills the other, and then turns into a dragon (using the magic helmet) and hoards all of the wealth. In the meantime, the gods move into their new capital, Valhalla. What we have now is a social order that is built upon a corrupt foundation. Wagner's grand musical themes as the gods enter and assume control over Valhalla reflect all of the pomp of governing regimes, but also the illusion of power rather than its reality (Donington, 1969, pp. 98-101).

At some point, Wotan travels on Earth and fathers two twin children, a boy and a girl, Siegmund and Sieglinde. The twins are separated and grow up not knowing one another. They also do not know that Wotan is their father. When Siegmund grows up, he rescues his sister from an evil husband, and in the process obtains a magical sword left by his father. They fall in love, and Sieglinde becomes pregnant. The evil husband returns to kill the man who stole his wife, and Siegmund would kill him with the magical sword except that Wotan is threatened by his jealous wife not to allow it. Wotan initially wants to make an exception regarding the social rule forbidding incestuous marriages. He loves Siegmund, but selfishly wants him to have the magic sword so that he can kill the dragon that is hoarding the ring of power and return the ring to Wotan. His wife's refusal to allow this forces him to obey the rules of society rather than fulfill his plan, and this requirement becomes a self-reflective turning point in Wotan's psychology.

Brünnhilde, another of Wotan's illegitimate daughters (this one the product of his rape of Erda, the Mother Earth goddess), wants to help her half-brother, Siegmund. But she is stopped by Wotan, who shatters the magic sword, thereby allowing Siegmund to be killed by Sieglinde's husband. Brünnhilde collects the pieces of the sword and takes Sieglinde away. She manages to help her half-sister escape before Wotan catches up with them. Wotan, angry at the rebellion/disobedience of Brünnhilde, places her in a sleep state on the top of a mountain ringed with fire, where she can be rescued only by a man who knows no fear. The fire is a trick (in the sense that it is not real) created by Loge, and it represents the fabrications that civilization uses to conjure a controlling fear (as in the fear of Hell) in the minds of the masses. Later, Sieglinde gives birth to a son, Siegfried, who will re-forge and use Wotan's broken sword.

Siegfried's mother, Sieglinde, dies during childbirth in the wilderness, and Siegfried is raised by Mime, Alberich's brother. Siegfried grows up hating Mime. He is never introduced to society, so he remains in what one might call an angry state of Nature. Because he never knows how society forces people to obey its rules, Siegfried knows no fear (although he eventually wishes to experience it). Shaw has noted that Siegfried as a character personifies Wagner's anarchist friend Michael Bakunin (Shaw 1966, pp. 47-9). Siegfried finds out from Mime that the broken sword that was left in Mime's care is the sword of his true father, and he manages to re-forge it. Mime tries unsuccessfully to kill Siegfried, but then decides to try again later after helping him experience fear by letting him fight the dragon who hoards the ring of power. Siegfried ends up killing the dragon and retrieving the ring of power as well as the magic helmet. He disappointingly never experiences fear, but he does discover Mime's treachery and kills him.

Throughout these events, Siegfried obtains information from a bird, from which it can be deduced that communication with Nature offers a natural form of espionage (as compared with the technology of the magic helmet) that one might parallel with the idea of intuition. Siegfried hears about Brünnhilde from the bird and finds out that only one who does not know fear can save her. He follows the bird to Brünnhilde's mountaintop prison, and along the way encounters Wotan. In a brief conflict, Siegfried shatters Wotan's staff with his sword (the same sword that Wotan originally shattered with his staff). At this point, it is obvious that Wotan is impotent as a leader. If Wotan represents the government of a civilized state, this government no longer has the energy to rule. Allegorically, Siegfried, personifying the thirst for revenge sought by an angry Nature, is too powerful to be stopped by any corrupt leader who no longer has the moral authority to rule. Siegfried goes on to awaken and love Brünnhilde.

The end of the "Ring" is long, and the plot is complicated. But in essence, Siegfried is tricked and drugged by some who are involved with the son of Alberich. Siegfried is killed, and Brünnhilde ends the opera burning up in the flames of Siegfried's cremation. The ring of power is returned to the water nymphs of the Rhine (the same nymphs that open the first of the four "Ring" operas), and Valhalla burns and crumbles simultaneously with the cremation of Siegfried's body. The preparation for the burning of Valhalla is made by Wotan himself, who has abandoned all pretense of continuing his corrupt reign. The revolution of Siegfried and Brünnhilde is now complete. Nature's power (the ring) has now been returned to it, and the rule of the gods (that is, corrupt civilization) is ended. Nature, in all its anarchic splendor, has reclaimed its rightful stewardship of life on Earth.

Alberich, Wotan, and the Babylon System

Both Marley and Wagner were revolutionaries in a very real sense, and both Marley and Wagner believed that they could help initiate world-healing revolutions through their art. While Marley's revolutionary tone is explicit in his lyrics, such as when he encourages his listeners to "Rebel" in the song, "Babylon System," Wagner's intent needs to be interpreted from the perspective of his own world view.

Clearly the most important philosopher to have influenced Wagner, especially with regard to his writing of the "Ring" operas, was Ludwig Feuerbach (see especially, *The Essence of Christianity*, and *The Principles of the Philosophy of the Future*.) Feuerbach was hugely influential in the development of German thought in the 1840's and 1850's. Both his views and style of writing contrasted with a previously dominating Hegelian approach to philosophy, and intellectual circles found his ideas to be as exciting as they were new. Wagner wrote the libretto of the "Ring" operas around 1850, and his autobiography clearly describes Feuerbach's influence on the ideas that he imbedded in these operas (see also, Magee 2000, chapter 4).

Feuerbach—and thus Wagner—saw religion as a way of personifying solutions to the troubles that are natural to the human condition. God (or gods) are not real things in places like Heaven. Rather, humans invent these things as intellectual constructs as a means of placing order on otherwise chaotic and terrifying lives. Religion is not something to be ridiculed by philosophers. Rather, religion is a window into which it is possible to see deeply into the mysteries of the human psyche. Wherever there is need, there is a god invention. To calm the fear of death, we have an immortal God, and an immortal soul. To free us from panic with regard to human misery, we have an omniscient and omnipotent God. To cover our particular needs, we have either gods for those needs (e.g., love, war, etc.) or saints to whom we can make particular requests for help and guidance. Thus, Wagner (through Feuerbach) is not a spiritual man in any true sense of the word, but he respects spirituality as a real organizing construct that is fundamentally needed by the masses to sustain them amidst lives of strain.

Thus, in the "Ring" operas, Wagner's gods are quite human in character. These characters tell us not about divinity, but about human nature. Indeed, Isaiah Berlin once characterized the gods in the "Ring" as "just a lot of gangsters" (Magee 2000, p. 54). Importantly, the chief god, Wotan, is quite comparable in many respects with Alberich, the evil dwarf. In the end, both are found to be hopelessly corrupt, and both are defeated (and *need* to be defeated). Neither Wotan nor Alberich produce any lasting good for society or for Earth. That one is more evil in method than the other is surprisingly irrelevant in the "Ring" universe. The trouble with both is that they equally represent deviations from what Wagner might call the order of Nature.

For Wagner, the state of Nature is not the feared chaotic state from which man needs government and social order to free us from the ever-present risk of anarchistic war where all are against all, as Arendt (1958, p. 32) has described this 17th Century Hobbesian view (Leviathan, Part I, ch.13). Rather, Nature provides a supportive environment that would amply provide for the needs of all humans if only humans would live in harmony with Nature. But humans decide by themselves to live in a state of disharmony with Nature. The greatest offenders of this are elites who consciously choose to wage a war of control with their fellow man, trying by any available means to amass wealth and power. These elites compel others through coercion of various means to work for them, and in the process the elites steal the fruits of these labors.

For both Marley and Wagner, the key to living in harmony with Nature is love. With respect to Wagner, we know that he held this personal view from his letters to August Roeckel (n.d., pp. 82-7). Those who exploit others for their own benefit are incapable of loving those whom they exploit. But those who choose love over exploitation can also choose to make love the principle by which all human interactions are governed. In a very real sense, government in the perfect state of Nature is not the rule of law or force, but the rule of love.

Returning to the contrast between Alberich and Wotan, at first they appear to represent two ends of an opposing spectrum. The former represents government by theft, torture, and cruel exploitation. The latter represents the rule of law as seen in a more civilized state. But the human desire to amass wealth and power corrupts the rule of law so that, in the end, its outcome in terms of its effect on the masses is no more internally liberating than that of a totalitarian system. This is seen in the attempts by Wotan to find loopholes in the contracts that are written on his own staff. The original promise of these contracts is entirely unimportant to Wotan. What is important is that he achieves what he wants regardless of the interests of others, which is, of course, the driving motivation of Alberich as well.

At this point, it is useful to suggest an element of correspondence between Marley and Wagner, in particular with respect to Marley's portrayal of the Babylon system itself. Babylon is a consequence of the desire of man to organize his political and social world. The organization can be brutal, as with an authoritarian regime, or relatively benign, as with a modern democracy. But the result is the same regardless; with either system people are mentally and spiritually enslaved. Here it can be seen that the similarities in political outcome that exist despite the contrasting governmental approaches represented by Alberich and Wotan suggests a commonality between Wagner's ideas and Marley's Rastafarian view of the Babylonian system. For both Marley and Wagner, outside of a state of Nature, all forms of governance lead to the same condition of alienation for the oppressed masses.

In his song, "Babylon System," Marley takes aim at both explaining the nature of the Babylon system explicitly and the need to rebel against it. Here Marley clearly explains that the elites of society want to control the very nature of the individual, and he expresses his defiance of this effort by declaring, "We refuse to be what you wanted us to be. We are what we are. That's the way it's going to be." He declares that the elites cannot control the masses any longer through a corrupted educational system that gives only lip service to the concepts of equal opportunity, freedom, and liberty. Sympathizing with those masses he states elegantly, "We've been trodding on the winepress much too long" before explicitly encouraging his listeners to "Rebel."

The significance of the winepress metaphor is important in this context since it references the idea that the fruits of the labor of the masses are enjoyed not by the masses themselves but by the elites of society, which seems somewhat correspondent with Wagner's view as seen, for example, with the enslavement of Alberich's fellow dwarfs. Marley explains in "Babylon System" that the system itself is a vampire that sucks the lifeblood out of people who are enslaved by it. As with Wagner, the system explicitly includes both "civilized society" with church and university as well as societies with more authoritarian regimes. Marley does not hesitate in stating in the song that the educated graduates of the system act to reinforce the Babylon system through barbarous acts of coercion—including theft and murder—by merely participating within the system. The rules of civil society are not designed to assist the masses to "organize out" the chaos of anarchic Nature. Rather, the rules are made by elites to assist those same elites in maintaining control over their wealth and power. With regard to Wagner, theft by brute force is the norm for Alberich, which includes stealing physical wealth as well as the idea of rape (theft of physical pleasure). For Wotan, theft by legalistic trickery is the method of choice. However, Wotan will also resort to more blunt means (read in this, "militaristic means") of achieving his aims if his primary method of legalistic trickery is not feasible, such as when he rapes the Earth Mother goddess, Erda, as a means of obtaining information from her.

Intriguingly, the solution to all of this abuse by the elites of a corrupt society appears somewhat similar for both Marley and Wagner, a two-step process that must begin with revelation. Marley orders his listeners to "Tell the children the truth.... Somebody got to pay for the work that we've done. Rebel." For Marley, revelation is found in his songs, whereas for Wagner the same is found in the "Ring" itself. Revelation followed by rebellion or revolution seems to be a common prescription for both Marley and Wagner, and I discuss this idea further below. While this may seem obvious from the tone of Marley's lyrics, it cannot be overemphasized at this point that Wagner consciously intended for the production of the "Ring" operas to act as the spark that would ignite this revolutionary transformation of society as well (Magee 2000, pp. 58-9).

Life without Fear, Siegfried, and the Rastas

Wagner portrays two "personalities" for the state of Nature. The first is a personality of naive innocence that is fundamentally at peace, even slumbering. This state of Nature has more in common with blissful anarchy than hateful chaos (which again contrasts with the Hobbesian view). This is most clearly seen in the opening scene of the first of the "Ring" operas, *Das Rheingold*, in which three water-nymph maidens are given the job of guarding a treasure of gold that is on the top of a rock resting in the water of the Rhine. The nymphs are pretty useless as guards, and much more adept at playing in the water while sensuously teasing the dwarf, Alberich. With Nature's guard down in this manner, it is no surprise that Alberich is able to steal the gold and from it forge the ring of power.

Nature's second personality is revealed in the character of Siegfried, and this is an anarchistic personality in which Nature is fully awake and very angry in a retaliatory sense. Here is where the full power of Nature becomes evident. As a youth, Siegfried, raised by the dwarf, Mime, interacts with no one but Mime and the surrounding forests. Since Mime is a liar and a brute whom Siegfried neither trusts nor loves, the result is that Siegfried is essentially raised as an angry but pure child of Nature itself, beautifully uncivilized yet motivated to find greater meaning in life regardless of the cost. Because Siegfried has never been exposed to the coercive and manipulative control of modern society, he has never been taught to fear. In Marley's sense, Siegfried does not hold any of the false beliefs that would sustain the Babylon system. Indeed, Siegfried does not know fear, which for Wagner is a characteristic of someone fully in synchrony with Nature. It is this lack of fear that gives Siegfried his great power, and it is this same lack of fear that forms a striking contrast with respect to the relative impotence of Wotan, Alberich, and Mime. Siegfried easily destroys Wotan's staff, the contractually laden phallic symbol of power. He is also able to break through the barriers of society in his search for life's meaning, as is symbolized by his easy walk through the ring of false fire surrounding Brünnhilde on her mountaintop prison.

With Siegfried, Nature's naivete is not completely erased, and this remains Siegfried's greatest weakness, and the cause of his downfall when he is tricked and killed by those more cunning than himself in the last of the four "Ring" operas. Nature needs the ally of wisdom in human form combined with revelation in order to overthrow oppression. To fulfill this revolutionary potential, the seductive power of Nature needs to attract the sagacity of others who are drawn to Nature through the power of love, as in the case of Brünnhilde. It is Brünnhilde who ultimately puts two and two together to figure out that corruption is the cause of misery, and it is her embrace of love for Nature (through love for Siegfried) that allows the power of Nature (now guided by wisdom) to flow through her own actions such that she initiates a successful revolution of existing society (see again, Wagner's letters to August Roeckel, n.d., pp. 82-7).

For Marley, the personification of Nature as a power with revolutionary potential is captured by the "Rastaman" or "Dready," the man of Nature (the parallel to Siegfried the anarchist) who stands defiantly in front of corrupt civilization with his dreadlocks in full glory. The dreadlocks themselves represent a return of man to this state of Nature. But they also represent the crowning assumption of Nature's full power (as we see in Siegfried's strength as well). Without ambiguity, this is revolutionary power. Perhaps no song captures this idea as well as "Ride Natty Ride," also in the Survivor album. In this song, Marley declares that "Dready got a job to do," indeed, a destiny that cannot be stripped from him by any element of society. As with Siegfried, Dready lives "having no fear, having no sorrow," for neither Siegfried nor the Dready regret the destruction of the old order. Marley explains that the elite of society openly fight against the Rastaman by building a world of confusion (Babylon), and he explicitly declares that this world is an illusion, with "illusion" conveying the sense of the Sanskrit term "maya."

Marley then makes a direct reference to a test of "fire," a fire that will destroy the old order of civilization and through which the Rastaman will pass unhurt. While one might naturally want to see a connection between this fire and the ring of fire that surrounds Brünnhilde as she lies asleep in her mountaintop prison (see below), the more direct comparison might be the fire that appears at the end of the "Ring" to destroy both the corrupt totalitarian world of Alberich as well as the more temperate Valhalla. With both Marley and Wagner, these are revolutionary fires that are set by those who are liberated from the tyranny of the corrupt world order. The revolutionaries are the Rastaman for Marley and Siegfried (and later, the Siegfried-liberated Brünnhilde) for Wagner. This apparent parallel between the two composers seems supported with respect to Marley's "Ride Natty Ride" when he sings, "Now the fire is burning. Out of control panic in the city, wicked weeping for their gold. Everywhere the fire is burning. Destroying and melting their gold. Destroying and wasting their souls."

Some readers may also perceive a correspondence between Marley's view of the spiritual goal of Rastafarianism relating to the treatment of fear and the dilemma Wagner poses in the "Ring" operas when Wotan punishes his own daughter Brünnhilde for acting out of love to try to save her half-brother, Siegmund. Wotan puts her to sleep on a mountaintop surrounded by a ring of fire that only one who knows no fear can penetrate. The sleep state can be seen as an allegorical parallel to the mentality of all in society who live under the control of rules and false beliefs that corrupt governments use to pervert a free existence that is indigenous to the normal state of Nature. Thus, one interpretation of the fire can be as the fear-based barriers to freedom that intellectually confine us in our prison of mental slumber. Only one who exists in a perfect state of rapport with Nature can break through those barriers since the barriers have no real power if one does not adopt the fear-based belief system that supports them. Again, this is the role of Siegfried, and, from a Rastafarian perspective, of Marley and all Rastafarians. While one should be cautioned against taking the Marley and Wagner comparison too far in this respect, the basic elements exist on both sides to at least support the potential of a correspondence with respect to the treatment of fear by the two composers.

With Marley, the Rastaman revolutionary does not have to physically attack the corrupt civilization or its institutions. Marley is not advocating guerilla warfare. Rather, the Rastaman simply has to exist, or rather to "Be." In Marley's world view, the corrupt society falls by itself when those who are controlled by it wake up and throw off the illusion of fixed order that is sustained by the Babylon system. The Rastamans, with all of their "dreadlock glory," announce the end of the Babylon system by virtue of their very existence. Their refusal to be controlled by the system, as evidenced by both their physical appearance as well as their intellectual enlightenment, immunizes them from the seductions of the system's keepers. Crucially, Valhalla also falls not by the acts of violence from the outside, but by virtue of its own corruption, and Wotan himself both acknowledges the inevitability of the collapse of his corrupt order and the imminent destruction of his capital. The element required for the collapse of Valhalla is the assumption of Nature's power combined with wisdom that is achieved by Brünnhilde through her love for Siegfried. Using a Marley term, it is love that breaks the cycle of Babylonian control and causes the fortress of Valhalla to crumble like a sand castle caught in a wave's wake. Similarly, it is the love of the Rastaman, Brünnhilde's Siegfried, that creates the condition of contagion that sweeps away the illusions without which the Babylon system cannot stand.

Historically, Wagner's approach to politics may be seen as more aggressive than that of Marley. Wagner was not hesitant either in his own life (as evidenced by his participation in the Dresden uprising) or in his music to embrace an active role in revolutionary politics. Recall also that Siegfried eagerly and successfully battled a variety of opponents in physical combat, including Wotan. This characteristic of Wagner's portrayal of revolution probably reflects the influence of anarchists such as the politically active Michael Bakunin, but one may also see here some of the incandescent fervor of Marx who also wrote in that time period of the need to use violence as a catalyst for revolution. Nonetheless, in the end of the "Ring" after all combat is completed, Valhalla causes its own collapse, and one is tempted to note the apparent parallelism between Marley's and Wagner's views of at least this final component of revolution.

Why does Wagner mix both violent and passive components

of revolution? Perhaps this is the result of the mixture of influences that acted on Wagner's thinking. Not all anarchists of Wagner's day were supportive of the violent overthrow of existing civilization. For example, Proudhon (whom Wagner read and admired), saw anarchy as a natural and peaceful evolutionary outgrowth of a "civilized" world in which order has been previously maintained through coercion. That is, society needs to be created by a coercive elite first before the more peaceful order of voluntary anarchism can take hold. Then, anarchy is not disorder, but rather a new and improved stage of social development within which people can sustain social orderliness through voluntary cooperation rather than as a consequence of the threat of sanctions imposed by a more powerful elite. While Wagner both read and was influenced by Proudhon (see Magee 2000, pp. 33-6), what we nonetheless see with Wagner is an embrace of both Proudhon's utopian idea of a peaceful anarchistic society based on voluntary cooperation as well as the use of force (one might say, the force of Nature) to kick the decaying hulk of corrupt government into its grave.

Marley, on the other hand, also sees the destruction of civilization, and similarly views its destruction through the use of the fire metaphor. But it is not the Rastaman who strikes the match or plants the bomb. Rather, the Rastaman is immune to the call of the Babylonian oppressors, and without such confused but willing servants, the Babylon system is no longer sustainable and simply collapses upon itself, just as a tall building will collapse with great force once its foundation is damaged. Thus, Marley's self-appointed role is to assist in the awakening of the masses, thus damaging the foundation of the exploitive system. Once awoken, the masses will no longer participate in the support of Babylon, and without their support, the system of oppression will self-destruct. While one can see these elements in Wagner's "Ring" as well, there is more ambiguity on the preliminary use of force with Wagner.

The Connection Between Love and Revolution

For Wagner, love can be viewed as the driving force behind the idea of revolution. Indeed, it is the renunciation of love that is the cause of oppression in society, as is seen forcefully with Alberich's actions when confronted by the need to choose between power or love in the opening of the "Ring", while it is the return of love within society that corrects this (see also, Donington 1969, pp. 46-48). In the "Ring" operas, this "return of love" theme is seen initially in the love of Brünnhilde for Siegfried. (Note that Wagner has explicitly stated in his letters to Roeckel that humans learn of love and its revolutionary power in an embryonic fashion through intimate contact [Wagner, n.d., pp. 82-7; see also Donington 1990, p.122]). The metaphor, of course, associates love of Nature through its representative, Siegfried.

It is important that Brünnhilde requires at the end of the final "Ring" opera the revelation that both she and Siegfried had been deceived, and that Siegfried was killed through foul play. This revelation triggers her anger, which is actually her assumption of Nature's anger that was formerly expressed through Siegfried, but is now made even more powerful with the addition of wisdom. Brünnhilde is the true revolutionary who acts not through instinct (as is the case with Siegfried), but through certain knowledge of what must be done. That which must be done is the destruction of evil, which is corrupt society. Her love for Siegfried is the ingredient that allows her to assume this power of Nature that is capable of such destruction.

Marley's approach to the issue of love and revolution is more delicate than that of Wagner, but no less real. Three songs show Marley's view on the issue of love in a heuristically useful fashion, "Wake Up and Live," "Redemption Song," and "Could You Be Loved." In "Wake Up and Live," Marley calls on the masses to rise from their "sleepless slumber," the slumber that is characteristic of all who are mentally trapped by the Babylon system (and recall with this the sleep of Brünnhilde when she was surrounded by a false fire). Over and over again Marley begs his listeners to wake up, to be alive. Once one awakes, living as Nature intended is normal, even automatic. Again, revolution is simply the awakening of those who are controlled, since the awakened masses will no longer support Babylonian oppression.

But what is the first step of the awakening process? Does one simply shout into the ear of the Babylonian captives? For Marley, the oppressed must free themselves. There is no savior that will accomplish the job of liberation without the help of those who are slaves of the system. Redemption is a three-step process. First one needs a prophet or teacher who is willing to reach out to the masses, and this is a role that Marley and other Rastafarians play. The second step is to awaken those masses by inviting them to act, and the first act is to get them to speak, or in Marley's case, to sing. This is the essential goal of "Redemption Song." Here Marley describes the role of song in the liberation struggle. He states that he too was mentally enslaved, but he was able to free himself with only the power of his "songs of freedom." Marley then asks his listeners if they will also sing these songs, explaining "Won't you help to sing these songs of freedom? Cause all I ever had, redemption songs, redemption songs." Indeed, for Marley, the songs themselves are both the vehicle and evidence of liberation.

Yet when people are captives of the Babylonian system, asking them to wake up and live may be more than they are capable of doing, even if their initial activity is only to sing. Here is where Marley reveals that the true power of revolution comes through love, the third step of the redemption process. No where is this more clearly heard than in his song "Could You Be Loved?" In this song, Marley gives his listeners the key to being able to rebel. He simply asks if they would allow themselves to be loved. From Marley's perspective, captives of the Babylonian system live totally without love, even for themselves. This is far worse than a plague of low self-esteem. These captives believe that their reality is their fate, and since they live lives in which they are constantly exploited, their value as humans must be equal to that which they experience in life. They live in pain because that is who they are.

But Marley takes the first step to break this destructive state of consciousness by simply asking them if they would allow love to enter their realm. He explains, "Love would never leave us alone. In the darkness there must come out to light." Love leads one out of the darkness of mental captivity; it leads those who live dark lives into the light. But the first step is not for those who are oppressed to love others or Nature. Rather, it is the step of allowing love from the outside to seep into the darkness of one's mental prison. Allowing someone to love you is the first stage to allowing you to love yourself.

Keenly, Marley ends this song with a request for action on the part of his listeners. After asking if they would allow themselves to be loved, he then tells them repeatedly to "say something." He asks for, perhaps even demands, an answer. He acts almost like a therapist sitting at the bedside of a near-comatose patient when he says the final words of this song, "Say something. Could you be loved?" It is the power of love that can seduce such a slumbering person to rise up. Love can break the mental barriers of pain and confusion with a directness that logic or reasoning lack.

In an intriguing parallel, is this not also similar to what Siegfried offers Brünnhilde when she suffers the forced sleep of Wotan? She is mentally disabled while she is surrounded by her prison of fire on the mountaintop, and it is perhaps not too much a stretch to say that this metaphor strikes at the meaning of Marley's diagnosis of those who are captives of the Babylonian system. Crucially, it is Siegfried's quest to offer love, matched by his lack of fear and his assumption of the power of Nature, that allows him to awaken Brünnhilde. Indeed, it is Brünnhilde's responsive and consequent love for Siegfried that bonds her to him so dearly, and which ultimately gives her the power to trigger the destruction of the corruption and evil from which the world suffers. Love awakens and empowers Brünnhilde as nothing else could, and it is love that similarly awakens and empowers the slumbering sufferers of Babylon.

For Wagner, awakening eventually leads to a refusal to participate in a corrupt system, and it is this refusal that leads to revolution. This idea of refusing to participate in a corrupt and enslaving system can be seen in Brünnhilde's situation near the end of the final "Ring" operas when she is forced to marry someone she does not love. When she discovers how her true love, Siegfried, was both deceived and killed, she throws off her oppression (her falsely contrived marriage) and re-asserts her claim—through love—to Siegfried before acting both to honor him in death and to destroy the system that oppressed them both (and the rest of the world).

A close reading of Marley indicates that he addresses this same issue in his own fashion; those who love—and who can be loved—will be drawn to the power of Nature, and no one who lives in a state of bonding with Nature can be bound by any human. Enlightenment (through education or revelation) combined with love of self and Nature yields a personality that is immune to the corrupted ways of thinking that the exploitive Babylonian system requires in order to operate. Again, one who cannot be controlled by the Babylon system destroys the system simply by not participating in it. One who lives in a state correspondent with Nature is one who is truly free, and such is one who lives and breathes love.

Love as an Engine of Political Change

It is important to note that revolutionary politics did not yield much practical fruit for Wagner, and we can acknowledge the truth of Shaw's observation that Wagner has not given us a post-revolutionary path to good governance (Shaw 1966, pp. 100-9). Wagner was disappointed by Bakunin's and Roeckel's experiences (both were imprisoned, and their imprisonments did not result in any social change). On the other hand, Wagner himself was professionally and financially saved not by a revolutionary but by "the establishment"—a king who was apparently more than a little psychologically unstable. Indeed, the left-wing anarchist Siegfrieds of 1848 did not succeed in politics, as is often still the case with utopian revolutionaries today. If success is measured by durability, the Wotans, Loges, and Alberichs of the world are often masterful politicians who survive extended periods of reign. Most modern established democracies still elect (and re-elect) their leaders just as they have done for many years, and some of the nondemocratic world leaders who survive the longest are ruthlessly authoritarian.

Marley similarly does not show us how to choose our leaders, how to govern ourselves, or even how to structure our governmental systems. In short, neither Wagner nor Marley offer a prescription for how to govern after a revolution. What they do offer are some ingredients along the path to revolution. Thus, it is a fair question to ask what we actually get by studying their politically-laden music. If revolution is associated with turmoil, do Wagner and Marley offer us little more than a path to non-ending unrest?

At this point it is necessary to synthesize ideas from the works of Marley and Wagner since they do not explicitly resolve an answer to the above question. Such a synthesis requires some degree of speculation, of course. But it also offers potential insight. Again, Shaw offers some useful direction regarding our current dilemma. "There is no such thing as Man in the world: what we have to deal with is a multitude of men, some of them great rascals, some of them great statesmen, others both, with a vast majority capable of managing their personal affairs, but not comprehending social organization, or grappling with the problems created by their association in enormous numbers.... The government is of course established by the few who are capable of government, though its mechanism once complete, it may be, and generally is, carried on unintelligently by people who are incapable of it, the capable people repairing it from time to time when it gets too far behind the continuous advance or decay of civilization" (Shaw 1966, pp. 67-8). If we, for the sake of argument, allow Shaw's critique of our variable ability as humans to govern ourselves competently on a continual basis to stand, then we can see a permanent contribution to our state of affairs via the political thought of both Wagner and Marley. The key is not to see Wagner and Marley as offering a path to permanent political salvation, but rather a path out of our moments of greatest governmental incapacity.

Life is not fixed, and revolution does not lead to a permanent state of affairs. This contrasts with, say, Beethoven's view of revolution as presented in his opera, *Fidelio*, in which the French Revolution can be seen as a defense of the more static (and thus permanent) idea of republican virtue (see Bokina 1997, chapter 3). What Shaw sees is a need for society to change constantly by cycling between governmental decay and its repair in an ongoing process of slow evolutionary growth. Humanity's experiences of social and political improvement span many centuries, and there is indeed no end to the ups and downs along this path. The recurring phenomenon for this evolutionary path is the punctuation of revolutions in order to get rid of that which is bad, or at least that which is no longer useful. Both Marley and Wagner seem to suggest that these revolutions can often produce the greatest good when they are fundamentally inspired by love rather than, say, a Machiavellian strategy (either "lion" or "fox" [see Lukes 2001]) to shift the causal focus of exploitation from one dominating agent to another.

It is of interest to note that social scientists have rarely examined love as an engine for revolution, despite the fact that a number of powerful revolutionary movements in our species's history have been driven by the concept of love. For example, certainly one can reference Gandhi, Martin Luther King, Jr., and even Jesus as leaders who initiated powerful social and (ultimately, at least in some sense) political movements, and who's followers saw non-romantic and universally directed love as a crucial component of their motivating belief systems. One can argue, for example, that passive resistance as a political strategy resulted from the importance of love in the philosophies of Gandhi and Martin Luther King, Jr., and that passive resistance was not by itself the bottom-line causal root of their beliefs. Indeed, if one tries to argue that passive resistance was the primary ingredient of their pragmatic liberation-oriented political strategies, is it at all convincing to claim that the underlying motivation for these strategies was merely the cold calculation of scheming resistance fighters?

Not all revolutions are driven by the idea of love toward fellow humans. Indeed, most revolutions—always messy—seem to be primarily angry affairs, and it normally takes a long time to resolve the collective trauma that appears inevitable with such epochal shifts in the social and political fabrics of human society. But when revolutions occasionally occur that are guided by leaders who see universally-directed love toward others as a primary engine in their own motivations, societies can benefit in ways that are needed by our species. In some cases, no solutions to ongoing social trauma may be possible in the total absence of love as an engine of change. For example, can a strictly mechanical solution be designed that will resolve the current violence in the Middle East without addressing the need for both Palestinians and Israelis to enjoy living near each other? When Islamic hatred is the dominating emotion directing terrorist revolutionary action against Western societies, can there ever be peace? Similarly, will the Hutus and Tutsis of Rwanda and Burundi ever stop killing themselves in the absence of Mandela-like leaders who preach love and its consequent respect for the individual rather than hate? Sometimes there is simply no alternative for stopping violence and abuse than to teach love in some manner or form, however concentrated or diluted the lessons may have to be within any given set of circumstances. One can say that political violence is stopped by good governance. But is not good governance driven by a desire to treat people equally, fairly, and indeed at least in some sense, lovingly?

Can music serve an effective educational role to influence the behaviors of a society to achieve these aims? First, consider the opposite. Music can teach people to kill, or at least to support killing. Consider the example of the popular songwriter, Simon Bikindi, a Hutu who composed and recorded the government-commissioned songs that were sung in the streets and jungles of Rwanda by thousands of Hutu militia members at the same moments in which they used machetes to hack nearly one million of their Tutsi and moderate Hutu compatriots to pieces during a 100 day genocidal rampage in 1994 ("Killer Songs: Simon Bikindi Stands Accused of Writing Folk Music that Fed the Rwandan Genocide," by Donald G. McNeil Jr., *The New York Times Magazine*, 17 March 2002, pp. 58-9). Consider also that music has been used indirectly to support violence and domination, as when Hitler heavily exploited a contrived Nazi association with Beethoven's music both before and during World War II to culturally support the ideology of German/Aryan superiority with regard to other races (Dennis 1996, chapter four).

If music can teach people to kill, cannot it also teach and inspire members of our societies to re-insert the idea of love into national debates during times of crisis? Are there not pregnant moments in the evolution of our world when the idea of love clearly threatens the continued control over our societies by harsh though established political hierarchies, especially when this idea of love is associated with one or more leaders who combine it with significant personal sacrifice? Is not the use of music to liberate the entrenched thinking of our human masses during these times revolutionary? If music laced with love is not so powerful a force that could threaten the power of political elites, then why were so many songwriter/activists of the 1960s, 1970s, and even 1980s (including Bob Marley) who critiqued society while singing of love and its child of peace watched and sometimes harassed by elements of the United States government during those tumultuous years of the Vietnam War, the Civil Rights Movement, and their aftermath (Kaiser 1988; also, White 2000, pp. xiv-xv)? And then why was Sting's song, 'They Dance Alone," that spoke of the widows and mothers of thousands who "disappeared" during the Pinochet years banned from being performed in Chile during that dictator's period of rule? Even if love is not the message, if music itself is so weak a political medium, then why did Salvador Allende connect so much of his campaign to mobilize peasant, Indian, and leftist masses with personal requests to songwriters such as Victor Jara, Quilapayún, Inti-Illimani, Violeta Parra and others to write and perform songs throughout Chile that taught his revolutionary message (Mattern 1998, chapters 3&4)? Similarly potent examples of music being used to present political messages can be found among the histories of most nations, with the best examples usually coming from the moments of greatest political and social change.

When societies change, music often matters. Wagner and Marley are telling us that the message of music during those times of great evolutionary pregnancy can be crucially enhanced with the empowering glue of love. But they are also telling us that love is a characteristic of our normal state, a state from which we become repeatedly alienated by the evolutionary path of market-based human organization, and it is not irrelevant to recall at this point Durkheim's ideas of anomie and suicide with respect to individuals most isolated from the nurturing bond of a supportive collective. To return to a healthy state of being, we need—at least occasionally—to revisit that almost embryonic status in which we exist in synchrony with Nature. Love—for ourselves and others—is the key to this return. It is a strengthening theme of liberation, in the sense that people who can authentically love others with universal direction (as compared with strictly selfish or romantic intent) are in correspondence with a supportive state of Nature.

Wagner and Marley obviously do not give us answers to all questions of serious social and political change. But they insert an element into the discussion of revolution that is too often lacking from our normal political debates. Perhaps social scientists are more cynical in their treatment of love as an engine of revolution (for reasons that may not be entirely clear), and thus we tend to leave such discussions to visionaries in the arts. But with potentially billions of people on this planet listening to (and learning from) politically potent music, can we afford to ignore the messages of this music? And if the messages sometimes deal with the idea of love as a revolutionary force, can we really afford to disregard this even if at first the idea does not seem practical? If we can examine the lethal role of military force in settling political disputes, is it not also appropriate to consider Lee's observation when he asserts that Wagner is telling us that "we are headed for world destruction if we cannot evolve a political system that does not use money for power, if we cannot develop an ethical system that recognizes and contravenes our self-destructive urges, if we cannot learn to love" (Lee 1990, p. 13). It is music that has often conveyed this idea so convincingly in our society.

Of course, by this time it is clear that I am arguing for a new effort among social scientists to examine the political content of music generally, and I see the efforts of both Marley and Wagner as offering exceptionally robust examples of music intermixed with important political ideas. The millions of people who have listened to the music of these composers and have dwelt on their associated political sentiments suggest by their shear numbers that we should examine the content of these ideas as seriously as we examine the equally important traditional foci of politics and its theory.

The idea of love as an engine of revolution is an idea that is perhaps more timely now than ever before. In some situations, militaristic approaches to political change have not succeeded and simply cannot work in the long run regardless of the effort applied, and the rise of leadership (political, spiritual, or musical) that reminds combatants of their rooted connectedness to all other humans—and especially to their enemies—may be just the ingredient needed to re-direct the potential for greater violence such that peace and tolerance are more likely outcomes.

Wagner portrays deep, bonding love among and between humans as a powerful evolution-correcting political force in his "Ring" operas, as does Marley in much of his politically driven music. It is not naivete that drives the political thoughts of Marley and Wagner. Combined with their critiques of human social and political organization, these are complex, coherent, and muscular ideas which we as social scientists cannot afford to marginalize through either cynicism or neglect. These are ideas that affect more than the intellectual debates of a handful of scholars. These are political ideas which millions of people are hearing regularly, manifestos of "living" political theory powerfully delivered to eager listeners in the form of rhythm, tone, and verse. It is no understatement to say that such ideas when disseminated widely have the potential to change our societies profoundly, especially in times of great stress and uncertainty. As scientists, our intellectual future may in part depend on our ability to understand the ever-more-frequent raging political debates that musically surround us. From time to time, we could do much worse than to turn up the speakers and listen.

Primary Sources for Further Reading

Berger, William. 1998. *Wagner Without Fear*. New York: Vintage Books.

Shaw, George Bernard. 1966(1898). *The Perfect Wagnerite*. New York: Dover.

White, Timothy. 2000(1983). *Catch a Fire: The Life of Bob Marley*. New York: Henry Holt and Co.

And on the web:

http://www.bobmarley.com (accessed December 2002)

CHAPTER 4

Nationalist and Patriotic Music

"Nationalist music" can trace its origins to composers of the Romantic Era, in large part spanning the years from 1820 to 1900. This period saw a rebellion from the prior overwhelming dominance of the Vienna school, and it coincided with a time in which nations were actively forming and consolidating within Europe. These new nations had boundaries, and these boundaries more often than not circumscribed societies with distinctive cultures and histories. Thus, the period essentially "demanded" that some composers embrace musical styles and content that reflected the cultural sensibilities of these new nationalities. Nationalist music is indeed defined by this characteristic of national self-reflection.

However, nationalist music is not limited to this early period from which it originated. A great deal of nationalist music continues to be composed today, and it can be identified as nationalist in as much as it serves the same purpose as the music from the earlier "definitional" time period. It is music that acts as a particularly potent window into a culture. This culture can be widely embraced by an entire nation, or it can be a subset of one or more cultures that are contained within a nation. But when one listens to nationalist music, there can be no doubt that one is experiencing a musical portrayal of a specific culture, a portrayal that is designed to both define and explain some aspect of this culture to a listening audience.

Nationalist music is sometimes confused with patriotic music, and indeed there are some similarities since patriotic music is a sub-genre within nationalist music. But while nationalist music tends to portray a culture, or at least some aspect of a culture, patriotic music has a somewhat different purpose. From *Funk and Wagnall's Standard Dictionary*, a patriot is "one who guards his country and zealously guards its welfare." From *Webster's Third*

New International Dictionary, a patriot is "a person who loves his country and defends and promotes its interest." Similarly from *Webster's*, a patriot is "a soldier who fights for love of country." Thus, patriotic music is not a relatively passive portrayal of a culture. Rather, it is an assertive and sometimes aggressive statement of national defense. Patriotic music is thus much more one-dimensional than the larger genre of nationalist music.

In general, nationalist music can convey a myriad of cultural perspectives, from portrayals of rural life to urban existence and anything in between. The key is that whatever is portrayed should be clearly seen as originating in whole or part from within a culture that exists within identifiable national boundaries. The significance of these portrayals on the development of a national identity within a populace can be appreciable. But patriotic music can be identified by its single-minded approach to the uncompromising defense of a nation. With respect to national development, patriotic music can sometimes be of great significance to a people after a nation has been consolidated, which implies that nationalist music would tend to precede patriotic music chronologically in the evolution of a nation's sense of self.

Sometimes nationalist music can appear to have patriotic overtones, especially when flags or other nationally-identifying symbols or monuments are connected with the music. But a close inspection of most nationalistic music will find the absence of the one-dimensional appeal to a nation's defense that is the single true identifying marker for patriotic music. A good modern example of nationalist music that is clearly not patriotic (according to the above definition) is Bruce Springsteen's song, "Born in the USA." Neither the song nor its accompanying video offer any hint of a one-dimensional defensive alignment with respect to the United States. Rather, the song is a portrayal of a certain cultural perspective found in many predominantly industrialized areas of the United States during the 1970s and 1980s, and it speaks of the psychological trauma of the Vietnam War felt by many young members of the working class who live in those areas. Yet the video that accompanies the song does prominently display the

American flag, and one might initially wonder if this (plus the song's title) tilts the song in a patriotic direction. But it is clear from both the song and the remainder of the video that the flag is used to convey the symbolic sense of national pride felt by many members of the communities who are portrayed in the song. It is not the song that is patriotic. Rather, it is the people in the communities about which the song was written who are proud of their nation that is being addressed in this instance, and the composition accurately reflects that sensibility of pride within that American sub-culture.

Perhaps the best way to describe nationalist and patriotic music is through examples. In the remainder of this chapter, I identify and describe a variety of nationalist and patriotic composers and artists across a few national settings. In some cases where warranted I list a number of works by one composer, whereas in other cases only one or two examples are presented. At the end of the chapter, I branch into a brief discussion of country music, which is an American nationalist musical form that is best discussed more broadly.

The Period of European Nation-Building

Early nationalist composers were largely influenced by Franz Liszt (1811-86). Liszt was born in Hungary, and in his very early youth he was attracted to Gypsy music. His interest in music that had a distinctive Hungarian style was particularly accented by an extended visit that he made to Hungary in 1839-40. As he later matured into a virtuoso pianist and a highly innovative composer widely acclaimed throughout Europe, he maintained this interest in musical themes derived from (predominantly Hungarian) Gypsy folk music. For example, he wrote a book on Hungarian Gypsy music, and this interest led him to compose his Hungarian Rhapsodies and other pieces with Hungarian themes.

During Liszt's time, Hungary also matured as a nation, as was the trend elsewhere in Europe during those years of revolution and national consolidation. This was an era in which the search for a meaningful and larger political framework encouraged many people to identify the connectedness between themselves and those of similar cultural origin. For example, in 1868, the so-called "Nationalities Law" extended the idea of Hungarian citizenship to all individuals of Hungarian origin regardless of their current nationality or place of residence. Franz Liszt assisted this process of reaching out to define what it means to be Hungarian—both as a nation and a people—by signaling his own break from the previously dominant classical musical forms of the Vienna school. This was a radical thing to do in his day, made more significant due to his own widely recognized importance throughout Europe as both a performer and a composer. The idea of crafting music to address nationalist and political ideas relevant to evolving European societies caught on, and it is noteworthy to point out Liszt's early contribution in this regard even though it was probably an inevitable phenomenon given the nature of the times.

Italian Nationalism

In Italy, no composer had a greater impact on the development of national identity than Giuseppe Verdi (1813-1901). (See especially the recent biography of Verdi by John Rosselli 2000.) As with Liszt, Verdi's impact on the development of Italian politics was aided by his already great reputation as a composer. During Verdi's early life, Italy as we now know it was a collection of separate states that were ruled predominantly by the Hapsburgs of Austria (French rule having ended with the defeat of Napoleon), the Bourbons, and the Pope. Yet pre-Napoleon French ideas of republican governance and political independence for a more broadly defined nation were popular then, especially among intellectuals.

Verdi's first overt foray into the political movement labeled "*Risorgimento*" which sought political unification among all of the separate Italian states was to write La battaglia di Legnano ("The Battle of Legnano") in 1849, the year that followed the revolutionary warfare of 1848 that spread to Italy from other parts of Europe. This opera is essentially a story set in the year 1176 C.E., and it involved the historic battle of Legnano in which an alliance of Italian cities (Verona, Vicenza, Padua, Venice, Sicily, and Constantinople) called the "Lombard League" defeated the German king Frederick I, whom the Italians called "Barbarossa." The political message of the opera is that Italians need to unite in order to resist the oppression of foreign (and emphatically Germanic) domination. It premiered just as the emperor of Austria (a political heir to Barbarossa) was planning on using his army to re-assert his rule over northern Italy. The opera was a huge hit at the time, and it was widely seen as a patriotic defense of Italian nationality.

As with many of Verdi's operas, the plots and songs (especially with the pre-*Legnano* operas) were often interpreted metaphorically. (See especially the detailed analysis by Julian Budden 1992.) This is particularly true when the operas suggested the political remedy of revolution and liberation. This is indeed the case of the song "*Va, pensiero*," which is a chorus sung by Hebrew slaves that comes from the opera *Nabucco*, written in 1841. This opera is based on the biblical persona King Nebuchadnezzar who ruled during much of the second Babylonian Empire from 605-562 B.C. *Va, pensiero* (still widely performed today as both a choral piece and solo, with variations in the lyrics) eventually became an unofficial national anthem after 1849 due to its allusion to politically potent images of fatherland that holds deep bonds to a remembering populace.

In 1859, with the help of Napoleon III and his large French army, Italy emerged as a nation. Although Verdi had little interest in becoming directly involved with politics, he was persuaded to run for parliament. Serving as a somewhat unenthusiastic representative, Verdi nonetheless did experience republican political life directly, however briefly. His involvement with opera was still the dominant factor in his life, of course, and he continued to compose operas that seemed to run into trouble with various censors throughout Europe. The problems with the censors usually involved dramatic moments or plots in which kings, aristocrats, or religious leaders were either killed or treated with significant disrespect. Verdi fought with the censors continually, but he was a pragmatist that made compromises when necessary to enable his productions to open. Yet he could rarely be explicit in conveying his political messages to his audience because of the influence of the censors. His audiences were nonetheless able more often than not to read between the lines, fully understanding the constraints of the day.

One of Verdi's early nationalistic operas is *I lombardi alla prima crociata*. While it was originally performed in 1843 in Milan (Lombard) at the La Scala theater, it was later re-worked as *Jerusalem* and performed in Paris. The opening scene includes the Milanese church of Sant'Ambrogio, and the plot is about the Crusades between 1095-1099 in Palestine. In the opera, the Lombards are victorious combatants who conquer Jerusalem. In its original form, this opera seems more oriented toward the Lombard audiences than those of wider Italy. However, the opera was widely successful in theaters throughout what we now know as Italy, and the basic propaganda message of the opera is that Italians have been great soldiers and conquerors in the past. This message was potent in the context of an Italian society that was unhappily ruled by a domineering Austria at the time of the opera's premiere.

Ernani is a Verdi opera that is actually cleverly subterranean political protest music. It was one of his early operas, premiering in Venice in 1844. Based on a play by Victor Hugo, the opera satirizes the aristocratic nobility. The plot has a bandit (Ernani, a tenor) for a hero who is actually a disguised nobleman whose father was killed by the King of Spain, Don Carlo. A woman, Elvira, is to be married by an old nobleman, Don Silva. But both Don Carlo and Ernani love her as well. Of all of the men, Ernani is the most noble, and he also is the one whom Elvira wishes to marry. In the end, Ernani succeeds in freeing Elvira from her captivity by King Don Carlo, but Ernani ends up having to commit suicide due to a cruelly applied promise that he previously made to Don Silva.

The political meaning of the suicide addresses the route of seeking freedom via a dramatic act of defiance. But it also addresses the idea that an easy route to freedom and happiness may be impossible to find, and that the ultimate sacrifice may be needed in order to choose freedom over surrender when confronted with intractable political corruption. This message was apparently well understood by Italian audiences of the time due to a novel written by Ugo Foscolo (from Venice) titled, *The Last Letters of Jacopo Ortis*, in which suicide is a response to personal tragedy and political impotence (see Berger 2000, pp. 118-119). But the opera also suggests that the elite will normally try to take advantage of those who are virtuous, and that the virtuous will be the only ones who will follow-through with their own promises (in this case, even the promise to commit suicide).

In this sense, *Ernani* is a strong critique of the morality of the ruling hierarchy that was contemporary to Verdi. This critique (again with a sexual motif) is repeated later in Verdi's opera *Rigoletto* (premiering in 1851), in which a rakish duke (with the cooperation of other corrupt nobility) takes advantage of every woman—innocent or not—within range, leading to the death or imprisonment of other less-powerful but more virtuous people. It was the censors who stopped the character of the duke from being a king, as portrayed in the French play "*Le Roi s'amuse*" by Victor Hugo on which the opera is based, a point which the Italian opera-goers most likely did not miss.

History is often a great motivator for some of Verdi's nationalist operas. Consider the case of Attila the Hun who launched an attack on the Eastern Roman Empire in 441 A.D. following the failure of the Eastern Romans to pay an agreed-upon annual tribute in gold. This was only the first of a number of westward invasions that more often than not involved disagreements over tribute. But in 451 he launched a major invasion of Gaul that was sparked by an incident that occurred in the year 450 in which Honoria, the sister of Emperor Valentinian III, wanted to avoid a forced marriage. She sent her ring to Attila and asked him to save her from this fate. Attila invaded Gaul, claiming he would marry Honoria and take the lands to the west as her dowry. He nearly succeeded in conquering Gaul before suffering his only defeat, forcing his withdrawal. It was soon after this in 452 that he decided to invade southward into Italy, and he sacked many cities, mostly in the north. To escape the invading Huns, many Italians fled to the swamps and lagoon of Venice. Thus, Venice rose like the Phoenix out of a situation of utter despair. Attila died in 453 on the night after his marriage, and the rise of Venice approximately coincided with the death of a hated conqueror.

It is through the lens of this history that Verdi's opera *Attila* must be viewed. The opera premiered in Venice in 1846, and it is easy to see this as a nationalist (even patriotic) appeal to the Venetians themselves. The *Risorgimento* was metaphorically connected to the rise of Venice following the decimation caused by conquering invaders. But the idea that foreign forces whose purpose was to dominate and exploit the nation should be defeated by both bravery and luck on Italian soil was unambiguously aimed at the contemporary Austrian rule over Italy. In the opera, Attila the Hun leads an invasion of Rome. Before the invasion, he is plagued by a dream in which an old man insults him and orders him to withdraw from sacred soil. When Attila actually does attack, he is confronted by an old man named "Leone," who uses the same words from the dream. The character of Leone was required to be portrayed in this way because the censors would not allow the opera to be more explicit. But the character unambiguously stands for Pope Leo, and the confrontation represents the idea that Italians seeking freedom from foreign domination have divine sanction. Indeed, current productions of this opera often have the character dressed in full papal white garb. In this scene, Attila prostrates himself before Leone, further enhancing the idea that even a barbarian cannot resist the deeply Italian embrace of the spirit.

In the opera, a woman named Odabella is eventually to marry Attila. Attila earlier killed her father, and Odabella actually wants to extract revenge by killing Attila. In the process, she foils an attempt by others to poison Attila, but eventually manages to kill him with a sword in a somewhat rushed ending. In this opera the parallels to history are very approximate. But the essential idea of the opera is that Italians can defeat any foe, however barbarous, if they will only unite in the attempt. Both divine providence and their own strength will guarantee the ultimate destruction of their enemies. Verdi was obviously required to disguise (and in some sense bury) this message in an opera about Attila the Hun, a consequence of the environment of censorship within which he operated. But the audiences understood the environment, and they were quick to draw the appropriate connections. This essential message was repeated in the later opera (1849), *La battaglia di Legnano*, in which the enemy was the brutal German King Frederick Barbarossa who similarly challenged papal authority.

By now it should be clear that Verdi approached nationalist music differently from the way Wagner characterized his political ideas in the "Ring." The political content in Verdi's music is typically tied to particular battles or events, whose portrayal can be seen as inspiring and sometimes prescriptive to the Italians of his day with respect to addressing their contemporary political troubles. Wagner, on the other hand, dealt with more universalistic themes in much of his politically rich music. This does not mean that Wagner was superior to Verdi as a political composer. But while Wagner's approach to political content in his music is more based on the identification of universalistic principles applicable to all humans, Verdi's approach is more particularistic since he remains focused on the pressing matters of the day. Analogously, it might be helpful to say that Wagner views politics in his music through a wide-angle lens, whereas Verdi's perspective is more narrow. Such analogies are never perfect, but there is nonetheless some heuristic use in making them. In opposition to this contrast, one can point to Wagner's intensely Germanic focus in his writings and personal interactions to suggest that he was just as nationalistically narrow in his political orientation as Verdi, and perhaps this is true with respect to Wagner as a person. But it seems clear that Verdi's approach to politicizing his music is more bounded than Wagner's. Evidence suggestive of this is that opera-goers today might find Verdi's political lessons as described above quite dated and no longer applicable to current political debates, whereas this would probably not be said of Wagner's political music.

Russian Nationalism

In the 1860s in Russia, a group of composers arose who consciously attempted to form a truly Russian form of music. This group of nationalist composers were named "*Moguchaya Kuchka*," which literally means "the mighty little heap," but is more commonly translated as "The Great Five," or "The Mighty Five," or "The Russian Five," or simply "The Five." The five composers were Aleksandr Porfiryevich Borodin, César Cui, Mily Balakirev, Nikolay Rimsky-Korsakov, and Modest Petrovich Mussorgsky. Of the five, Rimsky-Korsakov and Mussorgsky made the more fundamental and lasting contributions to Russian nationalist music. One of the goals of this group was to break away from the influence of Germanic and Italian musical forms, both contemporary and classical. They sought to do this both by incorporating traditional Russian folk melodies into their compositions, but also by infusing their works with new musical styles. These five composers were centered in St. Petersburg, and they were often contrasted with a rival nationalist faction based in Moscow and led by Pyotr (Peter) Ilyich Tchaikovsky. However, it was never a clear-cut case that the Five were any more or less nationalistic than Tchaikovsky, since Tchaikovsky often incorporated Russian folk melodies in his own compositions.

The origins of The Great Five can be traced to Alexander Pushkin (1799-1837) and Mikhail Glinka (1804-57). Pushkin was a writer whose work deeply influenced Glinka, his contemporary and friend. Pushkin's work, *Ruslan and Ludmila,* was his first venture into Russian nationalism, although its incorporation of Russian folklore is more limited than much of his later writings which also addressed a great deal of Russia's history and life

(Leonard 1957, p. 38). Glinka followed Pushkin's literary example with a desire to create a fully Russian form of music that was clearly distinguishable from its western European counterparts. His two most significant works were the operas *A Life for the Czar* and *Ruslan and Ludmila*, the latter of which was clearly inspired by Pushkin's earlier writing of the same name (see also Abraham 1982). While *A Life for the Czar* had a Russian theme and a possibly accurate historical story (see Leonard 1957, p. 44), it nonetheless was musically and structurally much like an Italian opera. It also incorporates some Polish components, including dances. But it was the Russian content that made the opera a success with both the Russian people and Czar Nicholas.

It is worthwhile to point out briefly how Glinka incorporated Russian musical content into *A Life for the Czar* since it is somewhat of a model for his later opera, and it illustrates some of the ideas used in creating nationalist music that was followed by The Great Five. In this opera, Glinka used Russian folk songs. In some instances, he used entire songs, whereas in other cases he used elements of these songs as themes. For example, in Act I the character Susanin uses words that come from a song commonly sung by cab drivers, and in Act IV a Russian song about a robber "Down by Mother Volga" is used as a thematic orchestral seed (Leonard 1957, p. 46). Glinka also created some Russian themes for this opera entirely by himself, such as when he imitates a Russian folk style using 5/4 time in the "Bridal Chorus" and the "Slavsya Chorus," which is a rhythmical setting common to Russian folk melodies. Glinka also incorporates *a capella* choral singing that follows a Russian folk style, as well as singing that resembles the antiphonal style commonly used by Russian choirs in the Orthodox Church in which one hymn or phrase would be a response to another.

Glinka's second opera, *Ruslan and Ludmila*, was composed after Pushkin was killed in 1837 at the age of 38 in a duel which was instigated by his enemies involving a defense of his wife's honor. During the six years when Glinka composed the opera, it is clear that he longed for his friend's guidance in designing the work. The overall plan of the opera was eventually sketched out by Constantine Bakhturin, who seems to have accomplished this in only a few minutes while drunk (Leonard 1957, p. 48). Additional help with the plot and libretto was offered by Captain Shirkov as well as Glinka's friend and poet, Nestor Kukolnik, before Glinka finally finished the libretto himself.

Ruslan and Ludmila was not well received in its original performances. The confusing way in which the libretto was written contributed heavily to the opera's general incoherence. The beauty of Pushkin's story was lost in the opera. The opera also contained a large number of very original and modern musical innovations, and the Russian audiences of Glinka's day were simply not prepared for this. While *A Life for the Czar* was predominantly Italian in structure and musical form, *Ruslan and Ludmila* was more thoroughly the work of a Russian artist who had reached his peak in being able to craft a nationalist form of Russian music. The opera contains a long list of musical details—including melody, instrumentation, rhythm, harmony, and overall style—that effectively initiated a new form of musical language that was explicitly Russian (Leonard 1957, p. 50).

After Glinka's death which was probably due to his syphilis infection, his sister, Ludmila Ivanovna Shestakova, carried on a personal crusade to support what she believed was her brother's vision for the creation of Russian nationalist music. First, she worked to create an ultimately successful revival of her brother's work in Russia. To do this, she employed musicians who were disciples of her brother, paid for new copies of her brother's music to be written (each by hand), and acted as a tireless propagandist for the cause of producing new performances of Glinka's operas and other works, all using money that was procured through the sale of her own land. But second, she acted as the unofficial head and protectress of the young musicians who would eventually become known as The Great Five. The Great Five met in her home as a group regularly, talking with her about everything from their personal lives to their professional problems. Mussorgsky and Balakirev were particularly influenced by her. Some of The Five had known each other for a long while, well before the group had consolidated under Shestakova's guidance. Indeed Borodin first met Mussorgsky when they were both in the Russian military. Yet when they did consolidate, it was Shestakova's role to maintain the cementing connection between the path that her brother had forged and the geniuses who would create the future that he had first envisioned.

While Ludmila Shestakova may have helped support The Great Five—especially in the beginning—both financially and as a propagandist, she nonetheless was not the intellectual mentor of the group. This role was held by Mily Balakirev. Balakirev (1837-1910) was both a disciple of Glinka and the lead organizer of The Great Five. In the early days, the group was also simply known as "The Balakirev Circle" (Leonard 1957, p. 65). Balakirev was also the musical tutor for much of the group, giving lessons on his own approach to composition and performance even though his formal training was not robust (Leonard 1957, p. 69). His group can trace its origin to a meeting in 1857 between Balakirev and César Cui, an officer in the Russian Army. Modest Mussorgsky joined the slowly emerging group in 1857, also as a piano student of Balakirev. Rimsky-Korsakov followed soon afterward, and the group was finally completed when Borodin joined in 1862.

Balakirev had an infectious impact on all of the members of the group. Mostly, his influence was a charismatic appeal to the idea of creating a new genre of authentic Russian music. This leadership was quickly tested in a struggle that the group found itself in that extended beyond its own boundaries. At the time that the group was active, there were two other visions of music that competed for attention on the Russian stage. One was lead by Alexander Serov, a composer and critic who idolized Wagner. Serov composed two popular operas, but his greatest influence was in his prose writings that ferociously attacked the emerging nationalist musical ideas of Balakirev's Circle. The other great influence of the time was orchestrated by Anton Rubinstein, a prodigious composer and pianist with hugely conservative musical leanings, which meant that he followed the musical path established by German composers such as Mendelssohn and Wagner. While his talents never equaled those of his idols, he nonetheless was a superb organizer. In 1859 he established the Russian Musical Society, and in 1862 he expanded this to create the Petersburg Conservatory. The idea of these institutions was to promote musical excellence in Russia that would be comparable with that found in Germany.

Driven by both the opposition of Serov and Rubinstein, the group of musicians in Balakirev's Circle responded to the creation of the Petersburg Conservatory by establishing their own competing school called the "Free Music School." It is hard to underestimate the level of harsh feelings that were held by both sides in this contest for the future of Russia's musical soul. To establish an immediate following, the Free Music School offered classes to talented musicians without cost. Also, the style of the instruction followed that of Balakirev's "free-form" approach. To finance this effort, Balakirev held public concerts, and these concerts inevitably contained performances of early works composed by the Circle members themselves. In 1866, the Moscow Conservatory was founded by Nicholas Rubinstein, Anton's brother. Peter Ilych Tchaikovsky was the new conservatory's first instructor, and he was also a recent graduate of the Petersburg Conservatory. Of course, Tchaikovsky eventually produced music that helped to define the Russian nationalist genre, even extending it to include some of the most sublime patriotic music ever produced. But the main point of 1866 is that the battleground between the conservatives (i.e., Western leaning) and the nationalists ("progressives" might be a useful descriptor) had expanded and was heating up. Much of the battle raged in diatribes appearing in the press.

The two most important propositions of The Great Five were that authentic Russian folk music should be treated seriously as a basis for future composition, and that the technical requirements of Western (predominantly German) music could be ignored if desired. But the group also desired to evolve in experimental and new ways, as was also being done by Liszt, Schumann, Berloiz, and Chopin. Thus, The Five were not so much anti-Western as much as they were innovators who did not want constraints to inhibit their spirit of experimentation.

In the end, Balakirev's musical contributions were not as great as was his early inspiration to his followers. Notably, he traveled up and down the Volga River collecting folk songs, and these songs became the themes in his symphonic work *Russia*. But eventually, others in the group resisted Balakirev's firm-handed control of their growth, and they broke off from him as they continued to follow their own evolutionary paths. Of the remaining five members, César Cui offered the least music fruit, although he compensated for this lack of compositional productivity by working as a propagandist for the Five and their ideas. His corrosive tone earned him many enemies, however, and even his efforts as a propagandist for the new movement were surpassed by those of the music critic, Vladimir Stasov. A final footnote on Cui is to observe that his harsh pen also targeted some of Mussorgsky's finest works, such as his opera *Boris Godunov*.

Borodin, a chemist whose work is in the area of aldehydes is still respected today, was the third most successful of The Great Five. His music offers a clear example of how The Five followed Glinka's early musical lead. He used traditional Russian melodies as well as the incorporation of new Russian musical forms in much of his composition (see especially Abraham 1974). For example, Act II in his opera *Prince Igor* (a work that was completed after his death by Aleksandr Glazunov and Rimsky-Korsakov) contains his well-known "Polovetsian Dances." Moreover he uses harmonies that are quite foreign to other realms of European music.

Modest Mussorgsky (1839-81) is perhaps the most innovative of all members of The Five, and indeed one can see the seeds of 20th century music in much of his work (see especially the biography by David Brown 2002). His influence is actually much greater than the quantity of his output would at first suggest. The reason for this is that he crafted his music so differently—and so boldly—as compared with other nationalist composers. The two most important works written by Mussorgsky are the opera *Boris*

Godunov (premiering in its final version in1874) and his *Pictures from an Exhibition* (1874) which was originally written for piano but later transcribed by Maurice Ravel for orchestra. *Boris Godunov* uses music and images that strongly identify both Russian symbols as well as its people. The opera is based on the tragic story by the Russian poet Alexander Pushkin involving the rise and fall of the Russian Czar Boris. As one of many examples of the use of accents that address some authentically Russian aspect of life, at one point in the opera the audience hears the orchestra sounding like the bells from the Kremlin that were heard when Boris was crowned. In other works, he incorporated (as did Glinka) rhythms using the 5/4 time signature that were common among peasant songs. This use of realistic touches in his music that originated from a Russian background (especially that of the Russian peasant) had a parallel with the school of Realism that was influential in the art world of Mussorgky's day.

Another of Mussorgsky's compositions, *A Night on Bald Mountain*, is a good example of how thoroughly he sought to incorporate ideas that realistically portray the lives—and especially the belief systems—of Russian peasants. This work is based on a mountain with three peaks (Mount Triglav) not far from Kiev. The mountain itself is named after a Russian pagan god with three heads. According to legend, each year at the time of the feast of John the Baptist, there would be a demonic festival of sorts on the top of the mountain in which Satan himself would join. One of the original titles for Mussorgsky's piece is "St. John's Night on Bald Mountain." In the original score, he described the work as "1. Assembly of the witches, their chatter and gossip; 2. Cortege of Satan; 3. Unholy glorification of Satan; and 4. Witches' Sabbath" (Leonard 1957, p. 100). This piece has been popularized recently with a new version of the piece made by Leopold Stokowski that is used in the Walt Disney movie, *Fantasia*.

Of all of The Great Five, Nicholay Andreievich Rimsky-Korsakov (1844-1908) had the longest and most fulfilling career (see especially Abraham 1975). At age 17, he was the youngest member of The Great Five. Despite a few ups and downs, he continued with the group, and when Balakirev had a nervous breakdown and had to withdraw from leading his nationalist movement, it was Rimsky-Korsakov who took his place. In his earliest years, he attempted to write music (even a symphony) at Balakirev's suggestion even though he knew very little about the formal structure or theory of music. He continued to compose constantly, taking a break only for a three-year assignment in the Russian Navy beginning in 1862 that allowed him to travel to a surprising number of diverse locations around the world.

Due to his growing reputation as a composer, in 1871 he was offered a professorship at the Petersburg Conservatory. This was a crucial moment for him. At that point he realized that his musical growth was being restrained by the influence of Balakirev, and he desperately wanted to learn all that he could of the standard methods of music composition. Yet these were the very approaches to music that Balakirev opposed. Moreover, Rimsky-Korsakov did not know this standard musical pedagogy, and he would be expected to teach it at the Conservatory. He accepted the professorship, and then set about secretly to teach himself the standard musical pedagogy and theory at a furious pace, keeping at least one step ahead of his own students at all times. He never ended this process of self-study. It was here that he learned how to compose fugues, the usage of counterpoint, methods of harmony, aspects of canon, and everything else that was part of the "German" musical toolbox. One cannot overemphasize the intensity of this program of self-study. For example, in a period of just a few months in 1875 he wrote approximately sixty fugues (Leonard 1957, p. 148).

All of this created a deep fissure in The Five, of course. Borodin alone defended Rimsky-Korsakov within the group. Indeed, Rimsky-Korsakov was quite open to beginning a new phase in his career in which he would compose more standard and conservative pieces that followed the structural orthodoxy of the day. But the truth of the matter is that either his heart was not in it, or he was simply not good at it. Yet when it came to using his new technical apparatus to compose nationalistic tone poems, symphonies or operas incorporating folk themes and stories, or romantic works with a Russian backdrop, things "clicked" and his music was no less than magical. He was a composer who mixed standard technique with a love of Russian nationalism, keeping a constant eye on fantasy, fairy tales, and Russian folklore as a source for some of his most creative works.

In the end, Rimsky-Korsakov never betrayed the vision of Balakirev; he fulfilled it by surpassing it. But also Rimsky-Korsakov did not limit himself to Russian themes for his music either, as is evidenced by his *Scheherazade* which is based on the Arabian story, "A Thousand and One Nights." This symphony is also a good example of how Rimsky-Korsakov was able to put entire stories into symphonic form, as compared with more common shorter musical pieces that followed some plot. For example, in *Scheherazade's* first performance, he included the following descriptions for the symphony's sections: "(I) The Sea and Sinbad's Ship; (II) The Tale of the Prince Kalender; (III) The Young Prince and the Young Princess; (IV) Festival at Bagdad—The Sea—The Ship is Wrecked on a Rock Surmounted by a Warrior of Bronze—Conclusion" (Leonard 1957, p. 154).

Yet most of Rimsky-Korsakov's work did involve themes of a Russian origin. For example, of his 14 operas, only two cannot be traced back to fairy tales, actual history, or literature coming from Russia or other Slavic countries or areas. (The two exceptions are *Mozart and Salieri* [1898] and *Servilia* [1902].) It is perhaps because of this that the operas are often performed in Russia to this day, although they are not often performed elsewhere. Examples of these are *Snow Maiden* (1882), *The Legend of the Invisible City of Kitezh and the Maiden Fevronia* (1903-4), *Sadko* (1896), *The Tsar's Bride* (1899), *The Tale of Tsar Saltan* (1899-1900), and *The Golden Cockerel (Le Coq d'or -* 1909). In the case of *The Golden Cockerel*, the story is based on one of Pushkin's poems dealing with an Arab astrologer as told in *The Alhambra* by Washington Irving, with Pushkin's treatment giving the story the Russian connection. On the symphonic level, his *Russian Easter Festival* overture (1888) is a work that extends well beyond the formal meaning of a Christian occasion to include musical images of starkly Russian pagan origin.

From a nationalist—and thus political—perspective, The Great Five should probably be considered as making more of a collective contribution than five individual contributions. In general, they excelled most often with vocal compositions, although there are notable exceptions to this. Despite the break between Rimsky-Korsakov and Balakirev, all five produced a body of work and ultimately successful propaganda that elevated Russian nationalist music to a level competitive with, or superior to, that found anywhere else. In broad terms, Rimsky-Korsakov's greatest contribution was on the level of fantasy and fairy tale, while Mussorgsky was predominantly consumed with his Realism-based vision of historically accurate music. Indeed, if one were to use both of these composers as models in an interesting comparison, one could say that Bruce Springsteen's composition "Born in the USA" (as well as much of his other work) is aligned in an American sense more in the direction of Mussorgsky's approach to nationalistic music than that of Rimsky-Korsakov, or any other member of The Five. Inspired by Glinka and led by Balakirev, The Five designed a future for Russian music that was wedded to the idea of creative freedom with respect to pre-existing musical forms, and thematically driven by musical notions, legends, history, folk art, and essentially anything else that is indigenous to the political and cultural realm within which the music is created.

One cannot end a discussion of Russian nationalist music without at least mentioning Peter Ilych Tchaikovsky (1840-93). Tchaikovsky is, of course, one of Russia's greatest composers. His work with ballet continues to be featured in dance companies worldwide, and some of his symphonies are sublime by any standard. But Tchaikovsky has not been widely recognized as a nationalist composer. He was one of the first students in Anton Rubinstein's Conservatory of Music in Petersburg, and he moved onto being an instructor at the Moscow Conservatory. Thus, he had all of the educational credentials of a cosmopolitan composer that would follow the German musical pedagogy. But

Tchaikovsky shared many of the musical instincts found among the members of Balakirev's circle. He had an interest in Russian folk music, and was fond of experimenting with new instrumentation. In short, he had a thoroughly Russian creative spirit, one which was recognized by Balakirev himself. In more than one instance, frequent communications between Tchaikovsky and Balakirev led to musical creations that remain among Tchaikovsky's most inspired, including his overture *Romeo and Juliet*. Tchaikovsky's nationalism was most apparent in his operatic compositions, however, and he does include Russian folk melodies and historical ideas as themes in some of these works. This is certainly true of *Eugene Onegin*, *Vakula the Smith*, *The Oprichnik*, and *The Voyevoda*. Nonetheless, Tchaikovsky's nationalism as expressed in his music never rivaled that of The Five.

Yet in one instance Tchaikovsky produced an orchestral work that clearly falls within the patriotic sub-genre of nationalist music, and that is the *1812 Overture*. This work was originally commissioned to celebrate the 70th anniversary of Russia's military victory over the invading French forces led by Napoleon in 1812. It was performed at the Moscow Exhibition in 1882 in a ceremony consecrating the Cathedral of Christ the Savior. The cathedral itself stood as a monument marking the Russian victory. The *1812 Overture* has since become a popular standard used in many patriotic settings, both in Russia and elsewhere, including 4th of July celebrations in the United States. Modern performances often include accenting touches, such as canons and fireworks, and the piece has lost much of its original meaning. Nonetheless, the overture remains one of the highest quality examples of patriotic music created by anyone, and it serves as a marker with respect to what is possible within this sub-genre.

While Russian musical nationalism was at its height, other Slavic nations also experienced their own versions of the nationalist phenomenon. In some instances, a single nationalist composer was the focus of attention within a nation, which differs strikingly from the Russian model in which an entire school of thought emerged from within a set of cooperating artists. In

Czechoslovakia, for example, one composer so significantly influenced the nation's expression of musical self-identity that the nationalist music of that country was essentially defined by that person's contribution. While in a strict sense, Czech nationalist music traces its origins to works by both Bedrich Smetana and Antonín Dvorák, by far the greatest contribution to the musical development of Czech nationalism was made by Dvorák. Antonín Dvorák (1841-1904) was born in Bohemia (now Czechoslovakia) in a village near Prague. Much of his music is unmistakably of Czech character, and it follows the general Russian pattern of relying on indigenous folk materials, especially melodies, rhythms (such as polka), and themes (including Bohemian dance traits such as the furiant and dumky).

Many people know of Dvorák as a musical propagandist of Czech identity through some of his popular (and relatively minor) works, such as the *Slavonic Dances* (1886 and 1887, and especially *Slavonic Dance*, opus 46, number 8) and the *Gypsy Songs* (1880). Yet even his most internationally popular *Symphony No. 9 in E Minor* (also known as *From the New World*, 1893) has unmistakable Bohemian themes, even though it additionally incorporates musical ideas (including Negro spirituals) obtained from a trip to the United States. In Dvorák's symphonies, he often uses the third movements to most pointedly insert musical ideas with Bohemian origin. His *Symphony No. 7 in D Minor* is a good example of this. Other nationalist composers in nearby nations later followed a strikingly similar pattern as with Dvorák of pioneering the incorporation of indigenous folk musical ideas into their compositions, such as is the case with Béla Bartók of Hungary.

Finnish Nationalism: A Nation Musically Transformed

Again as with Dvorák's solitary initiating influence on Czech musical identity, Jean Sibelius (1865-1957) made a profound mark on the development of nationalist music in his own emerging nation, Finland. Indeed, Sibelius's reach into the Finnish psyche may have arguably exceeded that of any other nationalist composer anywhere. Sibelius never used indigenous folk songs, harmonies, or rhythms in his music, as did many other nationalist composers. But he did utilize Finnish legends and history in his works. This, combined with his own political views and activities as a fierce nationalist, helped transform him into a national hero on whose attention the Finnish public became—and remains—transfixed.

Before 1808, Finland was ruled by Sweden. Russia conquered Finland during a war with Sweden in 1808-9. After that, Finland was known as the Grand Duchy of Russia, a semi-autonomous region politically connected to Russia. The Russian Emperor was the Grand Duke who had ultimate authority in ruling Finland. Because the Russian Emperor Alexander I was quite liberal with his rule of Finland from 1809-25, Finnish autonomy was extensive, resulting in an almost independent Finnish state. Nonetheless, Finland remained part of the Russian Empire, a state within a state, complete with its own language, capital, and legislature, until its ultimate independence in 1917. Russian rulers after Alexander I did not continue to rule Finland with the attitude of a benign despot. Indeed, things changed dramatically with the rule of Alexander III (1881-94), and again with Nicholas II (1894-1917). Some elements within Russia resented Finland's special status, and the repression of Finnish nationalism became more the norm.

Because of Finland's earlier domination by Sweden, formal schooling in the Finnish language was unusual throughout much of the 1800s, even though only a small minority of Finns spoke Swedish as their first language. The first Finnish language school in Finland was the Finnish Normal School, and it was this school that Sibelius attended. While attending this school, Sibelius was introduced to Finnish literature. One work in particular made a large impression on him, the *Kalevala*. The *Kalevala* is a Finnish national epic compiled as a poem from many sources within Finland and Karelia by Elias Lönnrot in 1835 and 1849. Its origin can be traced to an extensive Finnish oral tradition previously transmitted in numerous songs, incantations, and verse. The *Kalevala* is important from a nationalist perspective because it spawned the idea of the Finnish language, oral history, and culture as being worthy of national and international respect, and its publication became a turning point in the Finnish nationalist movement. Sibelius directly incorporated aspects of the *Kalevala* in numerous works, such as *Pohjola's Daughter* (1906) and *Luonnotar* (1913). But the *Kalevala* was also an indirect musical inspiration to him throughout much of his career.

In 1899, Sibelius composed music for a November celebration marking the Finnish resistance to Russian influence. Again, this was a time in which Finland was experiencing increased repression from Russia under the rule of Nicholas II. The finale of the larger work that Sibelius composed for that celebration was titled "Finland Awakes," and it was popularly received as an inspiring patriotic work, due equally to the sound of the music, the nature of the celebration in which it was performed, and the pro-Finnish nationalist views of Sibelius himself. Sibelius soon revised the piece, re-titling it *Finlandia*, which to this day remains a hugely popular patriotic work within Finland, comparable in status to Tchaikovsky's *1812 Overture* in Russia. More generally, Sibelius's work throughout the 1890s can be characterized as strongly nationalist within the Romantic tradition. Examples include compositions such as the *Kullervo Symphony* (1892), *En Saga* (1892), and *The Swan of Tuonela* (the third part of the *Four Legends*, 1893).

It is no understatement to say that Sibelius was a unifying force in Finland's political evolution. He saw Finland as one nation with an identifiable culture and history. The fact that he was also a composer had a tremendous effect on the mentality of the nation's populace, a legacy that continues unabated today. Although Finland is a small nation of only 5.2 million people, it has a national tradition of music that is proportionally very difficult to find paralleled elsewhere. Within its borders are 150 music academies. There are also 45 annual musical festivals and 31 local and national orchestras. All of these academies, festivals, and orchestras are tied together into a national network that is directly supported by the government of Finland. The government subsidizes musical education and other elements of this network, including support for individual performers and composers. Indeed, Finland exports its musical talent much as India exports it highest quality engineering talent that graduates from its world-class Indian Institute of Technology. For example, the number of Finnish conductors who have led prestigious orchestras around the world is impressive by any measure. This group includes Jukka-Pekka Saraste (Toronto Symphony Orchestra, and various venues worldwide), Esa-Pekka Salonen (London Philharmonia Orchestra, Los Angeles Philharmonic Orchestra, and various venues worldwide), Osmo Vanska (Minneapolis Symphony Orchestra, and various venues worldwide), Sakari Oramo (Birmingham Symphony Orchestra, and other venues worldwide), Susanna Malkki (various venues in the U.S., U.K., and Europe, including the Birmingham Contemporary Music Group), Mikko Franck (the National Orchestra of Belgium, and various venues worldwide), Okko Kamu (Swedish Royal Opera, Symphony Orchestra of Singapore, and various venues worldwide), as well as others, nearly all of whom graduated from the Sibelius Academy in Finland. (Indeed, the "conductor's class" in this academy is so well-respected that having completed it is normally included on one's curriculum vitae.)

Overall, approximately 50,000 children in Finland currently receive professional music training, and it is estimated that 5,000 of these will become music professionals. But this only hints at how profoundly music structures the Finnish national agenda, from Helsinki to the rural villages. Even the national Parliament begins its year with an opera. A particularly useful summary of the manifestation of music as a political and cultural phenomenon in Finland can be found in an article by Warren Hoge in *The New York Times* ("Finland's Bold Musical Ambitions Produce a Multitude of Maestros," 5 January 2003, p. A4 [YNE]). In that article, the celebrated Finnish conductor Mr. Esa-Pekka Salonen is quoted as saying, "Finland was a totally divided country, and Sibelius was the first man to unite it.... The struggle for independence was in his first two symphonies, and the nation read so much into this that it became the focus of the hopes of the nation, the nation's subconscious." Some would even claim that Sibelius is responsible for music becoming a primary medium for expression in Finland, one comparable to the spoken word itself. When Finns think politically, they simultaneously think musically; when their children embark to contribute to the emergence of a new world order, their weapon of choice is sound. Few in Finland would dispute that Sibelius is ultimately the one who is responsible for all of this.

Spanish Nationalism

The father of Spanish nationalism is Felipe Pedrell (1841-1922). Pedrell received little formal education in music, but he nonetheless composed a large variety of mostly operatic works. He also wrote an important prose work, *Por Nuestra Música*, that argued the case for developing Spanish opera by incorporating indigenous folk melodies, rhythms, and themes. As with many other nationalist composers, however, he connected his work with innovations occurring elsewhere as well. For example, some of his own operas were produced in Spain with Italian librettos (e.g., *El último Abencerrahe*—Barcelona in 1874) even though they utilized Spanish musical ideas and also had indigenous-language versions. (*Los Pirineos* had both Catalan and Italian versions.) Also, Wagner's operatic ideas influenced him. Two of his most valuable contributions to Spanish nationalist music were the publication of a collection of Spanish folk songs in a four-volume set (*Cancionero Musical Popular Español*), and an eight-volume collection of Spanish church music (*Hispaniae Schola Musica Sacra*). He further assisted in the development of Spanish nationalist music through his teachings, and his students included Isaac Albéniz (1860-1909), Enrique Granados (1867-1916), and Manuel de Falla (1876-1946).

Among Pedrell's students, Albéniz also composed music that borrowed heavily from Spanish folk music. But unlike Pedrell, Albéniz had a great deal of formal musical training, both in

Leipzig and Brussels. He is best known for his piano solo compositions. Among his best known works is *Iberia* (1905-9). This collection of 12 compositions has a special focus on the Andalusia region of Spain. Other notable piano works with an unmistakable Spanish basis are the *Cantos de España* (with "Córdoba"), the *Tango in D Major*, and *Suite Española* (with "Sevillana").

The most well-recognized of all Spanish nationalist composers is Manuel de Falla, and as with Albéniz, it was Pedrell that first inspired him to want to work with music of Spanish origin. Manuel de Falla composed songs, operas, ballets, and works for piano and harpsichord, although much of his work has since been transcribed to be played on guitar. As with many other nationalist musicians, he utilized Spanish folk music as a basis for many of his compositions, as with the ballet *El Amor Brujo* (premiering in Madrid, 1915) which incorporated folk music from Andalusia. One of his most internationally recognized works (*El Corregidor y la Molinera*) is used in Léonide Massine's ballet, *The Three-Cornered Hat*, which premiered in London in 1919. Another of his major works for piano and orchestra, again one with an Andalusian flavor, is *Noches en los Jardines de España* which premiered in 1916 in Madrid.

Musical Nationalism in England

During the Romantic period, there was a musical renascence in Great Britain led by composers such as Sir Hubert Parry, Sir Charles Stanford, and Sir Edward Elgar. This renascence was marked by a new wave of bold experimentation. But these composers nonetheless tended to follow the musical ideas current in Europe, and the German influence dating back to Handel was still mainstream. The nationalist movement in England arrived relatively late, long after Mussorgsky had made his mark in Russia. The nationalist movement in English music began with Ralph Vaughan Williams (1872-1958). As with Mussorgsky and other nationalist composers, Williams used folk songs and other indigenous materials for his inspiration (see especially Heffer 2001; also Ursula Vaughan Williams 1992).

Williams's special interest in English music was with the Tudor and Elizabethan periods, although English folk songs generally were a source of many ideas for him. This included his use of various modal scales, as compared with the standard chromatic scale. Such scales are commonly used in folk music found in many countries and are typically of medieval origin. Most folk music uses the Ionian, Mixolydian, or Dorian modes, although the Phrygian and Lydian modes are also occasionally heard. The music is normally sung, and the songs are commonly called "folk ballads" or "Child ballads." The latter reference is to Francis Child, the American 19th century scholar who compiled the definitive multi-volume collection of folk ballads, *The English and Scottish Popular Ballads*. Williams's first works to display the obvious incorporation of folk ideas are his *Norfolk Rhapsodies* (premiering in 1906).

One of his most popular symphonies is *A London Symphony* (premiering in 1914, but revised on multiple occasions until 1934). Also well known is his *Fantasia on a Theme by Thomas Tallis* (1910), a work for strings only. An interesting effect of *Fantasia* is to produce a very "English" feel by producing echoing sounds typical of those encountered in a large cathedral, not unlike Mossorgsky's approach to Russian realism in his own work (remember the Kremlin bells in *Boris Godunov*). Also, his ballad opera, *Hugh the Drover* (1924), borrows heavily from English folk songs. Williams also composed music for film, stage, and even radio. For example, he scored the music for the film *Scott of the Antarctic* (1949), and later adapted this music in his *Sinfonia Antarctica* (1953). As with many other nationalists, Williams also composed work that was inspired by the nonmusical works of other indigenous artists, such as *Riders to the Sea* (1937) which is based on the one-act play of the same name by John Millington Synge which was first performed in 1904.

American Nationalism

Due to the historical connection between the early colonists and Britain, early American music was dominated by English ideas, as reflected in the various anthems and hymns common to 19th century America. Eventually American composers traveled throughout Europe, bringing home the Continent's musical traditions with them. Once back in America, the European ideas were quickly blended with traditional indigenous musical forms, producing a diverse collection of hybrid music that has an unmistakably American feeling to it. The first composer to produce what we can now call an "American sound" was Charles Ives (1874-1954). (See especially the biographical account by Swafford 1998.)

Charles Ives did not make a living with his music, even though he was a truly prolific composer who tried constantly to interest musicians in performing his works. Rather, he made himself wealthy as an insurance salesman. Only late in his life was he "discovered," and only then did he have more frequent chances to hear his own music performed. Due to a heart attack which he had in 1918 when he was in his forties, he found it increasingly difficult to compose music. He stopped composing music altogether by 1930, still not having found an audience for his works. In 1947 he finally won a Pulitzer Prize for one of his compositions, his *Symphony No. 3*. The fact that this symphony was composed in 1904 is a metaphor for the delayed appreciation of his musical talents, and indeed it was not until the 1960s that the mainstream musical establishment finally and fully discovered both him and his works.

Ives's father (George Ives) was a talented musician who was once a bandmaster in the Union Army during the American Civil War. George was also instrumental in encouraging Charles to be experimental with music. Indeed, Charles's invention of what we now call "tonal clusters" began when he played the piano with a board in a manner reminiscent of his earliest musical experiences in which he pounded his father's piano with his fists. Charles

Ives's exposure to American church music was early in his life, and he was a salaried organist at a church at the age of 14. He also composed music early in his life, such as his *Variations on "America"* which was written when he was 17 for the organ (although later transcribed for orchestra). He studied music at Yale under the conservative and German-trained Horatio Parker. At Yale, Ives had to constrain his urge for free-wheeling experimentation that he learned from his father. It is said that Parker once crudely rejected one of Ives's early compositions, a *Fugue in Four Keys*, in large part because all four keys were played at the same time. Nonetheless, it was under Parker's tutelage that Ives obtained his background in formal composition, a background with which he profited enormously later when he began to re-integrate more adventurous ideas in his work.

In Ives's compositions, he tended to follow the nationalist pattern of incorporating indigenous music into his symphonies and other orchestral and chamber pieces. The indigenous music included religious hymns, traditional dance music, and popular songs. He sometimes radically incorporated new sounds into his works, such as when he places parts of a march played by a brass band together with a piano with unconventional tuning in the very beginning of "Putnam's Camp," which is included in the larger work, *Three Places in New England*. One of Ives's first pieces that integrates the European style of composition typical of the Romantic period with indigenous gospel music from America is the *First String Quartet*, a piece to which he later gave (with a "wink") the subtitle, *From the Salvation Army*.

There are other American composers of note that arose during the 19th century. Some of the better known of these are Scott Joplin (1868-1917), John Philip Sousa (1854-1932), Stephen Foster (1826-64), and Louis Moreau Gottschalk (1829-69). Indeed, elements of Scott Joplin's work with ragtime deeply influenced some of Ives's compositions, as found in Ives's *Ragtime Dances*, for example.

Modern Nationalist Hybrids

Strictly speaking, the nationalist movement is a sub-genre within the Romantic period, which usually means that the type of music considered "nationalist" is typically played with orchestral instruments within a symphonic, ballet, chamber, or other type of formal musical setting. But a basic tenet of nationalist music is that a sound which is recognizably indigenous to a particular nation is morphed into a musical hybrid that has a broader appeal than the original sound. The key is that the new sound must clearly reflect a unique national origin in some fundamental way. Whether or not the music is played by, say, a wind ensemble or a rock band, is really besides the point. Some may disagree, and that is fine, as long as one recognizes (for clarity) that my own view is one that includes modern sounds and instrumentation as being capable of producing music that falls within the political definition of the nationalist concept.

Some great 20th century composers continued the nationalist tradition of composing music that had indigenous folk inspirations. In the United States, one of the most important of such composers is Aaron Copland (1900-1990). (In particular, see the exhaustive study by Pollack 2000.) Copland was born in New York, and his sister was his first piano instructor. In 1921 he traveled to France to study under Nadia Boulanger at the Conservatoire Américain, a new music school for Americans. Copland was Boulanger's first American student, and she was also a pioneering female conductor and music instructor who broke many symbolic barriers. (For example, she was the first female to conduct the New York Philharmonic, the Boston Symphony Orchestra, and the Philadelphia Orchestra.) She was also the organist at the 1925 premiere at Carnegie Hall of Copland's *Symphony for Organ and Orchestra*. Copland was deeply influenced by Boulanger, and after returning to New York, he composed many works, some of which had a neoclassical orientation. But he eventually began to feel that he might be falling into a trap, one to which he perceived a great many modern composers were succumbing. He worried that his music might not be relevant to the masses. It was complicated and sublime, but perhaps too complicated and sublime. He then decided to try to simplify his music, and to ground it in ideas and themes that were understandable by the public.

This shift in heart led to a tremendous transformation in Copland's work. It was in this state of mind that he composed the three hugely popular ballets, *Billy the Kid* (1938), *Rodeo* (1942), and *Appalachian Spring* (1944). All of these works were inspired by music based on American folk concepts. Copland composed other Americana works as well, including his *Lincoln Portrait*, a piece he wrote during World War II.

Some nationalist compositions with folk roots inspire their own derivative works that are also nationalist in character. For example, Copland's ballet, *Rodeo*, was clearly influential in the creation of the video for Madonna's song, "Don't Tell Me," that is directed by Jean-Baptiste Mondino. The complexity of this video with regard to its portrayal of contemporary "cowboy" life can be quite striking when examined closely. The video begins with Madonna walking on a rural road in the American southwest. As a large truck passes her on the road, the music is interrupted in the manner of Internet streamed music when it is buffered due to slow transmission speeds normally associated with 56K (or slower) telephone-line modems. The camera then backs up, showing Madonna actually walking in front of a screen showing a previously filmed backdrop of the road scene. This, of course, points to the artificial and vicarious nature of the contemporary "Western" experience. Modern day cowboys (and cowgirls) experience the "Wild West" not by actually slugging it out on the range, but rather through visual and auditory media that offer a substitute and imitative experience.

Later in the "Don't Tell Me" video, dancing and bronco-riding cowboys are shown on a large projection screen that is placed in the same Western rural setting. Thus, people who are watching the video are actually watching a screen on a screen, further characterizing the "through-the-lens" vicarious nature of the

Western experience for most contemporary individuals. Finally, Madonna ends up riding a bucking bronco herself, an artificial one of course, one of the type commonly encountered in bars and some restaurants in Texas and other states in the American southwest. All of this does not pervert the presentation of the contemporary cowboy experience. On the contrary, the vicarious and artificial nature of this experience *is* the dominant contemporary cowboy experience, and the video's portrayal of that experience is quite authentic Americana. While the lyrics and the music of the song do not have an obvious nationalist foundation, in the context of the video, the overall work clearly conveys a nationalist orientation that connects viewers to an American folk heritage as it is currently experienced by the vast majority of American "pseudo cowfolks."

Nationalist and Patriotic Elements in American Country Music

While it did not develop from within the Romantic tradition of post-classical 19th century music, much country music in the United States nonetheless contains all of the essential political elements of the nationalist genre as defined in this volume. Modern country music has evolved from its indigenous folk roots formerly called "hillbilly music" which can be traced to the predominantly southern areas of the United States. Composers and performers of country music have traditionally been white. In the beginning, the music focused on the traditions of English, Irish, and Scottish descendants in the southern states, with perhaps the greatest geographical focus coming from the region of the Appalachian Mountains. Ballads were the norm of this music, and the lyrics of the songs traditionally conveyed stories which addressed the history and legends of the folk people and their ancestors. The instrumentation that predominated in such music was based on the fiddle and rudimentary percussion instruments.

During the 20th century, country music became much more complex musically. Some of the westward evolution of country music began when Gene Autry creatively altered country music to incorporate a cowboy flavor, a process which he continued throughout his productive singing and television career. Country music was also influenced by the swing rhythms of jazz, and new instrumentation helped transform it into an electronic phenomenon compatible with modern and popular dance venues.

Some of the country music that departed most significantly from the Appalachian-based country-folk form was called "outlaw music," and this was pioneered by Willie Nelson and Waylon Jennings. They blended rock rhythms with country's instrumentation while maintaining the intimate and reflective nature of traditional country lyrics. This has connections with musical styles called "southern rock" and "country rock." These latter styles originated on the West Coast of the United States (mostly Los Angeles), driven by West Coast immigrants from the South. To simplify the presentation in this volume, I refer to the entire genre as simply "country music."

As with much popular music today, most country music has a love orientation. However, a significant amount of country music continues to use the story format of traditional country music lyrics to convey political content. The result has been that country music now represents a large region and its highly patriotic culture within the United States. Essentially by definition, all nationalist music can be considered representational (minimally at the time that it is composed), and country music is no exception in this regard. However, a large proportion of country music can also be classified as representational in the patriotic sense as well.

The insertion of political content into country music was a direct outgrowth of country's traditional role as a venue for telling stories. Much country music traditionally represents an emotional outlet for people who are generally poor and who have relatively lower levels of education, income, and status. Country music tells the stories of their life experiences, and these stories are often filled with hardship or even tragedy. When country music acts as a representational venue for political content, it often has a patriotic flavor. In part this is due to the traditionally high level of involvement within the United States military among young people from the South. For many relatively less-well-off young people in the South, joining the military is a means of upward mobility. It offers employment with respect, a reasonable income, fashionable military-style clothing, and the promise of a better future (including educational benefits) after the completion of service. When a young soldier returns to his or her local community after military service, the neighborhood generally notes this arrival with the understanding that the person has matured and will likely make a positive contribution to society. This is a highly valued accomplishment for many such youth, and few other avenues so directly offer these same youths a similar benefit.

Yet this also points to a tension within the southern vs. U.S. musical dialectic. The edge to this political tension is due to country music's traditional role in representing people who have historically been marginalized in national U.S. politics. But this has changed in recent years. Since the election of Jimmy Carter, U.S. presidential contenders often come from the South. The South is now also a much more integrated, important, and industrialized economic region in the United States than it used to be. Thus, the "I've been marginalized but I'm fighting back" perspective of country music is not as relevant today as it once was, and country music has more recently taken on a much more assertive and clearly national patriotic role.

A useful example of country music's portrayal of the "marginalized but fighting back" outlook can be found in Tanya Tucker's song "I Believe the South is Gonna Rise Again." In this song, Ms. Tucker sings from the perspective of a white southerner who grew up poor. This southerner lived with her family in a rural shack next to other poor families, some black and some white. The song then goes on to profess a belief that the South will re-emerge as a place of power and respect, this time without the divisiveness of racial tension. One of the messages of the song is that the South's future is not going to be what previous generations of white southerners may have once envisioned. This implies that the former model of a rural economy and racial segregation will yield to a new reality that will merge more easily with a modernized perspective that is compatible with the overall evolution of the nation. This is representational political music, clearly. But this song is not patriotic per se, since the concept of a defense of the nation's interests is not present in either the lyrics or the melody.

On the other hand, Lee Greenwood's popular song, "God Bless the U.S.A." does convey the sense of a patriotic defense of the national interests. The song indirectly addresses the idea of relative southern poverty by arguing that freedom is a more valued commodity than material wealth. The song also claims a position of southern ideological leadership across all sub-regions of the United States, asserting indirectly that the southern flavor of pride in being an American is (or at least should be) a universally accepted characteristic of all citizens. This song was featured in a political television commercial for Ronald Reagan's re-election campaign in 1984, and it also received significant air play during the Gulf War against Iraq. Similarly, Elton Britt's hit "There's a Star Spangled Banner Waving Somewhere," written by Paul Roberts and Shelby Darnell in 1942, was popular during World War II, and it clearly fits the definition of a patriotic song with a southern country perspective that is projected across a national audience. This song indeed was a bit of a harbinger of country music's wider nationalist/patriotic appeal. The lyrics address the idea of relative southern backwardness via the metaphor of a "mountain boy" who wants to enlist in the Army to fight the Axis powers despite his having a crippled leg.

The degree of patriotic nationalism that exists within country music varies widely. Some country music is quite aggressive in its defensive posture, as with Toby Keith's song, "Courtesy of the Red, White, and Blue (The Angry American)." Mr. Keith wrote this song in response to the 11 September 2001 attacks on the World Trade Center and the Pentagon in the United States. The song begins with references to patriotic symbols, victims of the attacks, and a family background that values both peace and freedom. The song then takes a highly aggressive turn by celebrating the nation's strong military response when it was attacked unfairly (with a "sucker punch"). The remainder of the song is filled with deep anger and overt threats of violence against those whom Mr. Keith sees as America's enemies.

Some country patriotic songs are released to maximize their propagandistic effect, as with the song performed by Darryl Worley (written by Darryl Worley and Wynn Varble), "Have You Forgotten." This song was released as a single on 24 February 2003, less than a month before the invasion of Iraq by American and coalition forces in an effort to topple Saddam Hussein. The overt purpose of the song is to remind people of the September 11 attacks, and to argue explicitly that it is wrong to retreat from fighting now. The song contains direct criticism of those who argue that America is assuming a bullying international posture ("looking for a fight") by defending that very posture as correct given the nature of the attacks made on the nation. The song references "Bin Laden" explicitly, but it does not mention Iraq even though the association seems clear given both the timing of the song's release and the overall tone of the lyrics.

Alan Jackson took a more middle-ground approach to the September 11th attacks in his song "Where Were You (When the World Stopped Turning)." This song describes many common potential scenarios that ask the listeners to remember what they were doing on that Tuesday morning when the attacks occurred. The song also asks the listeners to recall their initial responses to the attacks. Mr. Jackson asks if you picked up a Bible, or perhaps felt guilty for being a survivor, or even if you went out to buy a gun. The purpose of the song seems to be to establish a sympathetic rapport with the listeners with respect to their emotional responses to those events, and this is a psychological approach that is aimed at healing. But Mr. Jackson does not go further by inciting anger or retribution.

Another psychological approach to the September 11th attacks and its aftermath is the song "John Walker's Blues" by the country singer and songwriter, Steve Earle. The song is included in his politically-rich *Jerusalem* album that was released in late 2002. The lyrics of the song are written from the perspective of John Walker Lindh, the American Taliban fighter known commonly as

"John Walker" who was captured in the American war in Afghanistan. As Mr. Earle portrays John Walker, he is a young man who could not relate to the Marin County/California culture that surrounded him. Looking for greater meaning in life, he found it in Islam, and then traveled abroad to find the purest version of this spiritual view.

Mr. Earl's song is highly controversial within the setting of the often stridently patriotic country-music milieu. But from Mr. Earle's perspective, the song may be seen as very patriotic in the sense that the song attempts to help others understand why John Walker acted as he did. Indeed, on his web site (www.steveearle.com, accessed July 2002), Mr. Earle has claimed that his *Jerusalem* album is "the most pro-American record I have ever made." On the other hand, Steve Gill, a radio talk show host based in Nashville was quoted by CNN as comparing Earle's work to Jane Fonda's anti-war activities during the Vietnam War (CNN, http://www.cnn.com/2002/SHOWBIZ/Music/07/23/walker.lindh .song/index.html, accessed July 2002). In this context, it is worth recalling that Ms. Fonda traveled to Hanoi in 1972 to denounce the bombing of North Vietnam by the United States, an act seen at the time as nearly treasonous by some. Such criticism about Mr. Earle reflects the high level of emotional intensity felt by some with respect to his perspective on patriotism. Exploring the psychology of those who attack America, and defending what Mr. Earle perceives as an American heritage of individual rights (something which he does elsewhere in the *Jerusalem* album), confronts a more one-dimensional approach to national defense as commonly voiced by many country singers.

Perhaps one candidate for the "classic" patriotic song with a southern country orientation is Elvis Presley's performance of "An American Trilogy." This is a composite song derived from folk melodies and hymns. It includes parts of "Dixie Land"and "Mine Eyes Have Seen the Glory," and the lyrics also reference the sacrifices that are required to defend a nation, as when a child loses a parent in battle. One of Mr. Presley's most noted performances of the song is during a concert in Hawaii that occurred near the end of his singing career.

National Anthems and Pseudo Anthems

Among all nationalist works, few are so undeniably patriotic as national anthems. Some national anthems are written by well-regarded composers and approach sublime art. For example, Joseph Haydn wrote "God Save Emperor Francis" in 1797, which was Austria's first national anthem. The anthem was modernized in 1929 when the text was changed to "Be Blessed Forever." This same melody was also used in the national anthem for the Weimar Republic, and it is currently similarly used by contemporary Germany. But more regularly, national anthems are dreary musical events whose only real reason to exist is the symbolic attachment that the music has to the process of national development. Yet regardless of their musical worth, national anthems typically remain powerful patriotic markers in the cultural tapestry of most nations for very long periods of time. Indeed, "God Save the Queen" has been the national anthem for Great Britain since 1825, which makes it the oldest such song on the planet. This is made even more remarkable by the fact that this national anthem was also a very popular patriotic song since the mid-1700s. Interestingly, the melody for "God Save the Queen" was also used in the German national anthem before 1922.

"The Star Spangled Banner," America's national anthem whose lyrics were written in 1814 by Francis Scott Key (1779-1843), follows the melody of the drinking song "To Anacreon in Heaven." The melody was composed by John Stafford Smith, and the song was used by the Anacreontic Society based in London. The new lyrics were written during the War of 1812 after Mr. Key witnessed the British attack on Fort McHenry, Maryland. The U.S. Congress voted to adopt the song as the official national anthem in 1931. Few people would argue that the melody of the song has much musical merit. Indeed, the song is quite difficult to sing well, and there is occasional talk of changing the national anthem to another song entirely. That the song remains the national anthem is largely due to its symbolic value.

There have been a few very notable renditions of this anthem that have been performed with such grace and/or originality that the song in those versions could be considered to have approached a more sublime level. An unusual and intriguing interpretation of "The Star Spangled Banner" was offered by Jose Feliciano. Mr. Feliciano sang the American national anthem in Detroit at Tiger Stadium during Game 5 in the 1968 baseball World Series. His version was slower than normal and clearly influenced by the blues. Mr. Feliciano's performance was quite controversial in its day, but it introduced the important idea that the song was open for interpretation, at least musically. In another instance, Marvin Gaye offered an unusual rendition of the national anthem in the opening of the 1983 NBA All-Star Basketball Game in Inglewood, California that incorporated a soulful rhythm and blues background produced by an accompanying drum machine. Also, during the 1990-1 Gulf War against Iraq, Whitney Houston sang "The Star Spangled Banner" at the Super Bowl football game. Her normally elegant voice has rarely been in such superb form as on that day, and copies of the video and audio versions of this performance continue to be popular items for sharing on the Internet. Also, Jimi Hendrix performed an extraordinarily unique and powerful interpretation of "The Star Spangled Banner" at the 1969 Woodstock Festival. Whether or not one considers Mr. Hendrix's version a patriotic rendition of the song is a matter of interpretation, as I discuss in significant detail later in this volume.

One of the most politically potent national anthems in the world today is the national anthem for France, "La Marseillaise," written on 24 April 1792 by Claude-Joseph Rouget de Lisle, an officer in the French corps of engineers based in Strasbourg. He never wrote any other song or poem of significance. The potency of this song is due to the history that surrounds it.

The French Revolution began in 1787 but peaked in 1789. The newly formed National Constituent was initially created as a modest concession from the king to the clergy and nobility, but it ended up acting quickly in 1789 to abolish feudalism and limit the powers of the aristocracy. By the summer of 1789, food supplies were very low. The peasants were the most affected by the food shortages, and they tended to suspect the aristocracy and king of foul play. This led to the tense period in July 1789 involving large numbers of panicking peasants called the "Great Fear." The famous French prison, the Bastille, was seized by the rioters on 14 July 1789, which is the origin of the national holiday, "Bastille Day." The prison was primarily seized on that day because the peasants wanted access to the weaponry in the building. But the seizing of the building also led to the release of seven prisoners who were then being held there at the time. In the past, many political prisoners and other important people had been held and tortured in that prison, and it was generally considered a building of huge symbolic importance to the revolutionary-minded French masses. This event changed the nature of the rebellion from one of a potentially controllable rebellion to full-powered revolution that threatened the continued reign of the French king, Louis XVI. The peasant rebellion quickly spread outside of Paris as well.

Elsewhere in Europe, many people (called "Jacobins") supported these revolutionary ideas. By 1792, this began to deeply distress the aristocrats throughout Europe, especially when the National Constituent Assembly began to involve itself with ideas of self-determination and international law. Suppression of the Jacobins became intense. Partially because Leopold II (Emperor of Austria) and Frederick William II (King of Prussia) were threatening France, and partially to support the Jacobins, France declared war on both Prussia and Austria on 20 April 1792. This was the event that caused Mr. Rouget de Lisle to write "La Marseillaise," and it was specifically written as a patriotic French marching song.

The initial few months of the war went badly for France, and there was concern that the Prussian and Austrian armies might conquer Paris due to traitorous actions of the aristocracy (especially the king). The National Constituent Assembly—which was populated by the bourgeoisie and nobles—saw the writing on the wall and decided to side with the peasants more forcefully, declaring full rights to all French regardless of status. In mid-August of 1792, volunteers who were on the way to the front lines to defend France first attacked the Tuileries Palace that housed King Louis XVI, killing the Swiss Guards. While en route to the palace, they sang "La Marseillaise," as did other military volunteers from Marseille a few days earlier when they marched to Paris.

"La Marseillaise" was adopted on 14 July 1795 as the national anthem of France by the National Convention, the legislative body that replaced the National Constituent Assembly. The text of "La Marseillaise" is very explicit in its call for a violent struggle, and future French authoritarian leaders wanted it banned. The words decry the bloody tyranny of the oppressors, claiming that they want only to cut the throats of beloved sons and companions. The song goes on to encourage the masses to arm themselves and to fight to protect the land by killing the enemy, watering the fields with the enemy's blood. Due to its revolutionary potential, this national anthem was banned by Napoleon Bonaparte, Louis XVIII, and finally Napoleon III. Only in 1879 was it officially reinstated as the French national anthem.

Few national anthems have as powerful a set of lyrics as "La Marseillaise." However, one such song is "The International." This song was the national anthem for the former Soviet Union between 1918-44. In leftist circles, it was also the official anthem for communists and many socialists. Following the collapse of the Soviet Union, a national anthem without words was briefly used, but it was soon replaced in the year 2000 with a national anthem with a benign (relative to "The International") set of lyrics.

Sometimes a national anthem contains content that is bitterly divisive. This is usually the case when the lyrics or music are supportive of only one side of a divided political society. An example of this is Israel's current national anthem. Israel's national anthem is "Hatikvah," or "The Hope." The anthem contains the words "nefesh Yehudi," or Jewish soul. The trouble with this is that a great many Israelis are not Jewish, and some have argued that the words "nefesh Yehudi" should be replaced with "nefesh Israeli" (see "New Lyrics For Israel," by Adam LeBor, *The New York Times* , 18 June 2007, p. A21[N]). Indeed, LeBor has noted that Raleb Majadele, a cabinet minister who is both Mulsim and an Arab, will not sing the Israeli national anthem because of its lyrics, although he will stand for the anthem out of respect for his Israeli nationality.

Occasionally songs emerge within a society which rally a nation in ways that might seem more appropriate for a national anthem. In some situations, the politics of the day are so deeply corrupted that the existing national anthem seems to represent more of the established and discredited political elite than the sensibilities of the masses. In these settings, new songs become symbolic of the politics of the time, as was the case with "Va, pensiero" in Verdi's day. Such songs are called "pseudo national anthems." They are not official national anthems, and they normally are not ever formally adopted as national anthems. But for awhile such songs reign in the hearts of the masses, and the lyrics often carry potent political messages that are reflected in the emerging politics of the day.

A good and recent example of a pseudo national anthem is the Kenyan song "Who Can Bwogo Me?" Kenya was ruled for many years by President Daniel Arap Moi who succeeded President Jomo Kenyatta after Kenyatta's death. After a 1982 attempted coup by the Kenyan Armed Forces (mostly the Air Force), President Moi's rule became increasingly authoritarian. With this increase in authoritarianism came a decrease in accountability and an increase in corruption, and eventually the nation became seriously economically depressed. During national elections in December 2002 in which President Moi's hand-picked successor lost to the opposition candidate, Mr. Mwai Kibaki, a political song was written and sung (actually, rapped) by two young Kenyans named "GidiGidi" (Joseph Ogidi) and "MajiMaji" (Jahd Adonihah). The song, "Who Can Bwogo Me?" was enormously popular and became an unofficial "replacement" national anthem that was heard just about everywhere.

The word "bwogo" is from the Luo language, the language of

a large ethnic group in Kenya. Roughly, it means "scare," and the song's lyrics gave birth to the cross-language new phrase "We are unbwogable." This phrase was even quoted by President Mwai Kibaki in a public appearance, and he translated it as "Nothing will defeat us." (See "To the Beat of a Hit Song, the New Kenya Sends Spirits Off the Charts ," by Marc Lacey, *The New York Times*, 16 February 2003, p. A8[N].) MajiMaji is quoted as saying about the song, "It means you can remove that fear in yourself and do anything.... It's about self-confidence toward the challenges of life. We wrote it about our own struggles, but I guess it captured the mood of this whole country" (*The New York Times*, 16 February 2003, p. A8[N]). Both in the streets of Nairobi and elsewhere, the song was widely referenced, albeit temporarily, as the new national anthem for Kenya.

The Psychology of Nationalist and Patriotic Music

These pages have repeatedly referenced the notion that there appears to be a general psychological need for both nationalism and patriotism in music among many—and perhaps all—nationalities. Music is nationalistic and patriotic not because it is "just that way." Rather, it is because the listeners of the music either want or need to hear a certain nationalistic or patriotic message at a distinct point in time, and they resonate with music that satisfactorily addresses that need. But what comes first, the need or the song?

Sometimes the music is composed first and then later "discovered" by a wanting populace, while at other times the music is composed at or after the time when it is first needed. It is normally not difficult to determine the sequence of events for any given situation. When the bonding between the music, the message, and the people is sufficiently profound, the music becomes a more or less permanent fixture in the psyche of a nation. This is the point at which the music takes on symbolic value, and it no longer matters whether the melody is an original composition or is borrowed from, say, a drinking song. It does not even always matter whether the song contains an explicit call to action, as with "La Marseillaise," or whether it is more general or vague in its meaning, as in the case of "Va, pensiero." What really matters at this point is that the people consider the music and its message to be a symbolic representation of themselves and their coherence as a national collective. This raises all sorts of psychological questions that will beg resolution in future research. But that political nationalist and patriotic music has the potential to make such deep impressions in the minds of a citizenry should now be abundantly clear. Patterns in the variations in these psychological impressions as they correlate with differences in the message of the lyrics or the social and historical relevance of the melodies will become more clear as scholars continue to probe into these arguably profound musical matters.

CHAPTER 5

Industrialization and the Emergence of Labor Music

This chapter outlines the genesis and development of political music that is associated with the labor movement in the United States. Without question music relating to workers in the industrial age has emerged in virtually every setting in which there are industries, and my focus on the American setting should in no way be interpreted as an indication of the absence of labor-related political music in other nations and cultures. Nonetheless, in a few instances I do extend the discussion heuristically to situations in which labor-related political music has emerged in other nations in a way that either closely parallels or interestingly diverges from that found in the American setting, allowing the reflections from these examples to further illuminate that which developed in the United States.

No single person contributed more to the development of the genre of political music in the American labor movement than Joe Hill. (However, some might argue that the *legend* of Joe Hill is the greatest contributor rather than Joe Hill himself.) His story continues to be legendary among labor organizers and their followers, long after his death by firing squad on 15 November 1915. His antagonists also remain equally passionate about this highly controversial figure. Indeed, one can still hear the influence of Joe Hill's music in contemporary works in this genre performed by groups and individuals as diverse as Billy Bragg and The Rolling Stones. The legend of Joe Hill also remains a popular topic of investigation and reporting. A useful account of his life and musical contributions to the labor movement can be found in the biographical treatment by Gibbs M. Smith (1984). Also, the Public Broadcasting Service in the United States has recently devoted resources to this story in an extensive report by Ken

Verdoia (http://www.pbs.org/joehill/story/index.html, accessed July 2002), a well-organized account which was particularly helpful in structuring elements of my own biographical summary below.

Joe Hill was born in Sweden on 7 October 1879, the child of Olof and Margareta Haggland. His original name was Joel Emmanuel Haggland. His father was employed as a laborer with the railroads, and Joel had eight siblings. Joel's early life was particularly difficult. His father died when Joel was eight, and by that time only six children were still alive. He and his other surviving siblings had to work as child laborers in factories. Joel contracted tuberculosis in his skin when he was 12 years old. To treat this illness, he had a number of skin operations that scarred his face, and these scars eventually became significant in the story surrounding his death. After his mother died in 1902, his nuclear family essentially disintegrated, and Joel decided to emigrate with one of his brothers to America, both arriving in New York that same year.

Finding employment and life difficult in New York, Joel and his brother quickly abandoned the city in favor of traveling. Splitting from his brother, Joel adopted what ended up being a pattern of continual migration that he maintained the rest of his life. There is historical evidence (usually postcards that he sent to relatives and friends) that he traveled throughout the Midwestern states as well as California and the Southeast. At some time between 1906 and 1910, he seems to have encountered legal difficulties and had to "disappear." This is when he changed his name to Joseph Hillstrom. It is not known why he had to change his name and temporarily disappear. Some people think he may have been engaged in criminal activity, while others argue that he had already begun to organize workers in the nascent labor movement of the day and had become a target of the exploiting employers.

During these years of drifting from place to place and shifting from job to job, he became deeply disillusioned with America. Long ago in New York he discovered that the image of America as a land of easy fortune was untrue. But now he also found that essentially all of the United States was far from a nation of opportunity and equality. Rather, he found in it a deep-seated pattern of ruthless exploitation of workers by wealthy capitalists. There were essentially no protections for laborers in his day, and the more he realized this the more he became profoundly influenced by some early labor-organizing activists in California.

By 1910, Joseph Hillstrom was in San Pedro, California. It was here that he was introduced to the Industrial Workers of the World (the I.W.W.), more popularly known as the "Wobblies" (see especially Renshaw 1999). It is probably best to think of the Wobblies as one of the more radical labor-related components of a larger social fabric of protest in the early 1900s that extended through the New Deal years of the 1930s and 40s, a fabric which included left-wing and populist politics as diverse as Governor and Senator Huey Long, Father Charles E. Coughlin, Dr. Francis E. Townsend, and even Father Major Jealous Divine. The Wobblies eschewed the idea of gradual improvement in the treatment of laborers, probably thinking that such improvement would always be more illusory than real. Rather, the I.W.W. sought a more complete overhaul of the economic system that essentially flipped the tables on the ability of the wealthy to control the lives of the working class. Joseph Hillstrom joined the Wobblies and soon became an active organizer for their cause. In 1910 he wrote an angry letter complaining about police brutality to the editor of the *Industrial Worker* (the I.W.W. newspaper) using the name "Joe Hill," and from then on he is known only by that name.

It is virtually impossible to trace Joe Hill's whereabouts accurately after this. Without doubt, he was always leading many organizational efforts of the I.W.W. labor movement. Reports have him participating in a great many events—often at the same time in diverse locations, and word-of-mouth reporting has not been successful in keeping the facts straight with regard to his actual travels. One of the reasons for this may rest in the fact that Joe Hill was such a prodigious composer of motivational labor songs, and laborers and their organizers so often sang his songs during their activities. Indeed, the I.W.W. printed many of his songs in what became known as the *Little Red Songbook*. Thus, even if Joe Hill was unavailable, this songbook traveled well, and it seems certain that many laborers felt a close tie to Joe Hill through his songs even if he was not physically present at a particular rally or event.

While Joe Hill was organizing for the I.W.W., he also had a significant number of encounters with the law. He was in and out of jail, and at least once was seriously beaten by the police. As with all events surrounding Joe, there is more than one side to these stories, with officials sometimes claiming that Joe was involved in all sorts of acts, including theft.

The beginning of the end for Joe Hill can be identified with his arrival in Salt Lake City, Utah in 1913. Approximately six months after he arrived, on 10 January 1914, there was an attack by two masked men at a grocery story in Salt Lake City around 10 p.m. The owner, a former police officer, was killed during an exchange of gunfire, as was his son. Nothing was stolen, and there was a vague report that one of the assailants may have been wounded. The police felt that this was an assassination attempt to "pay back" the owner due to his earlier work as an officer, and this is how it was reported in the next morning's newspapers. Apparently, one witness said that one of the robbers seemed to know the store owner, Mr. Morrison. The robber shouted something before shooting Mr. Morrison that suggested a desire to carry out an act of revenge.

Approximately an hour and a half after the time of the assault, Joe Hill went to a doctor's office with a bullet wound that he claimed he received while defending the reputation of a "virtuous woman." Joe Hill was also carrying a holstered gun at the time of his treatment, not unusual for a man who had just been in a duel. The following day the doctor saw the newspaper reports regarding the attack on the owner of the grocery store, and noted the request by the police to report anyone with any wounds caused by gunshot. After being contacted by the doctor, the police found Joe Hill sleeping in his room, and then shot him in the hand during the arrest when he tried quickly to grab his pants when they barged into his room.

The authorities in Utah did not find out until just before his trial that their suspect was Joe Hill, the well-known labor organizer. Since Joe had no past history with regard to the owner of the grocery store, the prosecutors dropped the idea that the attack was a revenge killing, and instead argued that it was a bungled robbery. The evidence tying Joe Hill to the case was circumstantial at best. There were no witnesses who saw an unmasked assailant clearly, although one witness suggested one of the gunmen may have had facial scars like those of Hill's. Hill claimed total innocence. He also refused to testify, and no one to this day knows exactly why. He likewise refused to be represented by an attorney (actually, he tried to fire and then ignored two volunteer attorneys). The jury found him guilty, and he chose to die by gunshot rather than by hanging.

While waiting execution, Joe Hill's case became a rallying cause for the Wobblies. Two I.W.W. organizers in particular were very active in speaking at rallies just about everywhere. The first was William D. Haywood, and the other was Elizabeth Gurley Flynn. Mr. Haywood was better known in those days as "Big Bill Haywood." He was involved in union and labor activities since his mid-twenties, working originally with miners. He himself was once exploited as a mine worker when he was only a child. His first union leadership position was with the Western Federation of Miners. Haywood tended to support conflict over compromise in his organizational activities. He felt that the mining employers simply would not offer significant compromises with regard to working conditions or wages for the workers unless they were threatened with work stoppages. Many skirmishes between the miners and their employers turned violent in those days. Death and disease due to working the mines in unsafe conditions was common, and the miners were naturally driven to extremes on many occasions as they fought for both their lives and the ability to feed their families. There were even fatal attacks on nonunion "scabs," as when a train transporting many such workers was bombed in 1904 outside of Independence, Colorado. Haywood himself was implicated in the 1905 assassination of a former governor of Idaho, Frank Steunenberg.

The authorities gave as good as they got in those days, and Haywood found himself illegally abducted from Denver, Colorado by Pinkerton detectives. These same Pinkerton detectives secretly took Haywood to Boise, Idaho where he was put on trial. Clarence Darrow ended up defending Haywood in a highly publicized trial. There was no physical evidence proving Haywood to be a part of Steunenberg's murder, and the prosecutor's case was built on the potentially forced confession of a person with a criminal past named "Harry Orchard" who had been considered suspicious by the Idaho police. In the end, the jury found Haywood not guilty, although there are many suspicions that the jury itself may have been tampered with in some fashion, including threats of death.

It is not my purpose here to side one way or the other with the outcome of Haywood's or Hill's trial. Rather, I seek to point out that union organizing was dangerous business in the early parts of the 20th century, and all sides—union organizers, business executives, and government leaders—played the game with iron-fisted gloves. Joe Hill's activities should be considered within this context. The union members of that period were used to violence, both against them and in retribution, and they were not easily swayed to abandon someone who fought for their cause just because he or she was accused of breaking the law. The workers could just as easily believe those who claimed that their union leaders were being framed, and in many cases they would have been correct. Moreover, these same workers were acutely aware that Joe Hill's prominence as a voice for their defense would have made him a likely target by his (and their) enemies.

In the years that followed his trial, Haywood helped to organize the I.W.W., eventually leading the organization by 1915, the year Joe Hill was executed. Hill had never met Haywood personally, but Haywood fought a fierce public battle to help Joe. Support eventually came from many corners, including President Woodrow Wilson and Helen Keller. But eventually, Joe Hill told

Haywood in a now famous letter not to mourn for him, but just to keep on organizing for the union. Joe Hill had become a martyr, a fate which he probably thought was a useful way to finish his life's work.

A Selection of Songs by Joe Hill

Joe Hill's songs are often passionate diatribes against the wealthy elite and their exploitive behavior. Joe pulled no punches in his lyrics, and his strong and graphic language remains a signature characteristic of his work. Since he had to be able to convey his messages in diverse organizational settings that often contained no musical instruments, he generally placed his verses in melodies that were well-known in his day.

Perhaps Joe Hill's most famous song is "The Preacher and the Slave." This song was first published in the 1911 edition of the *Little Red Songbook* with the author listed as F. B. Brechler. The author's name was later corrected to be Joe Hill in the 1913 edition songbook. The meaning of the song is tied to the complex environment of the times in which so many destitute people found themselves. The I.W.W. invested a great deal of effort recruiting migratory workers, especially those who took seasonal or temporary jobs in the lumber and construction industries. When the workers lacked employment, they would gather in the slums of major cities. The Salvation Army often went to the street corners in and near those same gatherings in the slums to recruit followers, and in this sense it was competing with the I.W.W. for the attention of the workers. "The Preacher and the Slave" is a satirical look at the efforts of those who tried to sell religion to these poor people, essentially arguing that anyone who followed the preachers was being deceived. This song is often popularly known as "Pie in the Sky," and the lyrics are well-worth a close examination. The song is sung to the melody of "Sweet Bye and Bye." Interested readers will find that this and many other songs by Joe Hill and other folk-writers of protest music have been collected by Edith Fowke and her colleagues (see especially, Fowke and Glaser, 1973; originally published as Fowke and Glaser, 1960).

"The Preacher and the Slave" by Joe Hill (1911)

Long-haired preachers come out every night,
Try to tell you what's wrong and what's right;
But when asked how 'bout something to eat
They will answer with voices so sweet:

    CHORUS:
    You will eat, bye and bye,
    In that glorious land above the sky;
    Work and pray, live on hay,
    You'll get pie in the sky when you die.

The starvation army they play,
They sing and they clap and they pray
'Till they get all your coin on the drum
Then they'll tell you when you're on the bum:

Holy Rollers and jumpers come out,
They holler, they jump and they shout.
Give your money to Jesus they say,
He will cure all diseases today.

If you fight hard for children and wife --
Try to get something good in this life --
You're a sinner and bad man, they tell,
When you die you will sure go to hell.

Workingmen of all countries, unite,
Side by side we for freedom will fight;
When the world and its wealth we have gained
To the grafters we'll sing this refrain:

    FINAL CHORUS:
    You will eat, bye and bye,
    When you've learned how to cook and to fry.
    Chop some wood, 'twill do you good,
    And you'll eat in the sweet bye and bye.

On more than one occasion, Joe Hill argued in favor of

including women in more union organizing activities. It wasn't just that women would increase the number of bodies involved in union activity, but that women would add a new and important social and cultural element to the overall worker movement. While in prison awaiting execution, Joe Hill began corresponding with Elizabeth Gurley Flynn, one of the most courageous women ever to organize for the I.W.W. She led strikes, gave countless speeches (often many in one day), was arrested on numerous occasions (once in the support of free speech), and she famously organized the 1912-3 evacuation of children from Lawrence, Mississippi during a period of brutal and violent confrontation between strikers and the police. She visited Joe Hill in prison in 1915, and Joe apparently idolized her as a role model for all women. Joe wrote a song which he claimed was inspired by Ms. Flynn, and he wrote that he hoped that the song would inspire other women to follow in her footsteps. The song, "The Rebel Girl," had its own music composed by Joe Hill.

"The Rebel Girl" by Joe Hill (1914-5)

There are women of many descriptions
In this queer world, as everyone knows.
Some are living in beautiful mansions,
And are wearing the finest of clothes.
There are blue blooded queens and princesses,
Who have charms made of diamonds and pearl;
But the only and thoroughbred lady
Is the Rebel Girl.

> CHORUS:
> That's the Rebel Girl, that's the Rebel Girl!
> To the working class she's a precious pearl.
> She brings courage, pride and joy
> To the fighting Rebel Boy.
> We've had girls before, but we need some more
> In the Industrial Workers of the World.
> For it's great to fight for freedom
> With a Rebel Girl.

Yes, her hands may be hardened from labor,
And her dress may not be very fine;
But a heart in her bosom is beating
That is true to her class and her kind.
And the grafters in terror are trembling
When her spite and defiance she'll hurl;
For the only and thoroughbred lady
Is the Rebel Girl.

One of the best examples of Joe Hill's use of satire and humor can be found in his song "Casey Jones—The Union Scab." The song was inspired by the large and long strike from 1911 to 1915 against the Harriman and Illinois Central Railroad System, a large corporation of which Southern Pacific was a part. The tune of the song is from the well-known melody "Casey Jones." In the song, the words "S.P." stand for Southern Pacific.

"Casey Jones—The Union Scab" by Joe Hill (1912)

The Workers on the S. P. line to strike sent out a call;
But Casey Jones, the engineer, he wouldn't strike at all;
His boiler it was leaking, and its drivers on the bum,
And his engine and its bearings, they were all out of plumb.

Casey Jones kept his junk pile running;
Casey Jones was working double time;
Casey Jones got a wooden medal,
For being good and faithful on the S. P. line.

The workers said to Casey: "Won't you help us win this strike?"
But Casey said: "Let me alone, you'd better take a hike."
Then someone put a bunch of railroad ties across the track,
And Casey hit the river bottom with an awful crack.

Casey Jones hit the river bottom;
Casey Jones broke his blessed spine;
Casey Jones was an Angelino,
He took a trip to heaven on the S. P. line.

When Casey Jones got up to heaven, to the Pearly Gate,
He said: "I'm Casey Jones, the guy that pulled the S. P. freight."
"You're just the man," said Peter, "our musicians went on strike;
You can get a job a'scabbing any time you like."

    Casey Jones got up to heaven;
    Casey Jones was doing mighty fine;
    Casey Jones went scabbing on the angels,
    Just like he did to workers of the S. P. line.

They got together, and they said it wasn't fair,
For Casey Jones to go around a'scabbing everywhere.
The Angels' Union No. 23, they sure were there,
And they promptly fired Casey down the Golden Stairs.

    Casey Jones went to Hell a'flying;
    "Casey Jones," the Devil said, "Oh fine:
    Casey Jones, get busy shoveling sulphur;
    That's what you get for scabbing on the S. P. Line."

Some of Joe Hill's songs point to the great emotional pain experienced in the lives of many exploited laborers. In some of his compositions he places the voice of the song in a worker who experiences this trauma. A good example of this can be found in Hill's sad song, "Down in the Old Dark Mills" which he wrote in 1913 to be sung to the tune of "Down By the Old Mill Stream." In this song, Joe writes about a man who met a girl while working in a mill. They fell in love and planned to marry, but tragedy struck of a type that was common for those who worked in mills. The dreams of a happy future were left unfulfilled.

"Down in the Old Dark Mills" by Joe Hill (1913)

How well I do remember
That mill along the way,
Where she and I were working
For fifty cents a day.
She was my little sweetheart;
I met her in the mill—
It's a long time since I saw her.
But I love her still.

CHORUS:
Down in the Old Black Mill,
That's where first we met.
Oh! that loving thrill
I shall ne'er forget;
And those dreamy eyes,
Blue like summer skies.
She was fifteen—
My pretty queen—
In the Old Black Mill.

We had agreed to marry
When she'd be sweet sixteen.
But then—one day I crushed it—
My arm in the machine.
I lost my job forever—
I am a tramp disgraced.
My sweetheart still is slaving
In the same old place.

But if Joe Hill was anything, he was a union organizer, and many of his songs were directed squarely at encouraging workers to join the I.W.W. The song "Everybody's Joining It" is a good example in this regard. Written in 1912 by Joe Hill, the song is sung to the tune of "Everybody's Doin' It" which was composed by Irving Berlin a year earlier.

"Everybody's Joining It" by Joe Hill (1911)

Fellow workers, can't you hear,
There is something in the air.
Everywhere you walk everybody talks
'Bout the I. W. W.
They have got a way to strike
That the master doesn't like—
Everybody sticks,
That's the only trick,
All are joining now.

CHORUS:
Everybody's joining it, joining what? Joining it!
Everybody's joining it, joining what? Joining it!

One Big Union, that's the workers' choice,
One Big Union, that's the only choice,
One Big Union, that's the only noise,
One Big Union, shout with all your voice;
Make a noise, make a noise, make a noise, boys,
Everybody's joining it, joining what? Joining it!
Everybody's joining it, joining what? Joining it!
Joining in this union grand,
Boys and girls in every land;
All the workers hand in hand—
Everybody's joining it now.

The Boss is feeling mighty blue,
He don't know just what to do.
We have got his goat, got him by the throat,
Soon he'll work or go starving.
Join I. W. W.
Don't let bosses trouble you,
Come and join with us—
Everybody does—
You've got nothing to lose.

Will the One Big Union Grow?
Mister Bonehead wants to know.
Well! What do you think, of that funny gink,
Asking such foolish questions?
Will it grow? Well! Look a here,
Brand new locals everywhere,
Better take a hunch,
Join the fighting bunch,
Fight for Freedom and Right.

Another notable pro-union song is "There is Power in a Union," written by Joe Hill in 1913 to be sung to the tune of the Christian hymn "There is Power in the Blood" composed by Lewis E. Jones in 1899. The title of this song has more recently been re-used by Billy Bragg in his own highly effective song that essentially offers an updated version of the same message as that expressed in Joe Hill's original verses.

"There is Power in a Union" by Joe Hill (1913)

Would you have freedom from wage slavery,
Then join in the grand Industrial band;
Would you from mis'ry and hunger be free,
Then come! Do your share, like a man.

> CHORUS:
> There is pow'r, there is pow'r
> In a band of workingmen.
> When they stand hand in hand,
> That's a pow'r, that's a pow'r
> That must rule in every land—
> One Industrial Union Grand.

Would you have mansions of gold in the sky,
And live in a shack, way in the back?
Would you have wings up in heaven to fly,
And starve here with rags on your back?

If you've had "nuff" of "the blood of the lamb,"
Then join in the grand Industrial band;
If, for a change, you would have eggs and ham.
Then come! Do your share, like a man.

If you like sluggers to beat off your head,
Then don't organize, all unions despise,
If you want nothing before you are dead,
Shake hands with your boss and look wise.

Come, all ye workers, from every land,
Come join in the grand Industrial band.
Then we our share of this earth shall demand.
Come on! Do your share, like a man.

Some of Joe Hill's songs called for direct action on the part of the laboring masses. In these cases, Hill voices passionate exhortations to break the bonds of servitude and to rebel. One can assume that the establishment of his day felt highly threatened by workers singing such songs, and Joe Hill's ability to voice these propagandistic ideas so forcefully certainly added to the sense of danger that he felt followed him. One of the best examples of this kind of song is "Workers of the World, Awaken," which Joe Hill wrote in 1914.

"Workers of the World, Awaken" by Joe Hill (1914)

Workers of the world, awaken!
Break your chains. Demand your rights.
All the wealth you make is taken
By exploiting parasites.
Shall you kneel in deep submission
From your cradles to your graves?
Is the height of your ambition
To be good and willing slaves?

> CHORUS:
> Arise, ye prisoners of starvation!
> Fight for your own emancipation;
> Arise, ye slaves of every nation.
> In One Union grand.
> Our little ones for bread are crying,
> And millions are from hunger dying;
> The end the means is justifying,
> 'Tis the final stand.

If the workers take a notion,
They can stop all speeding trains;
Every ship upon the ocean
They can tie with mighty chains.
Every wheel in the creation,
Every mine and every mill,
Fleets and armies of the nation,
Will at their command stand still.

Join the union, fellow workers,
Men and women, side by side;
We will crush the greedy shirkers
Like a sweeping, surging tide;
For united we are standing,
But divided we will fall;
Let this be our understanding—
"All for one and one for all."

Workers of the world, awaken!
Rise in all your splendid might;
Take the wealth that you are making,
It belongs to you by right.
No one will for bread be crying,
We'll have freedom, love and health.
When the grand red flag is flying
In the Workers' Commonwealth.

Joe Hill unabashedly compared the employment that many workers faced as equivalent to slavery. This idea re-occurs in a number of his songs. Sometimes the issue of slavery is approached more directly, however, as in the song "The White Slave" which Joe Hill wrote in 1912 to be sung to the tune of "Meet Me Tonight In Dreamland" which was composed three years earlier by Leo Friedman. In this song, Joe addresses the issue of sexual exploitation of the working class, particularly working women. He makes the argument that wages are so subsistence that working women earn only enough to barely feed themselves, but not enough to give themselves decent shelter. The result is that young working girls are tempted into prostitution in order to find a place to stay. This life soon breaks their health, their self-esteem, and their will to live. Mr. Hill makes no bones about who is to blame. It is the employers who refuse to pay their workers a decent wage.

"The White Slave" by Joe Hill (1912)

One little girl, fair as a pearl,
Worked every day in a laundry;
All that she made for food she paid,
So she slept on a park bench so soundly;
An old procuress spied her there,
And whispered softly in her ear:

> CHORUS:
> Come with me now, my girly,
> Don't sleep out in the cold;
> Your face and tresses curly
> Will bring you fame and gold,
> Automobiles to ride in, diamonds and silks to wear,

You'll be a star bright, down in the red light,
You'll make your fortune there.

Same little girl, no more a pearl,
Walks all alone 'long the river,
Five years have flown, her health is gone,
She would look at the water and shiver,
Whene'er she'd stop to rest and sleep,
She'd hear a voice call from the deep:

Girls in this way, fall every day,
And have been falling for ages,
Who is to blame? you know his name,
It's the boss that pays starvation wages.
A homeless girl can always hear
Temptations calling everywhere.

The I.W.W. also extended its propagandistic activities to the issue of the entry of the United States into World War I. This was a highly divisive topic at the time. Isolationist sentiments were powerfully represented in America in those days, and Woodrow Wilson led a country into war without the backing of a unified public. As an historical aside, it was precisely to avoid this same type of problem that U.S. President Franklin Delano Roosevelt delayed America's entry into World War II until the American public was unequivocally supportive of sending U.S. troops into battle. To make use of this delay, in a now famous battleship meeting in the North Atlantic in August of 1941, FDR agreed with Prime Minister Winston Churchill to complete the transformation of the American economy into a wartime economy that would supply Great Britain with the tools of war by signing the Atlantic Charter. (The "Lend-Lease Act," passed by Congress in March of 1941, was the first major piece of legislation authorizing FDR to direct large quantities of wartime supplies to the European theater.) FDR felt he had to wait for what he considered to be a nearly certain "incident" in the Pacific, one large enough to tip the balance of public opinion in the United States to favor a direct entry into the war. The Japanese attacked Pearl Harbor on 7 December 1941, and America's declared entry into both the Pacific and European war theaters began almost immediately thereafter.

The I.W.W.'s basic complaint about fighting in World War I was that workers were being used to defend a capitalist system that exploited them with essentially near-slave wages. To add insult to injury, the military forces paid these worker/soldiers poorly, fed them bad food, and gave them inadequate housing (i.e., tents). A powerfully satiric song that addresses these issues is "Stung Right," written by Joe Hill in 1913 and intended to be sung to the tune of the Christian hymn "Sunlight, Sunlight" composed by Winfield. S. Weeden in 1897.

"Stung Right" by Joe Hill (1913)

When I was hiking 'round the town to find a job one day,
I saw a sign that thousand men were wanted right away,
To take a trip around the world in Uncle Sammy's fleet,
I signed my name a dozen times upon a great big sheet.

> CHORUS:
> I was stung right, stung right, S-T-U-N-G,
> Stung right, stung right, E. Z. Mark, that's me
> When my term is over, and again I'm free,
> There'll be no more trips around the world for me.

The man he said, "The U. S. Fleet, that is no place for slaves,
The only thing you have to do is stand and watch the waves."
But in the morning, five o'clock, they woke me from my snooze,
To scrub the deck and polish brass, and shine the captain's shoes.

One day a dude in uniform to me commenced to shout,
I simply plugged him in the jaw, and knocked him down and out;
They slammed me right in irons then and said, "You are a case."
On bread and water then I lived for twenty-seven days.

One day the captain said, "Today I'll show you something nice,
All hands line up, we'll go ashore and have some exercise."
He made us run for seven miles as fast as we could run,
And with a packing on our back that weighed a half a ton.

Some time ago when Uncle Sam he had a war with Spain,
And many of the boys in blue were in the battle slain,

Not all were killed by bullets, though; no, not by any means,
The biggest part that were killed by Armour's Pork and Beans.

Another anti-war song written by Joe Hill is more broadly ideological and less satirical than the above example. In this song, "Should I Ever Be a Soldier," Mr. Hill explicitly states under what conditions and flag a worker should fight. It was written in 1913 to be sung to the tune for "Colleen Bawn," a song composed by J. Fred Helf and Ed Madden in 1906 about a young poor Irish girl who was murdered by her "higher class" husband.

"Should I Ever Be a Soldier" by Joe Hill (1913)

We're spending billions every year
For guns and ammunition.
"Our Army" and "our Navy" dear,
To keep in good condition;
While millions live in misery
And millions died before us,
Don't sing "My Country 'tis of thee,"
But sing this little chorus.

> CHORUS
> Should I ever be a soldier,
> 'Neath the Red Flag I would fight;
> Should the gun I ever shoulder,
> It's to crush the tyrant's might.
> Join the army of the toilers,
> Men and women fall in line,
> Wage slave of the world! Arouse!
> Do your duty for the cause,
> For Land and Liberty.

And many a maiden, pure and fair,
Her love and pride must offer
On Mammon's altar in despair,
To fill the master's coffer.
The gold that pays the mighty fleet,
From tender youth he squeezes,
While brawny men must walk the street
And face the wintry breezes.

Why do they mount their gatling gun
A thousand miles from ocean,
Where hostile fleet could never run—
Ain't that a funny notion?
If you don't know the reason why,
Just strike for better wages,
And then, my friends—if you don't die—
You'll sing this song for ages.

The Subsequent Labor Music Inspired by Joe Hill

Joe Hill's music inspired its own mini-genre of labor music that developed throughout the 20th century. Within this genre,"I Dreamed I Saw Joe Hill Last Night" was composed by Alfred Hays in 1925, and this song captures the general idea that Joe Hill's contribution was so significant to the early labor movement that his presence continues to be felt in his absence. The lyrics describe a dream in which someone sees Joe Hill by his bedside. The person then declares that he cannot really be seeing Joe Hill since Joe was falsely accused and then killed by the mining executives. Joe responds by saying that he never died because he continues to be with the workers in their hearts as they organize. Perhaps the most beautiful rendition of this song is one that was recorded by Paul Robeson, the leftist-leaning baritone whose U.S. passport was withdrawn by the U.S. State Department in 1950 at the outset of the so-called "McCarthy era." Robeson's passport was not returned to him until the Supreme Court ruled in his favor in 1958. Another notable rendition of the song is its performance by Joan Baez during the 1969 Woodstock Festival.

"I Dreamed I Saw Joe Hill Last Night" by Alfred Hays (1925)

I dreamed I saw Joe Hill last night,
Alive as you or me
Says I, "But Joe, you're ten years dead,"
"I never died," says he
"I never died," says he

"In Salt Lake, Joe," says I to him,
Him standing by my bed,
"They framed you on a murder charge,"
Says Joe, "But I ain't dead,"
Says Joe, "But I ain't dead."

"The copper bosses killed you, Joe,
They shot you, Joe," says I.
"Takes more than guns to kill a man,"
Says Joe, "I didn't die,"
Says Joe, "I didn't die."

And standing there as big as life
And smiling with his eyes
Joe says, "What they forgot to kill
Went on to organize,
Went on to organize."

"Joe Hill ain't dead," he says to me,
"Joe Hill ain't never died.
Where working men are out on strike
Joe Hill is at their side,
Joe Hill is at their side."

"From San Diego up to Maine,
In every mine and mill,
Where workers strike and organize,"
Says he, "You'll find Joe Hill,"
Says he, "You'll find Joe Hill."

I dreamed I saw Joe Hill last night,
Alive as you or me
Says I, "But Joe, you're ten years dead,"
"I never died," says he
"I never died," says he

The next most significant composer and artist in post-Joe Hill labor genre is Woody Guthrie (1912-1967). Mr. Guthrie had the same urge to travel as did Joe Hill. When he was only 15 years old, right before the onset of the Great Depression, Woody Guthrie left home and traveled across the country via freight train, carrying his guitar and harmonica wherever he went. During his

Depression-era travels, he stayed in the same type of camps filled with migrant workers and hobos that were previously a focus of I.W.W. recruitment efforts. Guthrie wrote songs that reflected his experiences with these groups of the dispossessed, and he performed these songs to these same audiences. Guthrie became a well-known and warmly-received visitor to these camps. His performances must certainly have been one of the high points of daily life in those communities of hardship. He composed in excess of 1,000 songs. Some of the titles of his labor-related songs are: "1913 Massacre," "Babe O' Mine," "Boomtown Bill, "The Dying Doctor," The Farmer-Labor Train," "Joe Hillstrom," "Keep that Oil A-Rollin," "The Ladies Auxiliary," "Ludlow Massacre," "Mean Talking Blues," "Talking Subway," "The Union Maid," "The Weaver's Song," "Weavery Life," and "Deportees." The last song, "Deportees" is about an incident involving a plane wreck and migrant workers.   Guthrie also wrote non-labor songs that addressed issues as diverse as the Dust Bowl, outlaw life, World War II, and even patriotic ballads. Woody Guthrie's most well-known song is "This Land Is Your Land."

Just as Joe Hill influenced Woody Guthrie, Mr. Guthrie himself similarly made a significant impression on those who followed him. Of all those influenced by Woody Guthrie, perhaps no one stands out as much as Bob Dylan. As with Mr. Guthrie, Bob Dylan performed many of his early songs primarily with guitar and harmonica. Bob Dylan idolized Woody Guthrie, and they finally met late in Mr. Guthrie's life before Guthrie died of Huntington's chorea. Bob Dylan made his most significant mark on the world during the days of the Vietnam War as a composer and performer of protest music, as did Arlo Guthrie, Woody Guthrie's son. (I discuss both of these composers in greater depth later in this volume.) Woody Guthrie also had a large influence on The Rolling Stones. Both Keith Richards and Mick Jagger wrote songs that reflect this influence, such as "Salt of the Earth" and "Factory Girl," both from the 1968 *Beggar's Banquet* album. Today, the labor-music genre is kept alive by a variety of lesser-known composers and artists, the most notable of which is perhaps

Billy Bragg.

Primary Sources for Further Reading

Smith, Gibbs M. 1984. *Joe Hill.* Layton, Utah: Gibbs Smith Publisher.

Verdoia, Ken.   http://www.pbs.org/joehill/story/index.html, accessed 2 December 2002.

CHAPTER 6

Protest Music: Movement and Non-movement Motivations

The dominant factor that influenced the genesis of the contemporary genre of political protest music in the United States, Britain, and much of Europe is the political tumult associated with the Vietnam War and the American Civil Rights Movement, both of which occurred in the 1960s and 1970s. It was during this period that the Beatles transformed themselves from a romantic "boy band" into a truly revolutionary musical powerhouse. They were quickly followed by The Rolling Stones, Bob Dylan, Joan Baez, "Peter, Paul, and Mary," the Smothers Brothers, Jimi Hendrix, Arlo Guthrie, many other individuals and groups, and even their own separated counterparts (such as Paul McCartney, John Lennon, and George Harrison). Collectively, these musicians both riveted and taught a large segment of an entire generation, as well as many others across generations. They taught their listeners both the value of questioning authority and the practical matters of how to do it, including the language to use. Moreover, they taught as they themselves learned, for no musician arrived on the scene with a clear blueprint outlining how to contribute to the transformation of a world.

Those were years pregnant with the seeds of change. And the period was not without victories for those who sought change. An American president fell through charges of an office misused, the Vietnam War—ultimately recognized to be an independence struggle—was lost (abandoned, or won, depending on one's point of view), and the Civil Rights Movement culminated with the end of racial segregation in the southern states in America and a real beginning to the long delayed process of national racial integration. Reading through a collection of the major documents of those days—as with the riveting collection offered by Unger and Unger

(1998)—can lead anyone to the conclusion that this was a time period in which American society in general was coming apart at the seams. But all crises come with opportunities for change and growth, and this tumultuous period in the United States was no exception in this regard. This was a period that defined the potential for political protest music. Music now had the demonstrated ability to accompany a political movement with a force that could not be ignored. The world of music changed in those years. The world changed in those years.

Once the die was cast and the model for the expanded role of music as a conduit for orchestrating political content was unambiguously apparent, the question arose as to whether or not music could remain such a potent political tool if it did not accompany a large-scale protest movement. That is, could music retain a powerful role as a vehicle of political protest for causes that did not carry with them the drama of a world-focused spectacle? This addresses the question of the range of use, and to some extent effectiveness, of political protest music within a large variety of protest settings, some involving widely recognized movements and others speaking to more isolated issues, events, and causes.

This chapter examines this diversity in the use of protest music. Beginning with the strongest case—protest music associated with the tumult of the 1960s and 1970s—I then turn to the issue of how the lessons of that period were utilized by artists and composers who sought to tilt public sympathy toward lesser known (or cared for) causes. While much of this discussion focuses on the interaction between music and politics in the United States, attention shifts eventually to examples of political protest music in other national and cultural venues, as with Chile during the 1970s and 1980s, before again returning to the case of the United States during the 1980s, 1990s, and finally the early years of the next century.

The Vietnam War and Its Effect on the Development of Protest Music

The Vietnam War lasted from 1955 through 1975. In essence, it was an unsuccessful effort to permanently partition North and South Vietnam into communist (North) and capitalist (South) areas. During World War II, the Japanese controlled Vietnam. After World War II, the Japanese left, and Ho Chi Minh became the leader of a populist and nationalist group called the Viet Minh, which had a strong presence in the northern areas. The group sought Vietnamese independence, and initially it was not communist, but it adopted a communist political orientation by the mid-1950s during their long confrontation with the French. Following the Japanese departure from Vietnam, the French wanted to regain its colonies in Indochina. They offered the Vietnamese a deal that was similar to that offered to French colonies in Africa. "Independence" could be granted only if Vietnam would become a state in the French Union.

The Viet Minh rejected this French offer as little more than a continuation of colonialism, and fighting began between the Viet Minh and French military forces in 1946. By 1954, after a stinging defeat for the French in the battle of Dien Bien Phu, the French negotiated a separation between their forces and those of the Viet Minh. The agreement was called the "Geneva Accords," named after the location where the negotiations took place. The agreement stated that the two sides would be separated by a demilitarized zone (the so-called "DMZ") which followed the 17th parallel while the French forces would move south. In the process of separating the forces, thousands of civilians were also relocated. According to the agreement, subsequent to the separation of forces, in 1956 there were to be internationally supervised elections throughout all of Vietnam. Since the Viet Minh was essentially an independence organization and movement, it was widely considered the most popular single political force in Vietnam at the time, and almost certainly would have won the elections.

During the negotiations between the Viet Minh and the French in Geneva, Ngo Dinh Diem became the prime minister of the South. Fearing a loss, Mr. Diem refused to hold the elections as promised, and the Viet Minh had no choice but to return to war. The United States feared the spread of communism throughout Indochina following the withdrawal of the French forces. Because of this, the U.S. supported Diem, despite the fact that he and his regime were both undemocratic and highly unpopular. Southern supporters of the Viet Minh traveled to the North to obtain military training, and they then returned to the South to continue the fight for Vietnamese independence (as they perceived it). These fighters were called the "Viet Cong." Diem asked for military support from the U.S., and the U.S. began by sending noncombat advisors and support personnel. The U.S. soon sent fighting forces as well.

In 1963, Diem was assassinated in a military coup. The U.S. knew he was a liability, and it failed to stop the coup even though it had advance warning of it. Despite the coup, governmental stability and popularity continued to be evasive qualities in the South, and the U.S. was looking for other ways to increase its presence in the country. While in the Gulf of Tonkin, the U.S. Maddox, a destroyer, was fired upon by patrol boats from North Vietnam on 2 August 1964. President Lyndon Baines Johnson falsely claimed that this aggression was repeated on 4 August. The U.S. Congress then passed the "Gulf of Tonkin Resolution," which allowed the president to prevent further attacks by using whatever military force may be necessary.

The Gulf of Tonkin Resolution is an important historical landmark. (See especially, Unger and Unger, 1998, pp. 257-258.) It was based on information given to Congress that was later unequivocally determined to be false. It has not been proven that President Johnson knowingly lied to Congress about the North Vietnamese patrol boat attacks on the U.S. ships, but it is possible that he did lie. The Gulf of Tonkin Resolution was used as the primary justification for the escalated U.S. intervention in Vietnam. It also confirmed an important principle that operated throughout the days of conflict in Vietnam (some would argue from Truman through Nixon), a principle of acting with hidden intent and (if needed) the uninhibited use of deception through the spread of falsehood—all for the purpose of obtaining support for a war effort that might otherwise not be publicly defendable. (Some readers may also find echos of this same principle with respect to the "weapons of mass destruction" rationale that was used by President George W. Bush to justify the U.S. invasion of Iraq.) This principle was later to haunt the U.S. government, although there is no evidence that the basic idea of deceiving the public to whatever extent may be desired or possible for the purpose of obtaining political or military goals was ever abandoned in later years. Much of the deception relating to the Vietnam War was described in "The Pentagon Papers," a long work commissioned by Robert S. McNamara, then the Secretary of Defense in the United States, and which was eventually leaked to *The New York Times* by Daniel Ellsberg. But other components of the evolving role of deception were also revealed by McNamara himself in his controversial memoir, *In Retrospect: The Tragedy and Lessons of Vietnam*, published in 1995. One of the most haunting aspects of the deception of those days was the misrepresentation of the casualty figures on both sides of the conflict.

Following the Gulf of Tonkin Resolution, there were increased Viet Cong attacks on U.S. military installations. The U.S. typically responded with bombing North Vietnam. By mid-1965, the U.S. had 50,000 troops in Vietnam, and the North Vietnam army begun formally to assist the efforts of the Viet Cong. 130,000 more U.S. troops were added by the end of the year. By 1967, the U.S. had 389,000 troops fighting the Viet Cong and the North Vietnamese. Nothing worked. No amount of troops, no amount of bombing, and no amount of effort short of a nuclear demolition of the entire country could have avoided the inevitable. The guerilla warfare tactics of the Viet Cong were enormously successful, even more so because of the hopeless level of corruption within the government of South Vietnam. In 1967, South Vietnam held presidential elections. But in those elections, all candidates who supported negotiating an end to the hostilities were banned from running.

In 1968, a major offensive against South Vietnam (the so-called "Tet Offensive") failed. But it nonetheless demonstrated that the war was not going to end soon. By 1967 (and especially after the Tet Offensive in early 1968), many Americans began openly to question the wisdom of fighting in Vietnam. Many felt that their government was lying, and that the Vietnamese opposed to the U.S. forces were stronger than the U.S. government was acknowledging. Many began to view the conflict as a war of independence that had been transformed into a civil war largely due to U.S. interference.

After a stunningly weak showing in a Democratic primary election in New Hampshire against Senator Eugene McCarthy (who was against U.S. involvement in the war), President Johnson decided not to run for re-election and began peace talks with the North Vietnamese. (Among the popular vote in New Hampshire, Johnson obtained 49% while McCarthy obtained 42%.) Richard Nixon won the 1968 U.S. presidential election saying that he had a "secret plan" to honorably resolve the conflict in Vietnam. He campaigned throughout the country without allowing reporters to question him about his "secret plan." Instead, he held public meetings, and in those meetings he allowed only members of the public to question him. The reporters were only able to watch and listen. Inevitably, individuals questioning him were nearly always exceptionally polite, and rarely did anyone reject his claim that if he were to tell them his secret plan, then it would not be secret any longer. The campaign worked, and in 1969, President Nixon began his program of "Vietnamization," which was to gradually replace U.S. soldiers with soldiers from South Vietnam. That was his "secret plan," something that the U.S. had tried to do for years. Nonetheless, the renewed effort at getting the South Vietnamese to fight for themselves seemed to have some initial success. By 1971, the South Vietnamese troops began to fight the ground war on their own, relying only on U.S. air support, and the U.S. began to withdraw some its 540,000 military personnel.

Nonetheless, the war heated up again, this time spreading into

Laos and Cambodia. U.S. bombing restarted with a vengeance, and harbors were mined. Forced by a lack of alternatives, an agreement was negotiated in 1973 that allowed for a cease-fire, a prisoner exchange, and the withdrawal of all U.S. forces. The agreement basically stated that the Vietnamese would be free to determine their own future peacefully. The U.S. Congress also banned any further U.S. military troop engagement in Indochina in August 1973. But corruption among the South Vietnamese governmental officials was rampant, and many military supplies sent by the U.S. to assist the South ended up in the hands of the Viet Cong. Nixon was pre-occupied with the Watergate scandal. North Vietnam began a full invasion of the South, and all prior arrangements were obliterated. In 1975, the South Vietnamese army and government collapsed, and the end of the war finally arrived.

In the end, there were 47,000 American casualties, approximately 200,000 South Vietnamese casualties, approximately 900,000 North Vietnamese casualties, and countless wounded on all sides. Financially, $200 billion were lost in the fruitless war. This is the backdrop against which protest music matured in the United States and Europe. It was a backdrop of death, deceit, and destruction, all of which was amplified domestically in the United States because of the forced nature of military service due to the draft.

Musicians had a captive audience during those Vietnam War years: young people and their loved ones who were going to be sent to fight—and possibly die—in a war no one really understood. The war tore U.S. families apart, very much as was depicted in the television series, "All In the Family." An entire generation of Americans had been created who no longer felt comfortable with the idea of blindly trusting their national political leadership. Before the Vietnam War, rock and roll was primarily an extension of rhythm and blues. But the Vietnam War changed this, and rock, folk, and their derivatives were forged into sophisticated mediums of protest music.

In this evolutionary sense, it is impossible to separate the current protest genres of rap, gangsta rap, and modern rock from the events of the Vietnam War. The Vietnam War enabled political protest music to evolve to a state of sophistication that it otherwise could never have achieved. Ironically, though much of the music of the 1960s and 1970s was composed as a reaction against the war, the very existence of this type of music might not have been possible without the war. Even racially driven protest music was raised to a new level of potency by the mainstream acceptance of the connection between protest content and contemporary music. In this way, the Civil Rights Movement of the 1960s and 1970s was amplified by the concomitant developments of the Vietnam War, leading to parallelisms in their growth. A useful and in-depth treatment of the entire period that combines a discussion of the Vietnam War, the Civil Rights Movement, and the music of the period can be found in the book, *1968 in America* by Charles Kaiser (Kaiser, 1988).

Protest Music of the Late 1960s and Early 1970s

Perhaps no single piece of music characterizes the crisis that America experienced during the Vietnam War days as powerfully as Jimi Hendrix's instrumental rendition of the "Star Spangled Banner." He played this on the Monday morning of the "Woodstock Music & Art Fair" in August 1969. He was the highest paid performer at the festival, receiving $125,000 for his two sets, and about 90% of the audience stayed through Monday morning in order to hear him perform. It is doubtful that the audience was prepared for what they heard when he played the American national anthem since it was certainly not a normal rendition by any means. The country was tearing itself apart, and it hardly seemed an appropriate setting for a straight forward rendition of the anthem with a one-dimensional sense of patriotism.

One way to introduce and to understand Hendrix's rendition of the national anthem is to examine how this artist has incorporated psychological insights into some of his other works.

A useful example in this regard is Hendrix's instrumental rendition of the song, "Somewhere Over the Rainbow," taken from the film *The Wizard of Oz*. From the story, that place of which the character Dorothy dreams is a happy and magical imaginary place that offers contrasts with the fearful realities of mortal existence. But when she concludes her mental voyage, she discovers the Wizard to be a fraud and her land of wonder to be a dream. Upon awakening, she finds herself in her "normal" grounded reality, surrounded by her family and friends. Yet she remains with something of value from her memories of her imaginary travels. Her fantasy helps her to appreciate her real existence in a new and meaningful way, and this gives her some measure of insight into a higher appreciation of life. Thus, when reality and fantasy collide as they do with Dorothy, the fantasy leaves a residual of experience that adds to the interpretive understanding of the reality.

This tension between the fantastic and the real is that which Jimi Hendrix captures in his rendition of "Somewhere Over the Rainbow." To begin the song, he uses a melodic—almost *bel canto*—style of guitar playing that preserves the idyllic fantasy aspect of the piece. Then the melody (representing the fantasy) is interrupted by interludes of wild discord that represent the inevitable clashes between fantasy and reality. (For everyone, such clashes are encountered in real life as a consequence of objections originating from, say, the school of hard knocks.) Then the melody of the song returns, followed by additional interrupting discord. Again and again the battle is waged, until the song finally ends.

But the song does not end on the note of discord. The harshness of reality does not win this battle. Crucially, the song ends with the melody still intact, triumphant although scarred. Reality does not banish the fantasy; rather, the fantasy colors the reality, instilling it with beauty in the process. When reality and fantasy finally meet, reality is psychically closer to full acceptance, although its interpretation has been altered with the grace of the dream. While the fantasy helps shape the appreciation of reality, it neither destroys the grounded necessity of unadorned perception nor numbs one to its lessons. Through the forge of conflict, the fantasy paints the reality the color of beautiful, and the reality and fantasy merge to form a greater creation in unity. As an artist who himself suffered through a number of nervous breakdowns, Jimi Hendrix offers a portrayal of inner struggle that is both inspiring and needed. For Mr. Hendrix, inner conflict leads to greater psychic understanding whereby human existence is understood no longer as a process of plodding dully through a sequence of birth, work, and death. Hendrix tells us that life is to be appreciated as beautiful, and that this appreciation is achieved through the tumultuous merging of the perception of mundane facts with the fantastic imaginings of dreams. This, indeed, is at least one view of Hendrix's concept of spirituality—a process by which human survival is transformed into that which is divine.

In Jimi Hendrix's rendition of the U.S. national anthem that he played at Woodstock, he follows a similar pattern as that described above by embedding a psychological meaning to the piece. The anthem begins in a normal fashion, not as smooth sounding as the introductory sound of "Somewhere Over the Rainbow," but nonetheless firm, distinct, and bold, as would be appropriate for a song that represents a great nation. But when the anthem continues, wild gyrations of pyrotechnic guitar tumult interrupt the melody of the anthem. The nation you see, was going through a form of collective nervous breakdown at the time, and Hendrix knew all too well how to map that deeply personal experience onto the collective soul of his country's citizenry. But following each cycle of daring plummet into chaos and despair, the anthem returns to recognizable form. From the metaphor of sound, the nation still stands despite its troubles. It is driven to its knees through internal and external conflict, but it rises to its feet, time after time, crisis after crisis. The discord portrayed in Hendrix's national anthem is more severe than that found in his rendition of "Somewhere Over the Rainbow," for this was no child's growing pain. This was a nation of adults repeatedly brought to its knees due to a wartime nightmare that seemed unwilling to end. Yet as the nation stood again from its knees after each pivotal collapse, it grew stronger.

Hendrix does not leave the nation in despair at the end of his rendition of the national anthem. In the end, the melody of the national anthem is still clearly recognizable, which means that for Hendrix the nation itself (and thus the enlightened principles for which it stood) is still recognizable despite the country's problems. Great nations do not forever exist without suffering. They grown through their conflicts, becoming even greater through the struggle. Hendrix's vision is not a one-dimensional portrayal of American patriotism. No one will ever accuse that former paratrooper of robotically waving a flag. His creative perspective of a nation in trouble is driven by a realistic appraisal of the state of America's collective consciousness at that moment in time. Yet his perspective is also deeply inspiring, and by means of this interpretation, sublimely patriotic. His America is not a country torn to pieces and left to die. His America is a body politic having a collective breakdown, an event that will leave the nation with a pain in need of synthesis, but also with a heightened outlook on life. From this view, the potential future contribution of such a country to a needy world is clearly greater than that which could be offered by a land that has never had to rise from its own desperate grief.

Then is this truly "protest music" if Mr. Hendrix does not explicitly shout that he opposes the war? Indeed it is. The very best protest music leads the listener to an understanding of a greater reality such that the listener participates in the discovery of this reality rather than simply being told to accept it as presented by someone else. What Mr. Hendrix is protesting is a simple-minded understanding of the national condition. What he gives us is political realism musically expressed. His approach to portraying the country's inner turmoil is not to hit listeners over the head with a simple political message, but rather to invite them to discover the complexity of this turmoil within the context of his music.

The strategy that Mr. Hendrix uses to teach his lessons is similar to the approach which Tony Schwartz has used in the past to create advertisements for political candidates. Mr Schwartz is the New York based political consultant who created the so-called "Daisy commercial" for television that was used in the 1964 Johnson campaign against the Republican candidate Barry Goldwater. In this commercial, a young girl is counting the petals on a daisy when she looks up and her voice is replaced by a military commander reciting a countdown that leads to the detonation of a nuclear weapon. After this, President Johnson's voice is heard talking about the need for people to love one another. No where in the commercial is Barry Goldwater's name mentioned, and the commercial is constructed so as to induce the viewer to make the connection between Mr. Goldwater and the irresponsible temptation to use nuclear weapons. Mr. Schwartz has labeled this approach to advertising the "voter as workforce" model, since the voters themselves have to make a conclusion based on the way the materials are presented. This approach to advertising has also been called the "deep sell," since the voter more intimately accepts conclusions that are a product of his or her own thinking. This is to be contrasted with an earlier approach to political television advertising pioneered by Rosser Reeves, another New York based advertising executive. Mr. Reeves helped develop the television commercials for the Eisenhower campaign, and his approach was to pound the viewer with the information that he wanted them to accept, just as he had done with commercials for other products, such as the Anacin pain reliever and M&M candies. One might call this form of advertising "hard sell." Extrapolating these advertising models to Jimi Hendrix's rendition of the national anthem, Hendrix's approach would clearly be more analogous to that of Mr. Schwartz's "voter as workforce" or "deep sell" model.

Some readers may worry that I could be reading too much into Hendrix's work. Such concerns are valid for all complex political music, including that of Wagner, Beethoven, and others. With respect to any composer of complex music, it may or may not be that the composer is consciously attempting to create such a complex portrait, which in Hendrix's case is a psychological portrait of America in its state of crisis. I tend to think that he was fully aware on the conscious level of the complexity of his work when he created his music. But it has long been recognized that artists can express complex ideas by internalizing their own experiences such that their art is (at least in part) a product of profound intuition combined with some degree of habitual or practiced expression. This does not require that a rational decision-making process fully control the creative process, an important point made by Martin (1995, pp. 215-6). Indeed, Martin is merely extending an idea into the realm of music that has long been argued more generally by Mead (1934), Becker (1974), and others. This raises the idea that music can be a form of social action that simultaneously accesses a more profound and deeper level of thought than mere rationality.

With respect to any piece of complex political music, readers may find it useful to debate the idea of whether or not a composer consciously infuses his or her music with meaning that is as complex as that which listeners may attribute to it. I tend to side with the view that anyone who creates complexity fully understands the meaning of that complexity. But others may argue that composers sometimes follow a more intuitive orientation toward composition with respect to music that subsequently lends itself to a complex philosophical or political interpretation. For example, I once saw an interview of Freddy Mercury, the late lead singer of the rock group Queen, in which he was asked to interpret his song, "Bohemian Rhapsody." After some reflection, he responded by saying that he did not know its meaning. Of course, this can lead to the question of whether that was a true response, or if he simply said this to avoid discussing the song's real meaning, thereby leaving it open for others to find their own meaning in the music. Indeed, the purpose of much art in general is to force the listener or observer to participate in the interpretation of the art by internalizing the complex nuances of the art while using those same nuances as a lens from which life and reality can be re-evaluated. An artist's description of the meaning of the art can potentially destroy this internalizing process and in a sense transforms the listener or observer into an interpretive stenographer, which of course defeats the transformative purpose of the art itself.

Political music, just like advertisements, is simultaneously both educational and propagandistic. Some of the best political protest music is that which generates a reaction within the listener that catalytically creates change in the listener's own thinking process. Of course, one should not be surprised that this can happen with music that contains no lyrics since this volume has discussed many examples of music that conveys political content without the use of accompanying words. It should also be noted that this "lyric-less" approach to political music continues within the contemporary rock genre. For example, Kelefa Sanneh analyzed instrumental music composed and performed by the group "Godspeed You Black Emperor!" in which the message is unambiguously antiwar with respect to the 2003 U.S./Iraqi military confrontation ("How to Make Antiwar Music Without Using Words," by Kalefa Sanneh, *The New York Times*, 4 April 2003, p E4[N]). The group uses both their music, the name and cover of their CD, and projected images at their concerts to issue an anti-war message. The name of their CD is "Yanqui U.X.O.," where "U.X.O" stands for unexploded ordinance (land mines and bombs). On the level of music, this group seems to take a page out of Jimi Hendrix's own method of interlacing melodies with discord and din. However, unlike Hendrix, the melodies utilized by Godspeed You Black Emperor! do not triumph in the end. Rather, this group's music descends into unambiguous strife, fear, confusion, and cacophony. The listeners are left not with Hendrix's hope of renewal, but rather with the pure anger of raw protest.

The quantity of protest music that appeared in the 1960s and 1970s is so great that it is impossible to describe all of it here. However, there are a few general types of protest music around which much of the larger genre may be organizationally grouped: (1) comic satire, (2) calls for peace, and warnings against taking protest "too far," (3) psychological portraits of profound and personal inner conflict, and (4) the fusion of political and spiritual

change. My aim here is to discuss one or more examples in each
of these general groupings, knowing full well that the inclusion of
much great music is being sacrificed for the prize of organizing an
otherwise unruly collection of passionately inspired composition.

Comic Satire:

Arguably the most potent song of satirical political protest to
come out of the Vietnam War era is Arlo Guthrie's "Alice's
Restaurant." The 18 minute piece is partly spoken and partly sung,
all with a guitar accompaniment. It is based on a mostly true story
(plus some inevitable artistic license) of how Arlo Guthrie and
Richard Robbins were arrested while trying to throw away some
garbage. In 1965 they were visiting some friends on Thanksgiving
who lived in a former church in Stockbridge, Massachusetts. One
of the friends was named "Alice," and she apparently cooked a
delicious Thanksgiving meal. The church was filled with junk, and
Arlo and Rick decided to clean up the place. They filled a VW
minivan with the garbage and then went to the local dump to get
rid of it.   Finding the dump closed on Thanksgiving, Arlo
remembered an out-of-the-way road where they then went,
eventually dumping the garbage over the edge of a hill. The local
police chief, Officer William J. Obanhein, found the garbage, and
he soon found who dumped it. The two youths were arrested, put
in jail, released on bail, put on trial, and ultimately ordered to pay
a $25 fine each and to clean up the garbage. Later, according to
the legend and the song, Arlo was going through a military
physical, and the arrest showed up on his record. The question
then became whether someone who was once arrested for littering
was suitable for military service.

This song portrays in hilarious detail how Arlo views the irony
of his experiences. However, the point of the song is serious. Arlo
Guthrie uses "Alice's Restaurant" to cast deep doubt on the
nonreflective implementation of society's rules. In the song, the
police chief ("Obie") is someone who is deeply disturbed when
confronted with people who do not conform in their behavior to his
understanding of the established norms, and he pursues these

perceived grievances with a near manic sense of determination. He sees his reality from the lens of these rules, and when someone openly deviates from the rules, his reaction appears to greatly exceed the magnitude of the deviation. Similarly, the military officers who are present at Arlo's military physical hold to the letter of their rules without a realistic reflection on their appropriateness in the given situation. This is the purpose of the song: to identify nonreflective thinking as a critical fault in contemporary society. For Arlo Guthrie, the Vietnam War was not so much a consequence of bad people doing evil things, but of nonthinking people following the dictates of their political leadership without questioning the rightness of their leaders' decisions. Guthrie uses satire as a catalytic tool to leverage change—through reflection—in his listeners.

Calls for Peace, and Warnings Against Taking Protest "Too Far":

The Beatles—both when they were together as well as separately—composed a number of political songs that fit in this category. John Lennon and Paul McCartney's appeal for peace in the 1969 song "Give Peace a Chance" is, of course, an obvious example. The song, performed by John Lennon and the Plastic Ono Band, is a critique of the intellectual, social, and political organizational elements of human society that divide and compartmentalize human existence, and thereby miss the essential common element required of any unified view of humanity. Cutting through the complexity of it all (i.e., all "isms," religions, political configurations, and philosophies), the song simply declares that peace is that essential element of our common existence, and peace transcends all other aspects of human organization, intellectual or otherwise. The 1971 song, "Imagine," takes a similar approach to this idea. In this case, Lennon asks his listeners to imagine a world in which all of these divisive organizational elements are missing. In such a world, there is "Nothing to kill or die for" as all humans share the planet while living in a state of peace.

An earlier song, "Revolution," by John Lennon and Paul McCartney and included with the Beatles *White Album*, is an especially interesting example of this category of protest music. Essentially, this song both acknowledges the revolutionary potential of the current world climate, but then cautions against letting revolutionary enthusiasms extend too far. The song claims that desires to change the world are common feelings for virtually everyone, and thus are hardly unique to the revolutionary. The revolutionary's desire to engineer revolutionary change is often mixed with destructive ideas and emotions that can produce as much damage as good. The song counsels listeners to turn inward and work on freeing their minds from rigid intellectual structures that inhibit their abilities to include moderation in their overall plans. In this sense, the title and lyrics of the song yield a dialectic tension; the song's title seems to superficially embrace the dissonance of revolution (further evidenced by the initial auditory ruckus of the song) while the lyrics profoundly discard the more extreme activities and ideas commonly included in the repertories of many revolutionaries.

Psychological Portraits of Profound and Personal Inner Conflict:

This category of protest music contains songs with some of the most complex and/or profound lyrics to emerge from the Vietnam War era. Bob Dylan is arguably the leading composer of this type of song. Bob Dylan's original name is Robert Allen Zimmerman. His father was a part-owner of Zimmerman Furniture and Appliance Co. Bob Dylan was raised in Minnesota, and he briefly attended the University of Minnesota in Minneapolis. It was at this time that he became attracted to Dinkytown, an off-beat area of Minneapolis not too unlike those frequented by Woody Guthrie many years before. Bob Dylan was attracted to poets such as Alan Ginsberg, and he was especially drawn to the music of Woody Guthrie. It was also at this time that he discarded his given name and began calling himself Bob Dylan. The name "Dylan" came from the poet Dylan Thomas whom he admired. Bob Dylan soon idolized Woody Guthrie, and feared that Mr. Guthrie (who was seriously ill) would die before they could meet. Thus, before finishing college, he moved to New York in the winter of 1961 to be near the New Jersey hospital where Woody Guthrie stayed.

It was in New York City that Bob Dylan was discovered. At first his Woody Guthrie-inspired music was an odd sell, and even those who liked his sound did not really know how to categorize it. There was an independence to his music that defied current trends. But Mr. Dylan was an active composer, and his first two albums were released in 1962 and 1963. His second album contained the hit song, "Blowin' in the Wind," and it was with this second album that his audience started to coalesce into a more clearly discernable "following." People liked his new sound, and they also liked his independent way of thinking. Back in those days, for a new artist to get a spot on the Ed Sullivan Show was somewhat comparable to winning a lottery. In 1963, when Bob Dylan was invited to perform on this show, he wanted to perform his song "Talkin' John Birch Paranoid Blues," Ed Sullivan demanded that he play another song. The Cold War was hot at that time, and the John Birch Society was an extremely conservative and anti-communist group that was named after an intelligence officer of the United States Army who was killed in 1945 by the Chinese communists. Quite frankly, Ed Sullivan kept his show focused more on entertainment than on politics, and he was normally careful to avoid serious controversies, political or otherwise. (Recall his famous decision not so allow cameras to capture Elvis Presley's body below the waist.) But rather than switch songs, Bob Dylan walked away from his appearance on the Ed Sullivan show.

It is interesting to note that Bob Dylan's sense of independence caused him frequently to upset his own established fan base on numerous occasions as he continually transformed both the content and the sound of his songs (including the use of electric instruments). Yet with each adaptation, and with each loss of prior support, he gained new supporters in numbers far greater than those who became disaffected.

Bob Dylan's music evolved quickly. He had another album in 1964, another in 1965, and yet another in 1966. Each album was markedly different from previous albums. But through all of this change, Bob Dylan's ability to penetrate deeply into the collective American psyche remained. In song after song, and album after album, Dylan became a sort of combined musical "shrink" and prophet who drew his listeners into a cerebral state of profound inner reflection. Simply, people in those days listened to his songs and labored over the meaning of his lyrics, and it is no exaggeration to state that large numbers of college students in America stayed up many nights in solemn discussion attempting to map his musical messages onto an understanding of the state of the nation and world.

Bob Dylan wrote over 500 songs, and his repertory is simply too large to discuss in significant detail here. But an interpretive discussion of a few examples of his compositions will serve our heuristic needs in this instance. A good example of Dylan's ability to weave potent messages into psychologically complex songs is "Like a Rolling Stone," a song which he recorded in 1965. Some people do not even recognize this song as political protest music. (See, for example, Al Kooper's informative entry for Bob Dylan in the *Britannica Encyclopedia*, 2003 edition.) Nonetheless, in my eyes the song is deeply political in its content, as I explain below.

On the surface, "Like a Rolling Stone" is about a woman who once saw herself as a safely embedded member of the financial and political elite, and who is now finding herself estranged from that sense of safety. Words in the song suggest that she no longer is certain as to where she will even obtain her next meal, or where she will sleep from night to night. She is cast adrift with no rudder in a society that offers her no safe harbor, and Dylan repeatedly asks her, "How does it feel to be ... like a rolling stone?" Dylan reminds her that those whom she once called friends were merely taking advantage of her, exploiting her for their own benefit. A reference to Napoleon suggests an aggressive war-embracing government that the woman might once have viewed as "lowbrow." But now Dylan taunts her to meet this government face to face, explaining that its ability and desire to rip through any prior-existing sense of privacy no longer mattered, for she no longer had anything to lose.

One interpretation of this song is that Dylan is addressing an entire generation of young people who may once have thought of themselves as economically and politically secure. But that era brought with it a tension that disabled the potency of any prior sense of safety. Note that the Vietnam War was still developing in the American scene at the time when the song was written, and Dylan was in this sense acting as much as a prophet as a psychoanalyst. Here he offers a devastating critique of the illusion of safety through material wealth and social status. Moreover, in his view as expressed in this song, government is little more than an exploitive predator waiting to take advantage of all those who come within range of its grasp. This interpretation of Dylan's lyrics may not be obvious for all readers, and many may want to put their own interpretive spin on this song. Much of the utility of Dylan's music for anyone is in making an argument for one's own interpretation of his meaning. Thus, what I offer here is not "the gospel," but a starting point from which to proceed.

When trying to understand any one of Dylan's most political songs, it is useful to compare it with some of his other songs. In my view, "Like a Rolling Stone" is best viewed from the lens of an earlier and equally prophetic song, "The Times They Are A-Changin'." This song, released in 1964, is far from a simple statement that Bob Dylan was living in times of flux. This song divides the populace along generational and political lines, declaring that a seismic shift in the structure of contemporary society was about to occur. Rather than counsel moderation, Dylan blatantly announces that the change will be both ferocious and inevitable, and like a tidal wave it will destroy all those who get in its way. To individual listeners he warns, "...you better start swimmin' or you'll sink like a stone." To members of the U.S. Congress he cautions, "Don't stand in the doorway. Don't block up the hall.... There's a battle outside." To parents he addresses a profound fear, "Your sons and your daughters are beyond your control." And to all he commands that they remove themselves from harm's way as the change in society transpires, less they be trampled underfoot of the advancing masses.

It is worth noting that Dylan's political warning to Congress is highly reminiscent of the warning that Senator Huey Long once gave to his senatorial colleagues during the height of the Great Depression when he announced in the Senate chamber that he was trying to figure out if he was going to continue to sit in that chamber or go outside and join the masses that were certain to destroy it one day. Long's colleagues may not have liked his tone, but they listened to him seriously.

"The Times They Are A-Changin'" is more than prophesy. It is a call to action. One might think of it as a bold statement of psychological warfare, one in which he threatens the established hierarchy of that day by claiming that their days of social and political dominance in society are numbered, and that they best move quickly to retreat before they are driven forcefully from their positions of power by a wave of change that only divine providence could stop. Dylan offers a similar perspective in some of his other songs, such as "It's All Over Now, Baby Blue." In each instance, the theme is the same: change is coming, and indeed it is upon us, and one cannot save the dead, so move on quickly. This is not apocalyptic change, but it is a transformation that is revolutionary in its effect on society. Dylan's importance to us is that he saw it coming, and he sang about it both bluntly and with passion. Deep inside, many people—mostly young, but not always—sensed it as well. To those people, he was a voice that expressed these perceptions with a transcendent clarity.

And what is to become of the local citizen who is employed to represent the authority of government (e.g., a law enforcement officer) in this time of profound change? This is the same question asked of Wotan when Siegfried smashes Wotan's staff. The staff—representing the power of governmental sanction to control the masses—is rendered impotent in one powerful stroke. In a more limited sense, Wotan's role is also that of the local sheriff in a small community, and the sheriff's badge is the symbol of power that allows him or her to extend the reach of government into the lives of a community's citizens. When revolution arrives, what becomes of the sheriff? Dylan's answer can be found in his song, "Knockin' on Heaven's Door." Here, Dylan begins, "Mama, take this badge off of me. I can't use it any more." The voice of authority then cries that he cannot see any longer, and that his role in society is dying. Begging his mother to bury his weapons, he again recognizes his increasing blindness as he recognizes his coming doom. Of course, Dylan is not saying that the symbolic sheriff is physically blind, but rather that the sheriff no longer can use his previously established mental template to interpret the world that surrounds him. He does not understand why his understanding of the norms and rules of society are no longer relevant, but he does recognize their impotence. Unlike "The Times They Are A-Changin'," "Knockin' on Heaven's Door" is not prophesy; it is an epitaph.

Was Dylan trying to cause the downfall of the old psychic order by predicting its demise, or was he simply the prophet carrying the news of impending transformation? It is not clear. Psychological warfare often blends with the news. Sometimes armies announce the routing of an enemy precisely to encourage the opposing troops to collapse or surrender. And when a war is over, it is often impossible to separate the statement of objective facts from the propagandistic messages that are transmitted in order to catalytically manifest those facts.

One of Dylan's more apocalyptic songs is "A Hard Rain's A-Gonna Fall," initially released in 1963. The song opens with the question, "Oh, where have you been, my blue-eyed son?" The words "blue-eyed son" most likely references the ideologically-defined "ideal type" (in a Weberian sense) image of an American male, the sort of image that the advertising and film media so often projected as a typically American masculine concept in those more segregated days. But Dylan contrasts this ideologically-defined image with a world that is sorely out-of-sync with that image. In each verse that follows, Dylan begins with a variation of the initial question, shifting the emphasis from where have you been to what did you see, what did you hear, who did you meet, and finally, what will you do now.

In each verse, the questions listed above are answered, one question per verse. The blue-eyed ideal-type American responds to each question with perceptions that do not match his own politically-laden rosy image. He has traveled greatly, seeing sadness, hardship, and death nearly everywhere. When Dylan sings in the refrain, "It's a hard rain's a-gonna fall," he addresses the explosive contrasts between hopelessly idealistic and false ideological constructs (as represented by the blue-eyed son's own image) and a world filled with ecological nightmares such as "sad forests" and "dead oceans," as well as a world filled with live people in pain ... and the ever-present dead. But the refrain also raises the prospect of an apocalyptic future. In the end of the song, the blue-eyed son has lost all attachment to the fantasy of ideology. He returns to the world of pain and despair, fully prepared to sink with the ill-fated fortunes of this world rather than to cling to the ideas of a false ideology. The painful realization that the ideology is false is one part of the "hard rain" that Dylan senses will fall on many dream-ensconced people. But the hard rain could also represent a future that is as real as it is bitter.

"Witnessing" is an important concept for Dylan. In a number of his songs, he returns to the idea that people learn through their frequently brutal interactions with reality, a reality that more often than not conflicts with their mental constructs of how that reality should be. For example, in "Blowin' In the Wind," Dylan asks how many times bad things need to happen before the human actions that cause these bad things are banned. These "bad things" include ecological horrors as well as human pain and suffering. The answers are not as concrete as the questions, since the answers themselves are "blowin' in the wind." More generally, Dylan offers few corrective prescriptions to the problems that he identifies in his political songs. He is not a prophet that brings the hope of renewal. Rather, he delivers a blunt confrontation with a reality that is stripped of blinding ideological fantasy. Analogously, Dylan is the doctor that announces the diagnosis of a disease, a doctor who meticulously describes to his patient each and every behavioral sin that led to that patient's current disease, and then he reads the bleak survival statistics.

In times of great turmoil, other societies sometime experience artists who embrace a Dylanesque approach to protest music, and some readers may be interested to note that the Vietnamese had an artist who could be described in this fashion. Trinh Cong Son is a Vietnamese songwriter and singer who died of natural causes in April 2001. Mr. Son was persecuted for his song-writing activities by both the South Vietnamese government as well as the subsequent Communist Vietnamese government. Many compared him with Bob Dylan during the Vietnam War due to the deep emotions which his songs evoked. Consider, for example, the words for "Ngu Di Con" ("Lullaby"), a song with lyrics voiced by a mother who is holding her dying son, a soldier: "Rest well my child, my child of the yellow race. Rock gently my child, I have done it twice. This body, which used to be so small, that I carried in my womb, that I held in my arms. Why do you rest at the age of 20 years?" (See "Trinh Cong Son, 62: Stirred Vietnam with War Protest Songs," by Seth Mydans, *The New York Times*, Thursday, 5 April 2001, Obituary).

The Fusion of Political and Spiritual Change:

Just as there is no one way to look at politics, there is no monopoly on spiritual perspectives. Artists have blended their spiritual and political views in nearly all music genres. But the way in which one examines the fusion of politics and spirituality is fairly constant across these diverse musical flavors. The fusion of politics and spirituality in general involves three separate ingredients: (1) the political context within which the music is created, (2) the political orientation of the composer, and (3) the musician's approach to spirituality.

An interesting example of protest music from the Vietnam War era that mixes both a political and spiritual perspective can be found in the work of George Harrison, the former Beatle. In particular, Mr. Harrison's organization of his music within the context of "The Concert for Bangladesh" that took place on 1 August 1971 is perhaps his most coherent statement of his hybrid political and spiritual views. The concert took place in Madison Square Garden in New York City with the Vietnam War as a backdrop. The event itself was inspired by the desires of Ravi Shankar (the sitarist) and George Harrison to contribute humanitarian aid to victims of the independence struggle that gave birth to the country of Bangladesh. The concert included performances from a long list of musical luminaries of the day, including Eric Clapton, Leon Russell, Ringo Starr, Bob Dylan, and others.

Bangladesh was formerly East Pakistan. West Pakistan and East Pakistan were a single country that was formed as consequence of Indian independence in 1947 following nearly 90 years of British colonial rule. The union was not a happy one. The two halves of Pakistan were separated geographically, and West Pakistan lopsidedly dominated the politics of the nation. Moreover, East Pakistan had to compete within the overall Pakistani political setting with four other Pakistani provinces, all of which were located in West Pakistan. Also, East Pakistan had a cultural heritage and history that was separate from that of West Pakistan. The historic area known as Bengal was considered one province during British rule, and it was composed of the area of East Pakistan as well as what is now the Indian state of West Bengal.

From 1947 through 1971, tension between West and East Pakistan continued to grow. A pro-autonomy political party from East Pakistan won majority representation in national elections in late 1970, but the West Pakistani dominated government refused to give up its ruling position. Eventually, an independence movement rose to a fevered pitch in early 1971, and West Pakistan invaded East Pakistan with large numbers of government troops who savaged much of the country. The United States supported the continuation of a unified Pakistan, as did China. But the Soviet Union and India favored East Pakistani independence. On 3 December 1971, India invaded Pakistan, the Pakistan military efforts collapsed, and the country of Bangladesh was created. During all of this tumult, large numbers of people from Bangladesh suffered terribly. Death and disease were rampant, and the world was horrified by the pictures of famine victims that were shown in the media.

The Concert for Bangladesh occurred in the middle of this turbulence. The original idea of the concert was formed when Ravi Shankar asked his friend, George Harrison, if there was anything that they could do to help the people of Bangladesh who were the victims of the political struggle. Years earlier, Mr. Shankar had been instrumental in introducing the Beatles to Maharishi Mahesh Yogi, an Indian monk who taught Transcendental Meditation (popularly known as "TM"), a mantra-based form of meditation that is historically linked to a pre-Hindu Vedic approach to spiritual growth. Of all the Beatles, George Harrison was the most consistent in the practice of this form of meditation, eventually practicing the TM-Sidhi Program, which is an advanced and extended version of TM. From this exposure to meditation, George Harrison developed a deeply spiritual perspective on life that affected much of his music. Indeed, it is not possible to understand Mr. Harrison's most political music without understanding how he looked at spirituality.

During the practice of TM or the TM-Sidhi Program, the awareness of the meditator gradually shifts away from the five physical senses of hearing, touch, sight, taste, and smell. Normally, a person practices this form of meditation twice each day, essentially "book-ending" the day with an experience that is much different from that of normal waking-state consciousness. One interpretation of the experience (not necessarily an "official" interpretation) is that during meditation there is a profound sense of quietness that allows (or perhaps causes) the conscious mind to shift its awareness to the level of one's "higher self." This process of shifting the awareness away from the five senses to the spiritual side of existence is said to be an automatic process that occurs naturally once one begins the mantra-based form of meditation. The basic idea seems to be that the conscious mind gets caught up in a "loop" so to speak, which is analogous to having a prison guard focus his attention on twiddling his thumbs. With the guard thus occupied, the otherwise captive awareness of the soul is free to perceive as it would naturally without the high-decibel attention-grabbing dominance of the five senses.

As one continues to practice meditation, the expanded level of awareness available while meditating is said to seep into the way one experiences the rest of the day, eventually leading to a state of "total awareness" all day. "Total awareness" seems to represent a level of consciousness that does not separate the perception of the five physical senses from the subtle perception of a more complete sense of reality. In this state, ideas and all thoughts are seen as a by-product of the electro-chemical activity of the brain. As with much of physical reality, ideas are one aspect of something called "maya," or simply illusion. Since one's higher self seems to function on the level of pure awareness or raw perception only, ideas are needed by physiologically-based consciousness to organize perceptions into "chunks" that can be labeled with words. Thus, ideas—and all words that express these ideas—are an interpretive step away from the original perceptions. One might say that a form of Wittgensteinian language game results, and in this state people eventually "lose" themselves, which means that individuals can no longer distinguish between their "real" selves as spiritual beings who experience reality via total perception and the organizational ideas that the brain uses to interpret these perceptions.

Since people often want external confirmation that their ideas which they use to organize their sense of self are in fact valid and worthwhile, they seek approval from others. An example of such a situation would be of a rock star who requires the continual praise of fans in order to maintain a sense of high self-esteem. Input from the five senses is used to support this false conception of self. Meditation thus allows one to break this vicious cycle, thereby freeing one's true spiritual self from a life in which one is essentially enslaved by an addiction to the ever-temporal pleasures of the five senses. This, in a nutshell, is my interpretation of

George Harrison's approach to his spiritual life. I must add that I have never communicated with Mr. Harrison, nor has he written extensively about his spiritual views. But this is nonetheless what I have been able to piece together from what I would consider a rather in-depth examination of both his spiritual background and his music. With this perspective in mind, we can now approach an understanding of the music which he included in The Concert for Bangladesh.

The Bangladesh concert began with an instrumental piece performed by Ravi Shankar and his colleagues. Mr. Shankar performed a form of music called a "rag," which comes from the Sanskrit word "raga" meaning passion or color. (The "a" in "rag" is pronounced as the "a" in "father," and the "g" is hard as in "get.") There are many rags, all of which are normally intended to be performed at certain times of the day or in the context of certain types of events. The idea is that the music is to assist the listener in blending one's perceptual consciousness into the overall sense of the moment, thereby adding an element of spiritual coherence to the daily experience. Thus, the rag musical form is designed to produce a "color" in the consciousness of the listener that is appropriate to the setting. When the British colonized India, the colonizers tended to insist that the musicians perform the colonizers' favorite rag pieces regardless of whether the setting or time of day was appropriate. This led to a perversion in the orientation of rag music. Ravi Shankar was a performer who generally attempted to correct this perversion of the rag musical form, and his choice of music for the opening of the Bangladesh concert should be seen in this light. In this sense, this very political concert began with a spiritual statement.

Following Mr. Shankar's introductory performance, George Harrison performed his song "Wah-Wah." In India and Pakistan, there is a form of poetry called a "ghazal." Ghazals tend to be performed in both Urdu (the language of Pakistan) and Hindi (the dominant language of India), but they are also performed in other Near East countries and in other languages as well. In India, ghazals are often sung. Ghazals normally are verses that hold wisdom, often but not always of a spiritual nature. During the performance of a ghazal, points arrive in which the audience reacts to a moment of profundity, at which time members of the audience say the words "Wah, wah," which roughly translates as "bravo." Essentially, the audience is praising the performer at these moments of spiritual pregnancy.

In George Harrison's song, "Wah-Wah," he acknowledges his position as a person offering knowledge (one might even say "teacher" in this instance). He also acknowledges his audience's appreciation of himself and his music, "You made me such a big star," and he adds the praise "Wah-wah" in his song as if to parallel the adoring screams of his fans. He then goes on to renounce the praise, saying "I don't need no wah-wah." When he then sings, "I know how sweet life can be if I keep myself free from the wah-wah," he is directly addressing the ideas discussed above with regard to the contemplative issue of becoming "self-referral," as compared with maintaining a reliance on others for an evaluation of one's self-esteem. In essence, George Harrison begins his performance by rejecting any focus on himself, thereby releasing both himself and his audience to center their attention on a deeper awareness of the true meaning of the event.

Mr. Harrison's next song is "My Sweet Lord." Here he openly embraces his sense of spiritual awakening. The song is both a hymn of praise and a somewhat complicated statement of his (then) current state of spiritual development. When he sings, "I really want to see you .... But it takes so long, my Lord," he is referencing the idea that meditation works gradually in transforming one's perceptual abilities. While even a beginning meditator can experience a shift in awareness that expands a previously more limited perceptual state, profound levels of penetrating awareness come only with time and repeated meditation experiences. In this song, Mr. Harrison is acknowledging that he has perceived enough to know the truth of a greater spiritual reality, but not so much as to quench his sense of spiritual thirst. The general tone of this piece is perhaps captured best in the Latin word, "Sitio," which is often used in a spiritual context to mean "I thirst." Mr. Harrison's own state of development is one of being strongly drawn in this regard, which is reflected in his repeated plea to his Lord, "I really want to be with you."

Mr. Harrison's next song in the concert is "Awaiting On You All." In this song, he posits that his audience has been spiritually and mentally "polluted," which has left them in a "mess." He then offers his listeners a method of cleansing, telling them, "By chanting the names of the Lord and you'll be free. The Lord is awaiting on you all to awaken and see." In a very real sense, Mr. Harrison is perceiving his audience as spiritual captives in much the same way Bob Marley saw his own audience. As with Marley, emancipation is both a political and spiritual journey, and it requires some activity on the part of those who seek this freedom. For Mr. Harrison, the idea of "chanting the names of the Lord" references the repetition of the mantra in his own practice of meditation. In Vedic philosophy upon which so much of the Sanskrit language is based, the mantras are sounds (one might even be tempted to say musical sounds) that produce a sense of spiritual resonance. Over the centuries, Hinduism has personified these sounds, some of which have now taken on an extra meaning of being names of deities. Mr. Harrison blends the contemporary Hindu phenomenon with the earlier Vedic vibrational concept when he sings about chanting the names of the Lord. His spiritual approach is quite broad-spectrum in this regard, even referencing the perception of Jesus. He also argues in the song that established religion is too closely bonded with the economic system to meaningfully address his audiences' profound spiritual needs. Instead he speaks in favor of a more personal approach to spiritual awakening, one which closely parallels his own meditation-inspired path.

One of George Harrison's most intense songs is "Beware Of Darkness," which he performs later in the Bangladesh concert. In this song, he warns his audience of others who create sadness throughout the world. These people control the masses by manipulating their thoughts, thoughts that Harrison says "linger" in one's head, creating a sense of hopelessness. He explicitly warns against "Maya," or the idea-based illusions of the "unconscious sufferers." The "darkness" in life is brought on by leaders who wish to grow at the expense of others, and he cautions his listeners to avoid this state of existence that rots in the absence of spiritual light. This is a song filled with foreboding.

Harrison's tone shifts to one of mourning in his next song, "While My Guitar Gently Weeps." In this song, he laments that controllers have perverted his audience, keeping them from learning how to love. He sings that these controllers "bought and sold you," and you were "perverted," "diverted," "inverted." No one warned you, and now it is your ability to love that is the true victim. Again, much as with Marley, Harrison acknowledges that his audience's ability to love is sleeping, suggesting that his own role is one that gently prods his listeners to awake. For Mr. Harrison, a truly awakened individual is someone who naturally experiences life as love. Through all of this, his music plays on sadly, and his guitar "gently weeps." It seems clear from Mr. Harrison's overall spiritual perspective that the sadness in this song is not a final statement; he is not singing a requiem. Rather, he is using his music to tell his listeners about their own state, thereby urging them to realize this condition for themselves. Seen in this way, George Harrison does not see his songs as pronouncements of death, but rather as catalysts of change.

Unlike Dylan, Harrison does not leave his listeners with a dire diagnosis of their condition. Harrison rounds out his musical journey with great hope, as is reflected in his song, "Here Comes the Sun," which he performs toward the end of the Bangladesh concert. This song is a vibrant embrace of renewal. Here he acknowledges the desperation of the past, but notes that this desperation is fading away when he sings, "I see the ice is slowly melting." Finally, Harrison gives clear direction to his now uplifted listeners with the final song of the concert, aptly named "Bangla Desh."

By the end of the concert, there were probably many in the audience who realized that they had experienced an original musical event that contained more than a casual level of political and philosophical content. Some future performances have tried to repeat the magic of that evening, such as the concert "Live Aid," the large collective performance of "We are the World," and even the concert "Farm Aid." But the spiritual and political scope of the Bangladesh concert was truly extraordinary, and it set a standard for other concerts of its type.

Protest Music and Other Wars: The Chilean and Northern Ireland Cases

During the 1970s, popular music was metamorphosing into a highly potent vehicle for political protest, and it was inevitable that the phenomenon would experience some degree of contagion across borders as new opportunities arose with respect to other conflicts. Two cases of protest music that occurred outside of the United States during the 1970s are of particular interest to include in this chapter: the leftist/peasant protest music that appeared in Chile during the presidency of Salvador Allende, and music that was focused on the politics of Northern Ireland with respect to the incident "Bloody Sunday."

From 1925 until 1973, Chile was a democracy, and indeed it is possible to view Chile as a democracy since 1830. There were basically two constitutions from 1830 until 1973, with the change from one to the other occurring in 1925. During the latter period, Chile experienced its share of political crises, including some moments of military influence in domestic politics. But Chile always seemed to bounce back, and its constitutional democracy endured. Also during this period, the lower, working, and peasant classes were not well-represented within the political establishment. There had been occasional attempts to address the needs of the under-served, but not much came of these efforts in real terms. This changed after 1964 when Eduardo Frei Montalva, a Christian Democrat and ideological centrist, won the presidency with 56% of the vote. President Frei tried to institute a social and economic program that partially took control of the copper industry which was largely owned by U.S. companies. His copper policies resulted in Chile claiming 51% ownership in that industry. His programs also attempted to reform the agricultural sector, mostly by seizing and redistributing some land that was uncultivated.

President Frei depended on the middle class for the bulk of his support. However, this class was alienated by Frei's support for the lower (including urban) and peasant classes. President Frei's attempt to reach out to the lower and peasant classes simultaneously activated the middle and upper classes as well as the lower and peasant classes. The middle and upper classes engaged in a variety of attacks on the lower and peasant classes, which further activated these poorer classes. The largest issue was President Frei's support of land reform, which was politically hot since so much of Chile's arable farm land was controlled by a wealthy elite.

All this political attention gave the lower and peasant classes a taste of real power, and the result was an enhanced sense of coherency to their campaign for representation. Beginning in 1969, a group of left-of-center parties and groups formed a "Popular Unity" coalition. Their presidential candidate was Salvador Allende Gossens. Mr. Allende was a Marxist, and he was elected president in 1970 with only 36.3% of the vote due to a split in the remainder of the vote across more centrist and rightist parties. Such low vote proportions were somewhat of the norm for Chilean politics from 1937-73 (see Mattern 1998, p. 37[N]). However, the low level of support for Mr. Allende turned out to be deadly for him given the radical nature of his agenda.

Following the 1970 election, President Allende instituted an economic reform program that was much more ambitious than that of his predecessor, former President Frei. Allende nationalized the copper industry completely, and without compensation. This, of course, was highly disliked by the government of the United States. He also accelerated the land reform measures by attempting to take over some large agricultural estates. Similarly, he nationalized a number of basic industries. To pay for all of this, he printed unsupported currency to erase the debts caused by his policies.

President Allende was not able to control the political and economic chaos that his rapidly instituted policies caused. There were strikes, a poor balance of trade, decreased investment, food shortages, and lots of protest. Against this backdrop, President Allende sought to maintain support for his policies from the peasant and lower classes. But since the mainstream media was owned by the wealthy elite who opposed his policies, he was forced to utilize other means to spread his message and unify his support. It was because of this that President Allende turned to popular musicians in Chile in a highly involved campaign that has been documented in considerable depth by Mark Mattern (1998, chapters 3 and 4).

President Allende asked many Chilean musicians to compose songs that explained his government's policies in a way that would be understood by the more poorly educated masses. The musicians quickly heeded the call, producing many songs that tended to be highly political and quite confrontational. The songs played both educational and political campaign roles, and the use of their music in this respect paralleled much of the way Bob Marley's music was used elsewhere. Important musical groups and singers for that time period include Quilapayún, Inti-Illimani, and Victor Jara. Much of this type of music contained traditional, folk, and Indian themes. There was a conscious desire in these songs to connect the cultural heritage of the common people with the government's reform policies. This musical political campaign included extensive efforts to utilize theaters and concerts in both rural and urban settings.

Victor Jara's song, "Preguntas por Puerto Montt," is a good example of how this type of music pulled no punches in the attempt to educate the masses with regard to the activities of their perceived enemies. This song was written to denounce a military attack on 91 peasant families who moved onto some uncultivated land. The attack occurred in 1968 outside the city of Puerto Montt, killing some and wounding many. The lyrics of the song even explicitly assail Pérez Zujović, the minister of the interior at the time of the attack, making it quite clear who and what are to blame. (See Mattern 1998, p. 41.)

Due to all of this political tumult in the 1970s, Chilean politics became highly confrontational. It is also now widely recognized that the U.S. government was involved in efforts to further destabilize Chilean politics during the period of Allende's presidency. On 11 September 1973, Chile experienced a military coup d'etat, and General Augusto Pinochet Ugarte was installed as president. It is claimed (and sometimes disputed) that President Allende shot himself during an attack on the presidential mansion. The highly prominent musician Victor Jara was arrested, tortured, and executed. Many other musical groups fled the country, and some groups who happened to be outside of Chile during the coup remained abroad. The dictatorship that followed the coup was brutal. Parts of the economy improved, but the lower and peasant classes experienced a steep decline in both their standard of living as well as their political access.

It was also during this time that Sting released his politically potent song and video, "They Dance Alone (Cueca Solo)," which voices the pain of the widows whose husbands "disappeared" during Pinochet's rule. It is interesting to note again as I mentioned in an earlier chapter, that this song was banned in Chile during Pinochet's time. During the mid-1980s, Sting and the Police (Sting's band) traveled to Chile to perform. According to Sting's web site, Sting asked Amnesty International whether or not he and the band should perform in Chile in the context of Pinochet's repressive rule. Sting reports, "Their advice was that the band should go, because rock'n'roll means freedom in these countries" (http://www.sting.com/discography/solo_discography/songthey.html, accessed July 2002). While touring in South America (and Chile), Sting met people who were victims of harsh political environments, including many political prisoners who had been tortured. He also saw a form of Chilean political protest about which his song is named. The word "Cueca" refers to a traditional courtship dance found in Chile. The "Cueco Solo" is a dance performed by Chilean widows, mothers, and daughters of "missing" men. They perform this dance while wearing pictures (attached to their clothes) of their missing male relatives. These dances often took place during Pinochet's time in front of police stations as a profoundly sad but powerfully chilling form of feminine political protest. Sting's song itself is also powerful in its depiction of this deeply disturbing form of protest, and as with the style of prior Chilean protest music that manifested during Allende's period, his lyrics are explicit with respect to the primary actor involved (in this case Pinochet) and the horrors for which he is responsible.

The conflict in Northern Ireland has similarly produced some highly potent political music. In this chapter, I focus on only one prominent example of this music, one more commonly available to international audiences. The song, performed by the band U2, is of sufficient importance that it can serve as a heuristic vehicle to understanding the painful dimensions of the political trauma that it addresses.

From 1800 to 1922, Ireland was part of the United Kingdom. In 1920, Northern Ireland was separated politically from the remainder of Ireland due to longstanding cultural and economic issues. After that, Ireland itself embarked on its own evolutionary path to independence from Britain. This path formally began in December 1921 with the creation of the Irish Free State. In 1937, a plebiscite led to a new constitution and a fully independent Irish nation. The final tie to the Commonwealth was abandoned in 1948. Yet Northern Ireland was still tied to the United Kingdom.

Over the decades, many Protestants in Ireland migrated to Northern Ireland, a true center for Irish industry. Catholics in Northern Ireland did not migrate to the south in a reciprocal fashion. The economy was stronger in Northern Ireland, and World War II only deepened Catholic economic dependence on northern industry because of the upsurge in war-related manufacturing. Earlier Catholic withdrawal from political involvement with local politics in Northern Ireland can be traced to a rejection of the original separation of the north from the south. But this enabled Protestants to dominate politics in Northern

Ireland, thereby enhancing their economic clout as well. Eventually, Catholics found themselves as economically disadvantaged second-class citizens in a state that seemed at best only remotely concerned with their welfare. This led to strained politics, and eventually political protest. The engine of stark inequality that was defined by religion but manifested by class eventually produced violence.

Britain sent troops to help keep the peace between the Catholics and Protestants in Northern Ireland in the early 1970s. On 9 August 1971, Britain established a policy of interment without trial. Then on 30 January 1972, members of the 1st Parachute Regiment of the British Army fired on civilian demonstrators in Bogside, Derry. The attack immediately claimed the lives of 13 civil rights protesters. All were Catholic. An additional protester died after some months due to wounds inflicted in the assault. Before the attack, the demonstration was peaceful, and the civil rights protesters were unarmed. The demonstration itself was called to protest the new interment policy. The British attempt to control the damage caused by the incident was immediate. It claimed that the demonstration was illegal, and it attempted to cover-up the details of the incident by sealing the results of its own investigation into the attack for decades. The day of the attack became known as "Bloody Sunday," connecting it in name to a massacre in St. Petersburg, Russia in 1905 in which 100 pro-labor peaceful demonstrators were killed (with hundreds more wounded) by police during the rule of Emperor Nicolas II.

In both the Irish and Russian cases, violent and mass protests increased as a consequence of the attacks. In Russia, this led to the so-called "Revolution of 1905." In Northern Ireland, the attack led to a long sequence of violent confrontations. The Northern Republican Army (the so-called "IRA") found new relevance in its more violent agenda aimed at protecting Catholics in the north. Its ultimate goal was to drive out all British forces and to reunite Northern Ireland with the remainder of Ireland. Similarly, Protestant paramilitary groups formed to combat the efforts of the IRA. All of this eventually became known in Britain and Northern

Ireland as the time of the "Troubles." In 1972 alone, 467 people died in these conflicts. Thirty years later, more than 3,600 people had died, and tens of thousand had been wounded.

U2 released the song "Sunday Bloody Sunday" in 1983 as part of their album *War*. In public statements by U2's lead singer, Bono has characterized the song as a protest against the revolutionary violence connected to the "Troubles." My own favorite performance of this song is U2's presentation at Red Rocks Amphitheatre in Denver, Colorado on 5 June 1983, where Bono tilted the interpretation of the song by introducing it with the words, "This is not a rebel song." Fans of U2 may also note that the song plays during the credits of the film "Bloody Sunday," which is both directed and written by Paul Greengrass. In the middle of yet a different performance of the song which occurred just after a significant bombing in Northern Ireland, Bono (who has a long history of political interest and activism) interjected the following words: "And let me tell you something. I've had enough of Irish Americans who haven't been back to their country in 20 or 30 years come up to me and talk about the 'Resistance,' the 'Revolution' back home. And the Glory of the Revolution. And the Glory of dying for the Revolution. Fuck the Revolution! They don't talk about the glory of killing for the Revolution. What's the glory of taking a man from his bed and gunning him down in front of his wife and his children? Where's the glory in that? Where's the glory in bombing a Remembrance Day parade of old-age pensioners, their medals taken out and polished up for the day. Where's the glory in that? To leave them dying, or crippled for life, or dead under the rubble of the Revolution, that the majority of the people in my country don't want. No more!" (See the video collection for *Live from Rattle and Hum*, 1987.)

U2's song, "Sunday Bloody Sunday," is a direct and passionate appeal to stop the violence associated with the Irish "Troubles." The lyrics lament about the length of the conflict as well as its savagery. Rather than picking a particular side in the conflict, the song posits that neither of the opposing forces have won. In one sense, one could argue that U2 has chosen to follow the safe political path by refusing to demonize one side at the expense of the other. This obviously begs the question of whether this implicitly endorses the status quo, which is continued Protestant domination and British rule in a Northern Ireland. Yet I think it much more likely that U2 is instead arguing for a more peaceful path to resolving the conflict rather than a military domination of one side over the other. This is a theme that has appeared in other songs by U2, such as the satirical "Pride (In the Name of Love)."

It is of interest to note that Sinead O'Connor released a response of sorts to Bono's claim that "Sunday Bloody Sunday" was not a "rebel song." In her 1997 release of her *Gospel Oak* album, she sang the song "This IS a Rebel Song." The song is a painfully direct and emotional appeal to what the song describes as an English cold, hard-heartedness. The song implies that the problems of Northern Ireland are a consequence of British domination more than anything else. The potency of this song is not a result of an angry diatribe, which does not even exist in the lyrics. Rather, this song has force due to the contrast that it establishes between O'Connor's voice which speaks of her own ability to love and a perceived English inability to reciprocate.

Protest Music with Non-Movement Motivations

While many people may think of protest music as normally associated with political movements that are connected to major events such as wars, much political music with a protest orientation results from a personal interest of the artist or composer. A good example of this type of music is the song "Russians," composed by Sting. Sting wrote this song in 1984 during the height of the Cold War between the United States and the Soviet Union. There was no strong anti-Cold War movement at the time. But Sting was concerned by the way each side of the "non-conflict" were portraying the other side, risking real war in the process. Apparently he was particularly concerned with how the Reagan administration was demonizing the Soviet Union as an "evil empire," and perhaps Sting felt that this was dehumanizing the way Americans felt about the Soviet people themselves. The song attempts to humanize the Russian people for a Western audience, explaining that both sides are equally concerned for the welfare of their families and friends.

Sting opened the 1986 Grammy awards with this song, and it was performed with the powerful addition of a doomsday clock ticking away in a countdown. The song was released in the album *The Dream of the Blue Turtles*. The music for "Russians" was largely borrowed from Sergei Prokofiev's "Romance," which is the theme from the soundtrack of the 1934 movie *Lieutenant Kij?*. The mixing of English lyrics with the musical work of a Russian composer in this song is significant, of course, capturing the need to bridge the two hostile political cultures.

"Russians" begins by recognizing that a climate of "Cold War" hysteria exists in Europe and America. Sting initially cites Nikita S. Khrushchev's threatening claim, "We will bury you," as rhetoric that does not make sense if "Russians love their children too." Khrushchev, who was the premier of the Soviet Union from 1958-64, often utilized a highly confrontational approach to America, both in the context of his speeches as well as in the way he interacted with U.S. presidents. Good examples of this approach can be seen with his worrisome public dialogue that he had with Vice President Richard Nixon at a World's Fair exhibit in Moscow, as well as his bellicose approach to President Kennedy in their first face-to-face meeting.

The song then goes on to address political comments made by U.S. President Ronald Reagan. President Reagan made what many people call his "Evil Empire" speech regarding the Soviet Union to the House of Commons in Britain on 8 June 1982. In this speech he said, "Our military strength is a prerequisite to peace, but let it be clear we maintain this strength in the hope it will never be used, for the ultimate determinant in the struggle that's now going on in the world will not be bombs and rockets but a test of wills and ideas, a trial of spiritual resolve, the values we hold, the beliefs we cherish, the ideas to which we are dedicated." During this period, the dominant defense orientation was called "MAD," which stands for "mutually assured destruction" through the use of nuclear weapons should either side launch an attack. President Reagan wanted to change this by creating a missile shield around the nation in a plan popularly called the "Star Wars Program" in reference to the popular movie in which energy beams and space weaponry were dominant tools in combat. Thus, President Reagan was suggesting that it might be possible to win a war involving a nuclear exchange, and Sting writes in the song, "There's no such thing as a winnable war. It's a lie we don't believe anymore." When Sting then rhetorically quotes President Reagan as saying, "We will protect you," Sting responds with disbelief that such a thing is possible.

A song that follows a similar theme as Sting's "Russians" is "Leningrad" by Billy Joel (video directed by Kathy Dougherty). Essentially, this song is about the ending of the Cold War. In the Cold War, both the Soviets and the Americans were long taught to hate each other, and the song tells about both peoples finally having the opportunity to see the other side in more human terms. More specifically, the Russians and the Americans physically interact with one another, and in the process find out that they have the same human qualities, from love of children to a desire to live peacefully. The city of Leningrad has now returned to being called by its original name of St. Petersburg, and the song title stands as a metaphor for the now silenced Cold War words that so distorted the human faces behind the national banners.

Some politically potent music coveys its message not so much in its lyrics or instrumentation, but rather in its use of the visual imagery that accompanies the music. An excellent example of such music is Madonna's "Like a Prayer" (co-written with Patrick Leonard). The lyrics of this song are more suggestive of a spiritual orientation to the music. But the video expands this to include a dramatic and quite complex set of controversial ideas. Directed by Mary Lambert, the video for "Like a Prayer" created a huge controversy when it was released in 1989. Pepsi announced an advertising deal with Madonna on 1 March 1989 in which the singer would be paid $5 million to appear in some soft drink commercials. Pepsi was also going to underwrite her upcoming tour ("Blond Ambition"). The next day, Pepsi released Madonna's first (and only) commercial which featured the song "Like a Prayer." The following day, Madonna's video for "Like a Prayer" was played on MTV. The Pepsi commercial, directed by Joe Pytka, was much different from the song's video. Some religious groups were offended by the imagery (religious and otherwise) in the video, and word of a boycott of Pepsi products began to float. The Pepsi commercial ran once more in the United States (although it ran only once total in Britain), and then Pepsi cancelled future showings. The contract with Madonna was dropped, although apparently Madonna retained her $5 million dollar payment.

Given all of the controversy that the video created, its interpretation is of particular interest here. As with interpreting many works of art, it is rarely clear that the artist consciously intended to insert all of the meaning that one can often find in such controversial pieces. Also, any interpretation of such art has to be made with the caveat that alternative interpretations are possible, and readers (or listeners, or viewers, as the case may be) are required to decide for themselves as to the merits of each interpretation.

The "Like a Prayer" video opens with Madonna running over a desolate hill past a fire burning in a discarded oil drum while a police siren is heard in the background. There is also the image of a burning cross and a jail door slamming shut. Thus, the video's introduction mixes the ideas of a dark message (the desolate hill), criminal activity (the police siren and the jail door), and racial injustice (the Ku Klux Klan imagery of the burning cross). A prophetic vision of an assault on a white woman (not Madonna) by a white gang then shifts to Madonna seeking refuge in a rural church. In the church is a statue of the black Peruvian saint, San Martin de Porres (1579-1639), a man particularly known for bridging racial injustice. The symbolism of the black saint is similarly associated with the idea of Jesus, with the connection being made by a series of flashed images of Christ. The saint (statue) is confined behind a metal cage. The statue cries, and Madonna lies down on a bench and begins to experience a vision.

Madonna opens the cage confining the black saint. The saint becomes alive and exits the cage and the church. Madonna then picks up a knife and accidentally cuts herself. The cuts on her hands resemble the stigmata associated with crucifixion. The symbolism here seems clear; the combined love and appeal from a worshiper (Madonna) activates a response from a spiritual source (the awakening of a saint), and her own stigmata suggests the need sharing sacrifice across both mortal humans and spiritual guides. A black choir then appears in the church, which may suggest the support of "heavenly hosts" buttressing the efforts of spiritual entities and mortal leaders who suffer while pursuing divine justice.

The camera then shifts to a scene outside of the church in which the white woman briefly glimpsed earlier is attacked by a white gang. Madonna is a witness to the assault. The approach of the police chase off the gang, and the black saint (now appearing as a normally dressed black male, but played by the same actor) goes to help the woman who was attacked. The police arrive and assume that the black man is guilty of assaulting the woman, and he is arrested and placed in jail. Note that the same black male (once as the saint and later as the falsely accused) is twice confined to a metal cage, the first instance suggesting spiritual bondage while the second pointing toward more mortal constraints. Next, burning crosses appear in the background as Madonna sings.

The camera again shifts to the inside of the church where Madonna is still experiencing her vision (indicated by her continuing to rest horizontally on the bench). She kisses the black man, who then returns to his cage and re-solidifies as a statue. At this point the vision/dream sequence ends, and Madonna wakes up to find the choir in the church, singing and dancing as before in her vision. The choir's role here is important since it indicates a continuity between the reality of the post-awakening material with that of the vision/dream sequence. Madonna then goes to the police and tells them that the accused black man is innocent. The man is then released.

In a superficial sense, the controversy over the video seems to be associated simply with the images themselves, not a deeper interpretive meaning. But sometimes people tend to leave the most profound meaning in art untouched when they object to certain types of controversial material. This does not imply that the more profound meaning is illusory. Rather, the suggestion made here is that the meaning may be too disturbing for some people to deal with on a conscious level. They reject the offending material while arguing that the work is simply in bad taste, thereby protecting themselves from experiencing an internal review of their own belief structures that are in fact the real target of the art.

In this case, I suggest that Madonna's video is making a clear statement about both race and spirituality. With respect to race, there is a clear message that pain and injustice have been inflicted on people of color. But there is a secondary and potentially more important message. From the video's perspective, the dominant culture of our society (which includes organized religion) acts to imprison that which is both good (in a moral sense) and Godly (in a spiritual sense). Love and spontaneous prayer (as compared with ritualistic prayer) leads to true communion with divinity. This communion presents itself as an altered state of awareness, which is represented in the video by Madonna lying down on the bench in the church and entering a trance-like state within which she perceives a vision. This spiritually expanded perceptual experience both reflects and interprets the real world in a manner which brings profound understanding regarding the hardships of physical reality (as metaphorically represented by the assault).

Clearly, the racial content in this video is designed to upturn conventional—and thus stereotypical—intellectual templates. One might think of this as comparable with the contrasting portrayal of Jesus as a "King" who is born within a family of low social status. The spiritual realm disregards the social priorities of the physical world, just as an adult disregards the fantasies of a child who clearly does not comprehend the greater complexities in life. From this perspective, true spiritual guidance crosscuts rather than parallels the malformed structure of human social organization. In a heuristic sense, teaching (which is one major purpose of such art) comes from confronting existing and common intellectual templates that harmfully structure relations among and between social groupings. Locating divinity within a black personage, and then awakening communication with that divinity through the power of a love that recognizes no racial boundaries, cuts through a host of preconceived and widely accepted social norms. This "theater shock" acts—at least in some instances—to dilate an otherwise constricted window into the viewer's mind, jarring loose the beliefs in obsolete social structures while opening the individual to new perspectives on life.

Madonna's role as a witness in this video is a crucial parameter in this interpretation. We all witness life. We watch it just as we simultaneously experience it directly. We also perceive that which is spiritual, particularly during moments of distress when our awareness is forced by trauma to transcend its more normal constraints. Our own spirituality emerges from its cage during these moments, just as the saint is metaphorically released from its confinement when uninhibited love intervenes. In this sense, our own personal growth is deeply dependent on our level of awareness, or perhaps, the quality of our perceptions. Thus, awareness—both spiritual and physical—is the engine driving this video. The expansion of awareness leads to deep reflections into the human condition, and ultimately personal healing, and divine redemption.

There are, of course, nearly countless other examples of political music that are not movement related. Such songs normally address particular causes in which the artist and/or composer is interested. For example, in the area of songs dealing with the environment, Michael Jackson composed and performed "Earth Song." While the video for this song (directed by Nick Brandt) shows dramatic footage of a damaged planetary environment, it nonetheless suggests in the end that such damage is reparable given a change in the attitudes of humans with regard to their perceived relationship with the environment.

In another subject area, Billy Joel's song, "The Downeaster 'Alexa,'" is an interesting example of political music directed toward the plight of a relatively small community under stress. This song is about the fishing community in the northeastern United States, and more specifically about the fishing men and women who can no longer make a living at sea. The video for the song (directed by Andy Morahan) incorporates shots that effectively accent the lyrics with footage of fishing people and their communities struggling unsuccessfully to survive economically in a difficult and unsupportive environment. The song decries governmental regulation that restricts what fish can actually be caught and sold. But the song also laments the fact that the fishing stocks are depleted. The fishing people are caught in the middle between the governmental actions that are designed to protect what is left of the fishing stocks, and the fact that there are already far too few fish left. The problem is amplified by the fixed nature of economic dependence within the fishing community. The children of those who live from the sea still need clothes and food, the mortgages still need to be paid for both houses and boats, and bills in general follow monthly cycles that are not tuned to the vagaries in the size of fish populations. There is no easy answer to this dilemma, and Billy Joel does not seek one. Rather, as with a classic folk song model, he sings simply to tell the story of the fishing people, and to help express their emotional frustrations with regard to life's complexities. In this sense, "The Downeaster 'Alexa'" is a true protest song, but its protest has a highly restricted range.

The long Iraqi war that started as an effort to remove Saddam Hussein and destroy his (nonexistent) weapons of mass destruction has become fertile territory for political music that is not yet movement related. Originally, much political music following the 9/11 New York and Washington, D.C. terrorist attacks contained a great deal of patriotic fervor. But by 2007, the general tone of political music had turned to resignation. (In particular, see "Pop Music and the War: The Sound of Resignation," by Jon Pareles, *The New York Times*, 2 January 2007, pp. B1&B5[N].) It is unclear how this music will develop. The absence of a military draft has made a large segment of American youth more detached from the war than was the case with respect to the Vietnam War. Perhaps a draft, or something like it, would be necessary to force this political music to mature in such a way that its general tone conveys a unified voice with a clear and politically potent message. The evolution of this music is something all those who are interested in political musicology will want to follow closely. Given time, the anti-war music related to the Iraq war may become a movement.

On the 7th of July 2007, Al Gore and some entertainment executives organized the largest entertainment event (in terms of audience size) ever. The worldwide concert, "Live Earth," took place on all seven continents (including Antarctica) over a 24 hour period, and it promoted a theme of saving the Earth's environment, with a focus on global warming. A terrific number of music luminaries took part (all *pro bono*). At the time of publishing this book, it is not yet clear whether or not this is the beginning of a full-fledged musical/environmental movement. Those who are interested in such movements will want to watch the development of this closely over the next few years.

Regardless of whether or not protest songs parallel a significant social or political movement, they nonetheless have a common characteristic. They voice objections to a state of affairs that is somehow connected to a level of dysfunctionality between the state and its citizens. In real political terms, when this dysfunctionality manifests, those who are affected most tend to lash out at others who seem to control their fate, or at least they attack those seemingly weak-kneed leaders who could intervene on their behalf should they only be sufficiently wise or courageous. If they do not lash out at their leaders, then the victims of this dysfuntionality protest their situation in more general terms. The key to success with regard to their protests, of course, is for their voices to have both a message and a level of coherence that resonates with other citizens in the body politic. A successful protest song will initiate a reaction among the masses that will be sufficiently noticeable such that politicians respond out of fear of losing their influence, and possibly their jobs. This forces politicians to support policies that address the relevant issues. Here I am not arguing that protest songs always create political change. But sometimes they help do this, and when that happens, it is because the songs themselves represent the issues at hand in powerful ways. Through the musically focused attention of a demanding populace, these issues are endowed with enhanced power to change the evolutionary course of political development.

CHAPTER 7

Politics and Hip-Hop

Over the recent past, hip-hop has become a major forum for music that conveys political content. While it is beyond the purpose of this chapter or volume to offer a detailed history of the development of hip-hop, a brief outline is useful at the outset as a means of setting the stage for the subsequent discussion of hip-hop's political messages.

In a most general sense, "hip-hop" is a form of expression. But more specifically, it is a cultural movement that emerged predominantly from African-American urban culture in the 1980s. (See Neal and Murray [2004] for a discussion of greater diversity in hip-hop's origins, including Hispanic contributions.) It has since spread to be widely embraced by a variety of cultures and races, both within the United States and internationally. While it is often thought that the term "hip-hop" is synonymous with "rap music," this is not the case. Hip-hop refers to a broader range of four interlocking cultural characteristics, of which rap music is just one. Indeed, rap music is the largest component of hip-hop music, but hip-hop also extends to other musical varieties, such as "gangsta rap music." In this chapter, I often follow the more colloquial usage of "hip-hop," in the sense that I use the term often to refer to rap music. While this is technically not a correct usage, readers who want more precision should be able to identify my meaning from the context of the text with little difficulty.

In the broadest terms, hip-hop music is poetic speech combined with driving rhythms. This signature characteristic of hip-hop is generally known as "rapping." Alternatively, rapping is sometimes referred to as "rhyming" or even "MCing." Rapping sometimes utilizes very strong language, both in terms of profanity as well as ideas and imagery. Hip-hop music is primarily percussive, even though melodic insertions are commonplace.

The three other signature characteristics of hip-hop are

"deejaying," "b-boying," and graffiti, and it is worthwhile spending a moment on each of these. "Deejaying" identifies the origin of hip-hop as a musical form. The original hip-hoppers were African-American deejays who were interested in creatively enhancing the dance floor experience. Their instruments were turntables used for vinyl records in the 1980s and early 1990s. They observed that the short break between songs in a dance setting would lead to an intermittent collapse of the occasionally frenetic energy of a club. To avoid these pauses, the deejays began to experiment with ways to play music nonstop that used percussive beats as a transition between songs (and later to create breaks within songs). These were called "break beats," and they generally matched the tempo of a previous song, continuing its rhythm in the absence of the other instruments.

Among the most influential of the early deejays in hip-hop were DJ Kool Herc (originally Clive Campbell), Grandmaster Flash (originally Joseph Saddler), Africa Bamtaataa, and the Grand Wizard Theodore. While he did not invent the idea, Kool Herc was the deejay who largely popularized the idea of talking to the audience both during the break beats and while the other music played. All of the deejays experimented with new sounds, like "scratching" (invented by Grand Wizard Theodore), which predominantly involves the hand manipulation of turntables (although elbows and other body parts can be employed as well). In a very real sense, these deejays invented a new form of music based on new instruments, primarily turntables and (later) rhythm machines. Grandmaster Flash and The Furious Five were among the pioneers who assertively used this new musical form to mix strong social commentary into the rapping repertory.

"B-boying" refers to a multifaceted phenomenon of dress and body positioning. Greg Tate, the long-time critic for the *Village Voice*, has noted in his frequently cited overview essay on hip-hop that appears in the *Britannica Encyclopedia* (2003 edition) that b-boying is a form of communication that is as subtle as it is complex, and Tate notes that the philosopher Cornell West has referred to this phenomenon as "postural semantics." The general tone of all b-boying is one of defiance combined with an expressive and assertive attitude. Common representations of b-boying include the placing of carefully framed hands in front of one's face while rapping, unorthodox arrangement of clothing (such as the wearing of pants backwards as with the group Kriss Kross), and highly energetic dance known as "break dancing" which includes the now widely recognized signature move of spinning upside down and vertically on one's head with one's legs spread out horizontally—the so-called "helicopter."

Graffiti is the final element of hip-hop expressionism, and the term is the plural of "graffito." Graffiti is casual writing, of which cave drawings are among the earliest known examples. These writings are normally placed on surfaces exhibited in public places, ranging from exterior walls of buildings to the sides of trains. Graffiti can be painted, drawn, or scratched, and its quality can range from crude language roughly applied to sublime poetry and art painstakingly created. While public officials generally regard graffiti as a nuisance, connoisseurs of this art value it as a distinctive form of expression that is not captured in more formal public writings, such as that found on plaques or monuments. Graffiti acts as a window into a sometimes difficult to perceive urban culture that daily wrestles with extremes of poverty and violence.

According to legend, modern graffiti as it appears in the hip-hop culture was initiated in New York City by a Greek American teenager named Demitrios in approximately 1971 or 1972. His "tag" was "Taki 183." "Taki" was his nickname, and "183" was the street number where he lived (183rd Street) in New York. He generally wrote his tag on the exterior sides of New York's subway cars, but he also utilized the subway system's walls as well. Inevitably, this caught on, and lots of teenagers began painting their tags all over the place, but especially on the sides of subway cars. It was a way to become famous, in a very real sense, at least among teenage youth. But it was also a way to compete, and it soon became obvious that just placing your tag somewhere was not enough. This led to a creative surge in the mid-1970s in which teenage youth began painting increasingly more meaningful and beautiful murals, often using spray paint applied surreptitiously in the middle of the night. Subway cars continued to be premiere venues for this art, since the cars guaranteed a continually changing and larger audience for the art. The best creators of graffiti were able to capture significant levels of recognition not only among their peers, but also among an increasingly respectful community of serious connoisseurs of art. Indeed, some graffiti were displayed in important art galleries in the major cities of the world, and these shows were occasionally reported and reviewed in the international press.

Businesses, of course, had long used the walls of buildings and subway cars to display their own advertising. But the creators of graffiti were not paying for the space to display their art, and their paintings did eventually eliminate the transparency of the subway windows as well as cover the paid-for advertising. Thus, in the 1980s, public authorities tried to crack down on the spreaders of graffiti, which amplified an already existent climate of rebellious defiance among the teenage youth who resented having to give up their newly-found capabilities and venues of expression. While the attitude of defiance had its origin in the social conditions that plagued the inner-city youth, its migration into hip-hop music is one of the most catalytic events in the evolution of rap. A pointed example of this migration is with the increasingly visible DJ Kay Slay (formerly Kenneth Gibson) who entered hip-hop culture as a graffiti artist. His graffiti was shown in the films "Style Wars" and "Wild Side." The crackdown on graffiti forced Mr. Gibson to re-direct his creative efforts to the art of turntabling, and he is now well-known as a central archivalist of hip-hop verbal "battles." (See especially "Hip-Hop's One-Man Ministry of Insults," by Lola Ogunnaike, *The New York Times*, Sunday, 4 May 2003, Arts section.)

While hip-hop music is now a world-wide phenomenon, it began in an area of New York City known as South Bronx during the 1970s. While hip-hop music is clearly one of many distinct forms of African American music, such as the blues, jazz, bebop, and technofunk, numerous parallels between hip-hop music and these other forms have often been made, and there is a clear lineage to hip-hop music from these earlier forms, a point made in the early 1980s by Cornell West (West 1999[1982], chapter 40). There were also numerous political legacies to hip-hop music. For example, the political turmoil of the 1970s involving the Black Panther Party later became one (of many) focuses of hip-hop awareness. For example, Afeni Shakur, the mother of the late rapper Tupac Shakur, was a member of the Black Panther Party, and some have argued that her politics had an influence on that of her son. (See "Hip-Hop Requiem: Tupac Shakur is Mourned, His Legacy Mined," by Neil Strauss, *The New York Times*, Wednesday, 11 April 2001, The Living Arts section, p. B1&3[N].) Some early political influences on hip-hop politics can also be traced to Malcolm X as well as other even more radical African-American political leaders.

When hip-hop quickly spread to the West Coast (primarily Los Angeles), competing venues emerged. Both subtle and major differences in the political stances of these coastally-defined venues became an important ingredient in hip-hop development. Some early hip-hop artists mixed social and political messages in their lyrics, as with the studio album *The Message* released in 1982 by Grandmaster Flash and the Furious Five. The title track for this album talks bluntly about the painful and violent aspects of ghetto life, and it set the stage for future efforts by hip-hop artists to blend these descriptions of social adversity with pointed advice to their communities, as with Tupac Shakur's discussion of teenage pregnancy in "Brenda's Gotta Baby." But it was with the group Public Enemy that hip-hop turned more aggressively in the direction of more radical political rhetoric.

By the mid-1980s, hip-hop had crossed racial lines entirely as it began its rapid spread into mainstream American culture. Interestingly, the medium of rap remained largely constant, but the message morphed into whatever was appropriate for each new setting. The Beastie Boys was one of the first white hip-hop groups that began to speak directly to a suburban white young audience, and the growth of hip-hop as a form of musical expression among white youth continues even now. Eminem became, of course, one of the most influential of these white rappers. The reasons why hip-hop has so profoundly influenced white suburban youth has been widely debated, and this group is beginning to add its own unique signature to expanding hip-hop culture. (See especially the front-page article by N.R. Kleinfield, "Guarding the Borders of the Hip-Hop Nation," *The New York Times*, Thursday, 6 July 2000, p. A1&18-9[N].)

Hip-hop has experienced two primary periods in its growth (although it should be noted that other authors have sometimes identified alternative temporal distinctions). The first is from 1973-93, and this is hip-hop's so-called "classical period." This period includes artists such as De La Soul, M.C. Hammer, 2 Live Crew, Queen Latifah, Salt-n-Pepa, N.W.A (Niggaz With Attitude), Dr. Dre, and others. The post-1993 period (also known as the "post-classical period" of hip-hop) includes artists such as Wu-Tang Clan, Puffy Daddy (later P. Diddy, and originally Sean Combs), Lauryn Hill, Mase, The Notorious B.I.G., Tupac Shakur, and others.

It was from within this later period that "gangsta rap" emerged, and it remains among the most verbally violent forms of rap music. Gangsta rap in particular has an "outlaw" flavor that has directly appealed to large numbers of emotionally alienated suburban white youth, even though its origin strictly reflects the more violent elements of inner city street life. It is difficult to isolate the purely political elements from within gangsta rap due to its overall rebellious tone. While its hyperrealism is often dominated by the issues of sex, drugs, and violence, there is nonetheless a widely apparent political aspect to much gangsta rap. This hyperrealism also signals a more poignant shift in the sensibilities of much of the African American lower class. As Cornell West has phrased it, "(T)he roots of the Afro-American spiritual-blues impulse are based on the supposition that somebody—God, Mom or neighbors—cares. Some expressions of black rap music challenge this supposition" (West, 1999[1982], p.

483). Gangsta rap thus announces a challenge to the utopian aspirations of the ghetto-stricken African American poor that had previously been expressed in its deep musical spiritualism as well as its positive—even cheerful—African-derived rhythmicality.

While my arguments here focus mostly on the political content of rap and gangsta rap music, it should also be noted that a great deal of political content can be also found in the work of other rappers that come from diverse orientations. For example, important political statements have been made by Muslim and feminist rappers.

The best way to understand the politics of hip-hop music is through an examination of various examples. The discussion below is hardly complete; there are simply too many political hip-hop songs for any one chapter (or volume) to cover in encompassing depth. Yet as with the other chapters in this book, I take the path of making heuristic choices among the extant works in order to illustrate primary types of political music, thereby helping to establish a "lay of the land," so to speak, which will hopefully assist readers as they pursue their own investigations of this continually evolving and highly dynamic musical genre. In general, I discuss four primary types of socially and politically rich hip-hop music. These are highly general categories, and some readers will certainly want a greater degree of differentiation across the spectrum of political hip-hop. Thus, my categories are not posited here as exhaustive, but rather as starting points from which more subtle levels of analysis can fruitfully emerge. The four general categories discussed below are: (1) the emergence of socially relevant hip-hop messages with and without prescriptive advice, (2) the radicalization of political hip-hop rhetoric, (3) class warfare and the rise of ghetto-centric gangsta rap, and (4) the transformation of hip-hop into a vehicle for white rebellion.

The Emergence of Socially Relevant Hip-Hop

Grandmaster Flash and his group, The Furious Five, pioneered the channeling of hip-hop into discussions of social causes. The composition of The Furious Five had two primary incarnations, but in the first instance Melle Mel (formerly Melvin Glover) was one of Grandmaster Flash's most creative rap collaborators. The group became hugely popular in New York City beginning in the late 1970s due to the combination of Flash's skill as a DJ as well as the Five's ability to deliver subtle rap lyrics. Two of their songs are markers in the evolution of hip-hop into a vehicle for social content and commentary. The first is "The Message," released in 1982, while the second is "White Lines (Don't Do It)" which was released a year later.

In "The Message," Melle Mel's voice foreshadows the hyperrealism of gangsta rap with lyrics that describe the horror of inner city ghetto life. The song begins with graphic descriptions of the assaults on the senses as one walks through the ghetto, "Broken glass everywhere. People pissing on the stairs, you know they just don't care. I can't take the smell, I can't take the noise. Got no money to move out, I guess I got no choice." The song then moves on to describe the rats, the roaches, the neighborhood junkie selling drugs, and even a person repossessing a car. The chorus then begins with the now famous lines, "Don't push me, cause I'm close to the edge. I'm trying not to loose my head. It's like a jungle sometimes, it makes me wonder how I keep from going under." These lines have been mirrored in approximation in countless other rap songs since then, and they even find a loud resonance (although with a different intent) with the lyrics of "Scream" performed by Michael and Janet Jackson. The remainder of the song is a poetic description of a long list of ghetto realities, including pimps and prostitution, pawning a mother's television set, harassment from bill collectors, inadequate educational opportunities, violent assaults, incarceration, and premature and tragic death.

To the listeners of the day, "The Message" was a graphic verbal acknowledgment of the quality of life that was common for so many inner city African American youths. It is very interesting to note that the song's hyperrealism with regard to the description of life at its worse is an ingredient that has continued to reappear in some of the most dynamic venues for rap music, including international venues. For example, Peter S. Green has reported that this type of rap music is the rage within the slums of post-communist Poland (see "Polish Hip-Hop Rocks the Homies in the Blok," by Peter S. Green, *The New York Times*, Friday, 5 April 2002, p. A4[N]). The breeding grounds for this music are the government housing projects called "blokersi" (bloh-CARE-zhee). The teenage youth, faced with few if any prospects, turn to hyperrealistic rap to obtain expressive release as well as to fill time. The Polish hip-hoppers are mostly males who are as angry with their situation in life as many inner city African Americans are with theirs, even though the issues for each culture are different. Poland is essentially all white and Catholic, and police violence and racial injustice are simply not issues there. But the lack of an avenue out of poverty combined with the stresses of opportunity-free high density living creates a culture that lives and breathes discontent. The Polish youth also benefit from being able to cheaply produce their own rap CDs on personal computers, selling them on the street later in an attempt to recover their costs. Readers may also be interested in following a similar phenomenon that is currently taking place in Cuba, a country that now even sponsors its own rap festivals (see "Rap Takes Root Where Free Expression Is Risky," by Brett Sokol, *The New York Times*, Sunday, 3 September 2000, p. 28&32, Arts Section). In a very real sense, Grandmaster Flash and The Furious Five paved the way for this increasingly international phenomenon, although it is hard to imagine that anyone could have understood the pivotal nature of their efforts when they first recorded "The Message."

With "White Lines (Don't Do It)" written by Sylvia Robinson and Melvin Glover (Melle Mel), Grandmaster Flash and The Furious Five took the social commentary concept embraced by "The Message" one step further and produced a song that added a prescription. "White Lines (Don't Do It)" is a song about cocaine abuse. The song describes the lure of the cocaine high as well as the implications of drug use. Graphic lyrics make the counseling message clear, "My white lines go a long way. Either up your nose or through your vein. With nothin to gain except killin your brain." As the chorus satirically urges the drug user to "Get higher, baby!" other verses describe the bitter consequences of cocaine use. The song's prescriptive solution to this problem is as impossible to miss as it is simple, and it is captured with the oft-repeated lyrics, "Don't Do It." As an aside, it is interesting to note that this song presaged Nancy Reagan's "Just Say No" campaign against drug use which she initiated in 1985 in a speech which she gave in Oakland, California at an elementary school.

The Radicalization of Political Hip-Hop Rhetoric

Hip-hop extended well beyond the realm of social commentary when a group of suburban-raised African American students with a connection to Adelphi University were brought together to form the group Public Enemy in 1982. The members of this group were Chuck D (the leader of the group, formerly Carlton Ridenhour), Professor Griff (Richard Griffin), Terminator X (Norman Lee Rogers), and Flavor Fav (William Drayton). With this group it is also important to note their production team, members of which wrote many of their most radical political songs. The production team is called the "Bomb Squad," and its members are Hank Shocklee, Carl Ryder, Eric (Vietnam) Sadler, and Keith Shocklee. Public Enemy was a primary influence in the emergence of radical hip-hop, and their popularity in the late 1980s continued into the early 1990s until controversies involving charges of anti-Semitism combined with their support for the radical leader of the Nation of Islam, Louis Farrakhan, led them away from their earlier messages that dealt primarily with racial, anti-government, and extreme leftist issues.

It is hard to exaggerate the radical tone of Public Enemy's rhythmically embellished politics. For example, the subtitle of their 1990 album *Fear of a Black Planet*, is "The Counterattack on World Supremacy." Titles from that album include "Welcome to the Terrordome," "Meet the G that Killed Me" ("G" means gangster), "Anti-Nigger Machine," "Burn Hollywood Burn,"

"Power to the People," "Who Stole the Soul?," "Revolutionary Generation," "War at 33⅓," "Fight the Power," and, of course, the album's title track. The track "Burn Hollywood Burn" is a good example of how the group can use their lyrics to target a specific institution. In this track, Hollywood is demonized as projecting both news and images through television that stereotype African Americans as violent gang members. For example, and from the track, "Get me the hell away from this TV. All this news and views are beneath me. Cause all I hear about is shots ringin' out. About gangs puttin' each others head out...." Public Enemy's other albums contain a similar tone. One of their most noted albums is *It Takes a Nation of Millions to Hold Us Back*, originally released in 1988.

Public Enemy was not a ghetto-centric hip-hop group. The political content conveyed in the lyrics of their songs can be ideologically located in the center of the most radical leftist traditions. Indeed, it is the relative absence of a ghetto focus that caused Public Enemy to be replaced in the minds of the next generation of hip-hoppers who sought to connect their politics with the plight of urban African Americans, and then again later with alienated white suburban youths. That is, the broadly leftist ideological approach to radical politics that was embraced by Public Enemy eventually gave way to political music that was more clearly tied to the social milieu and local political context of hip-hop's primary audiences. In a sense, Public Enemy was an anomaly in the evolution of political hip-hop. The group took the idea of politicizing hip-hop lyrics from the earlier social commentaries of Grandmaster Flash and The Furious Five as found in "The Message," but then framed their politics within a larger and more international ideological perspective. The political hip-hop artists that followed Public Enemy returned to the earlier rich descriptions of social contexts, and then interlaced these descriptions with more narrowly focused and socially connected political themes.

Class Warfare and the Rise of Ghetto-centric Gangsta Rap

Technically speaking, gangsta rap was born in the East Coast due to work from artists such as Schoolly D (from Philadelphia, and arguably the inventor of gangsta rap) and the group Boogie Down Productions (from South Bronx in New York City, see especially their album *Criminal Minded* with tracks such as "9mm Goes Bang"). These artists produced rap music that was clearly tied historically to "The Message," but which showcased a graphic level of descriptive bravado mixed with violence in inner-city ghetto life that was absent from the work of Grandmaster Flash and the Furious Five. For example, in Boogie Down Productions's song, "9mm Goes Bang," group member KRS-One (formerly Lawrence Krisna Parker) raps a story that reads like a TV drama about how he shot a crack dealer and was later himself shot at by police, from whom he had to escape with the daring help of DJ Scott LaRock (formerly Scott Sterling, another group member).

Yet despite its East Coast birth, gangsta rap became a national sensation only after it migrated from the East Coast to Los Angeles in the late 1980s. The West Coast emergence of gangsta rap began in 1989 (technically 1988) when the group N.W.A. (Niggaz With Attitude) released the album *Straight Outta Compton*. (However, note that some argue that Ice T's earlier release, "Six N the Morning," is the true beginning of the West Coast phenomenon.) It is of historical interest to note the N.W.A. later worked with Public Enemy's production crew, the Bomb Squad. The tracks in *Straight Outta Compton* defined a new era in rap music. The songs are filled with descriptions of violent life in the ghetto that are as casually stated as the reality is lived on the streets. Profanity is also inserted into this music in a big way, again reflecting street language among a class of ghetto youth. One should make no mistake about the interpretation of this music. Life was dangerous in certain areas of Los Angeles and its neighboring Compton, and the artists themselves claimed that their gangsta rap music depicted the reality of street life, not an exaggeration of it. The group's misogyny can be traced back to this as well, in the sense that women are often seen as an exploitable commodity in situations of poverty permeated by extreme community violence. With the hyperrealism of gangsta rap, N.W.A. allowed its listeners an uncomfortable window through which to view the depths to which ghetto life had sunk.

N.W.A. disbanded in 1992 due to internal disagreements, but its original members were Dr. Dre (Andre Young), Eazy E (Eric Wright), Ice Cube (O'Shea Jackson), MC Ren (Lorenzo Patterson), Yella (Antoine Carraby), and Arabian Prince (Mik Lezan). A number of these members pursued solo careers that exponentially amplified the original influence of N.W.A. In particular, Dr. Dre formed Death Row Records, a pioneering label in hip-hop. In 1992, Dr. Dre released the album *The Chronic* with his new label, and this seminal release essentially canonized gangsta rap as a new sub-genre within hip-hop. In this release he also introduced a new sound called "G-funk" which dominated much of hip-hop for years. Dr. Dre's influence as a producer extended far beyond his own work as a rapper, however. He was fundamental in assisting the careers of Snoop Dog (formerly "Snoop Doggy Dog," and also Calvin Broadus; featured in *The Chronic*) as well as Eminem (Marshall Bruce Mathers III), one of hip-hop's most influential white gangsta rap artists.

In a very real sense, gangsta rap largely addresses class warfare. This warfare is intimately connected to what Cornell West refers to as black nihilism, which is "primarily a question of speaking to the profound sense of psychological depression, personal worthlessness, and social despair so widespread in black America" (West, 2001[1991], p. 20). The level of violence depicted in gangsta rap is comparable to some low-level wartime situations. In part, the warfare involves inner-city youths who feel heatedly repressed by a racially discriminating police force. For example, consider the verse rapped by Daz in "The Day the Niggaz Took Over," a track from *The Chronic*. The song begins by asking why the "voice" of the song is so violent, and why he takes the law into his own hands by possessing a gun and using it to protect himself. He complains that the police do not protect him, and in fact shoot and harass him and his colleagues. There is rioting and looting in his neighborhood, and the situation is similar in some respects to, say, wartime Beirut. What remains is no love, but rather a desire to fight back, gun in hand. It is hard to imagine a song like this portraying anything except a war, at least a war as it is perceived to be by the ghetto youth. The gangs of the ghetto are the armies in this war. Later in this same track, Dr. Dre explicitly references these gangs as military "squads" engaged in looting and other wartime chaos.

These types of war-like messages are quite common among gangsta rappers. For example, interested readers might enjoy a close examination of many songs by Tupac Shakur, such as the song "Violent" from his 1992 album *2pacalypse Now*, a song which deals with the violent tension between ghetto youth and the police. Anger, violence, and the sense of war permeates many of these hyperrealistic gangsta rap tracks. It is music that should be listened to precisely because of what is being said. This is not merely "theater shock." It is all too real to be theater.

But gangsta rap is not just about warfare between inner city youth and what they perceive to be a repressive police force. It is also about warfare between status-differentiated African Americans themselves. One might call this "intra-class warfare." Within the gangsta rap hip-hop community, a great deal is made of African Americans who manage to leave the ghetto in their drive for upward mobility. These African Americans become successful business people and professionals, including doctors, lawyers, and academics. Some of the hip-hoppers of gangsta rap perceive that these higher status African Americans look down upon those who remain in the ghetto. Moreover, when a person from the ghetto achieves financial success through dubious means that are available to members of that social strata, higher status African Americans with more normal credentials fail to recognize a higher level of status in the now financially better-off ghetto residents.

Such individuals proclaiming ghetto "success" are called "playas" (also, "players"), and their means of financial success can involve virtually any means available to them, including pimping and drug-running. "Playas" express a distinctive persona that involves elaborate clothing, jewelry, and ostentatious cars as well as a highly visible night life. While most playas are men, there are also women playas. Often rappers like to refer to themselves as "playas." But successful rappers who call themselves "playas" normally earn their money quite respectably through the sale of their own music CDs. Their point in calling themselves "playas" is to re-enforce their perceived connection to the ghetto origin of gangsta rap hip-hop.

Violence, of course, is a fact of life among the real playas of the ghetto. Women who are successful as playas in their own right sometimes refer to themselves as "gangstresses," which is also the name of an important documentary on the female element of inner-city gangsta life by Harry Davis. The documentary features such hip-hop greats as Mary J. Blige and Lil' Kim, and it describes in stunning visual detail the difficult nature of the female experience in such settings.

Thus, often in gangsta rap hip-hop there is a flavor of resentment (sometimes underlying, but other times explicit) toward African Americans—both male and female—who appear to distance themselves from the pain of the ghetto experience. Cornell West has discussed this by identifying what he calls "contemptuous black middle-class attitudes" as a significant contribution to the collapse of hope among the ghettoized poor (West 1999[1982], p. 483). As with so much of hip-hop, new language is developed to express these and other ideas, and indeed this has resulted in the recent publication of a dictionary of hip-hop terms that has been compiled by Alonzo Westbrook called a "Hip Hoptionary" (Westbrook 2002). When African Americans achieve higher status through the path of education, they obtain college degrees that many ghetto-bound playas cannot match. The playas view these degrees with resentment, calling those who hold them "P.H.D.s," where "P.H.D." stands for "playa-hating degree." Westbrook's *Hip Hoptionary* defines a "playa" as "one who can get a girl/guy to do what he/she wants him/her to do," which implies that a crucial characteristic of being a playa is the ability to exert authority over others. African Americans whose higher level of status is based on education clearly do not recognize this authority, and it is this lack of recognition and respect that appears to be the focus of playa resentment. This can be seen, for example in the lyrics for "Been Around the World" (original version, not the remix) performed by Puff Daddy (formerly Sean Combs, and now P. Diddy), Mase, and the Notorius B.I.G. In that song, Mase raps, "Then you got niggaz that just don't like me. You know, the, those P.H.D. niggaz."

This is, of course, a war of words in the world of hip-hop. Certainly the intra-class war between ghetto-centric African American youth and their older, better educated, and higher status counterparts is not shot out on the streets. The higher-status African Americans do not live in the ghetto, and thus they are essentially inaccessible to the ghetto youth. However, the conditions within the inner city itself can be quite war-like in a real shooting sense. America is a nation with a race problem, one with which it has failed to resolve or even understand. Ghetto youth know full well that African American males are either incarcerated or killed at literally astounding rates. These same youths also know that their main contact with the government is through the legal system, the same legal system that uses predominantly white juries to impose the death penalty on impoverished African Americans who are often not given an adequate legal defense. Indeed, the recent upsurge in DNA testing is demonstrating that many of the inmates awaiting execution on death row are completely innocent of the crimes for which they were convicted. Moreover, there is a long backlog of DNA testing, and no one is conducting DNA tests in cases for which the accused have already been executed, implying that the government is guilty of murdering large numbers of men for which biased judicial and social systems have failed completely. Moreover, because of incarceration records, large numbers of African American urban males in some states cannot even vote in elections, let alone obtain productive employment and educational opportunities. There are reasons underlying the anger of gangsta rap, and these reasons are tied to real social and political problems in the African American community.

There should be no doubt that many ghettoized African American youth really see the world this way. Consider Tupac Shakur's song, "Words of Wisdom," a track from his *2pacalypse Now* album. In this song, Tupac Shakur talks about how America is collectively killing the black ghetto youth in what amounts to be nothing less than genocide. The ghetto youth are made to feel inferior by the same system that demands allegiance to a nation state that offers no respect to its poorest members in return. He calls on members of these repressed masses to break the chains of psychological bondage. When he states, "Lady Liberty, still the bitch lied to me," he unambiguously argues that America's claim of freedom and justice for all is a sham. When he claims, "Amerika, you reap what you sow," he leaves no doubt that the troubles of violence in the inner city are the country's own fault.

These inner city youths see a social and political fence surrounding themselves and their communities. Their anger comes out in their hip-hop voices. And for a nation that turns its head away from its own internal social issues while it actively engages international problems of violence (such as terror), there may be little chance of near-term change in the fortunes of these youths. The inner-city ghetto is a cauldron within which the creative energy of hip-hop is generated. Without this pain and suffering, perhaps some of the musical genius of the African American urban community would be diverted into other realms. In a cruel sense, we have the suffering of many to thank for some of the musical and poetic gifts of expression that now surround us.

Years ago, few might have imagined that the gangsta rap anger of urban hip-hop would or even could be translated into something relevant to millions of relatively well-off suburban white youth. But that is exactly what happened.

The Transformation of Hip-Hop into a Vehicle for White Rebellion

To be quite honest, no one yet totally understands all of the reasons why white youths have been so strongly attracted to hip-hop, and especially gangsta rap. One penetrating and long report and analysis of this phenomenon has been offered by N.R. Kleinfield ("Guarding the Borders of the Hip-Hop Nation," *The New York Times*, Thursday, 6 July 2000, pp. 1A&18A-9A[N]). It is clear that the magnitude of this phenomenon is huge. Indeed, approximately 70 percent of all rap albums are bought by whites. But Kleinfield's essay is not a philosophical analysis of white hip-hop. Rather the article describes how hip-hop has affected the ways some whites and blacks think about race. The premise of the article seems to be that hip-hop is fundamentally a black phenomenon, and that it has remained a black phenomenon even as it has crossed into a white audience. In some respects, this is correct. A great deal of hip-hop is still Afro-centric. But I suspect that something else is ultimately going on with large segments of the white listeners of hip-hop, and my approach in this chapter is to portray the complexities of this phenomenon from a psychological perspective.

In the few pages that follow in which I discuss the white focus on hip-hop, I make no attempt to fully explain the phenomenon. Here my aims are more limited. I heuristically focus on a content analysis of the lyrics and video of "Stan," a song rapped by Eminem. I believe my interpretation of Eminem's song is arguably correct (at least to my satisfaction), but again there can be no certainty in the interpretation of art. One of the purposes of art is to elicit individualized interpretations of inspired expression, and hip-hop is no exception in this regard. One cannot resort to the statement, "The artist certainly meant to say ...," for the artist's intent in the creation of art is often peripheral to the meaning that the art ultimately has on those who appreciate it. Moreover, while it is also the case that artists express themselves both intuitively and intellectually, others may find ideas within the art that are extrapolated beyond those ideas originally intended by the artists, an important point made by the sociologist Martin (1995, pp. 215-6).

I do not see Eminem as "the New White Negro," as he has been described by Carl Rux (Rux, 2003). On the surface, Eminem might seem to some to fit the description of a derived product of hip-hop derogatively labeled a "wigga"—a white person who, as Tate describes, "apes Blackness by 'acting hip-hop' in dress, speech, body language, and, in some cases, even gang affiliation" (Tate, 2003, p. 8; see also the above reference to Kleinfield, 2000, p. 18A[N]). Yet even Rux also argues that Eminem is much more than a white copy of a black persona. It does not seem reasonable to infer that Eminem's popularity is simply a result of his race combined with his ability to perform in an African American dominated genre. His "whiteness" does not automatically make rap music relevant to white audiences. Something much more profound is at the root of Eminem's appeal to both white and black youth.

Of course, my true aim in this instance is not so much to understand Eminem, or any white hip-hop artist. Rather, my purpose here is to suggest through example that at least some of Eminem's music is so complex in its psychological content that it acts as a vehicle for the expression of emotions, symbols, and issues that are very relevant (or at least subconsciously understandable) to many elements in a mass audience regardless of race. It is within this complexity that I find much of the appeal to Eminem's style of hip-hop. This is indeed to what Charles Shaar Murray is referring in a British review of Eminem when he writes that "troubled pop kids unable to identify with the shiny, happy dummies wheeled out by the industry will be ready and waiting the next time Eminem stands up" (*The Observer*, 12 May 2002).

If the key to understanding Eminem's hip-hop attraction to both white and black audiences is the way this artist embeds complex social and psychological commentaries within a musical frame, then a useful heuristic approach to "Stan" can be to compare the lyrics and video images for that song with a different work that similarly embeds complex psychological ideas. Of particular interest in this regard is Sylvia Plath's poem, "Daddy." "Daddy," published in 1966 three years after her death, is an elegy for her father, Otto Plath, who died in 1940 when Sylvia was quite young. Otto Plath migrated to America from Grabow, Poland, and eventually worked at Boston University as an instructor in German. "Daddy" is a torrential assault on Sylvia's father, and it is not clear from the historical record what Mr. Plath might have done to his daughter between the time when Sylvia was born in 1932 and the moment of his death to deserve such a lashing. Sylvia had a psychologically troubled life, having tried to commit suicide more than once, eventually succeeding. Her poems often seem to be composed from the perspective of a victim, and it is somewhat interesting to note that her husband, Ted Hughes, is an English poet who tended to write from the perspective of a predator.

Sylvia Plath feels trapped by her relationship (imaginary or real) with her father. In the beginning of the poem, she refers to her father as a "black shoe," and to herself as a foot "barely able to breathe." Moreover, this relationship is clearly not limited to the years in which Otto Plath was alive, since she refers to this confining relationship as having spanned "thirty years." A shoe, of course, is supposed to protect the foot, just as a father is supposed to protect his child. But the protection can turn to harm in certain circumstances, and it is the element of harm that dominates "Daddy." As a result, Sylvia declares, "Daddy, I have had to kill you," although in the next breath she laments that her father died too early.

Ms. Plath enhances this idea of psychological imprisonment by comparing herself with a Jew sent to a concentration camp while reminding the reader of her father's Nazi-like and militaristic Germanness. Eventually comparing her father with a cleft-hoofed devil, she declares how she fought a desperate mental battle to find him even though he was dead, saying "I thought even the bones would do." Failing to find solace, she attempts suicide. Failing even that, she states, "If I've killed one man, I've killed two," suggesting that she blames herself for her father's death and her own consequent abandonment, as well as for having to kill any idealized memory of her father. But here the reference also addresses her failed relationship with Ted Hughes, her husband, since the second death can be seen as her blaming herself for having killed the internal possibility of a shared love with a spouse. She is abandoned, alone, and defeated when she finally declares, "Daddy, daddy, you bastard, I'm through."

In its essence, and speaking broadly, "Daddy" is about a dysfunctional relationship with a father figure, and with men more generally. The father is absent, since he is dead. For years the child (Sylvia) imagines both good and evil of her father, eventually tumbling into a pit of perceived evil when he does not respond to her desperate psychological cries for help. She demonizes him for staying aloof, and for ultimately failing her. Her eventual response is to kill herself, an act that not only silences her own inner turmoil, but which also assigns the ultimate blame for her death on the non-responding object of her failed relationship. It is as if her father may at last awaken from the grave to react, finally, to Sylvia's ultimate attack with a twinge of guilt. The attack is, of course, as impotent as is her father's ability to rise from the dead, and Ms. Plath is truly finished.

My own preference is to approach Eminem's song "Stan" from the perspective of the work's accompanying video which was directed by Phillip Atwell and Dr. Dre. In the video, the fanatical fan named Stan is played by the actor Devon Sawa, although Stan's voice in the song and video is always that of Eminem. Stan has a pregnant girlfriend who is played by the singer Dido. Stan is infatuated with Eminem. He bleaches his hair to match that of Eminem, and he has decorated his basement with wall-to-wall pictures of his idol. In his basement, he takes a picture of himself and his girlfriend and then places a picture of Eminem over the side of the picture that contains his girlfriend, making it seem as if it is a picture of himself and Eminem rather than a picture of Stan and his girlfriend. At the time that he does this, he voices his words that he writes in a letter to Eminem, "My girlfriend's jealous cause I talk about you 24/7 .... We should be together too," all of which implies that Stan is experiencing some degree of repressed homosexual attraction toward Eminem. He indeed has a sexual relationship with his girlfriend, which is demonstrated by her pregnancy. It is the replacement of his girlfriend's image by that of Eminem that suggests an emergent homosexual orientation to Stan's attraction to his idol. This interpretation is amplified by the dysfunctional and angry relationship that Stan has with his girlfriend, ultimately resulting in Stan's attack on his girlfriend and his suicidal car crash which also kills his girlfriend, and his unborn child. Stan's male/female relationship simply is not working, and he is inwardly seeking an alternative form of relationship. Stan's underlying homosexual approach to his idol is both detected and ultimately rejected by Eminem in the song when he later raps, "And what's this shit about us meant to be together? That type of shit'll make me not want us to meet each other."

The above elements of the song and video have certain parallels with Plath's work. Sylvia Plath was also unable to achieve a successful relationship with her husband. The couple were separated at the time of her death by suicide, and her reference to her having killed a second man (partially implying her husband) in the poem "Daddy" evokes the same idea as in "Stan" of the main character both killing the spouse (also internally with respect to any true possibility of sharing love) and killing one's self through suicide. But at the core of the troubles for both Stan and Sylvia Plath is the dysfunctionality between each and their fathers. Stan also describes his father in brutal, authoritarian, and uncaring terms when he states to Eminem in the song, "I'm just like you in a way. I never knew my father neither; he used to always cheat on my mom and beat her. I can relate to what you're saying in your songs." In a very real sense, both Stan (in the song) and Sylvia Plath (in "Daddy") are psychologically destabilized because of a gaping vacuum in their own mentalities that is caused by that absence of a caring father image. But while Sylvia Plath describes her attempts to correct that imbalance in the past tense,

Stan is engaged in an on-going battle to use Eminem to resolve his own psychological father-imbalance. In the end, Stan is as unsuccessful as Ms. Plath, however. Eminem is not physically present for Stan, and Stan complains bitterly throughout the song of Eminem's failure to act in what he considers a supportive role, such as to sign an autograph or answer a letter. Eminem's failure to fulfill this role is caused by happenstance not disregard, and it is worth noting that Otto Plath's failure to be present during Sylvia's adolescence is similarly not due to his own design but to the unfortunate consequence of his death. But the tortured minds of Stan and Sylvia do not always see things in their logical places when internal pain requires the allocation of blame regardless of the explanation for the pain.

It is interesting to note that Stan takes this theme one step further by suggesting that the problem of having a psychological imbalance related to a father image is to be repeated with his 6 year old brother Matthew who turns up at Stan's grave in the end of the video looking a lot like a young and defiant Eminem with bleached hair. In this latter case, Matthew will grow up not knowing a father figure, or even a substitute father figure that a caring brother (Stan) could have offered. As with Sylvia Plath and Stan, the supportive male figure will simply be absent, and in this absence, fantasy and idolization will act as a poor and ultimately unsuccessful substitute.

How does all this relate to suburban white youth who do not have a ghetto-centric cultural orientation? Just as one does not have to be suicidal to understand and appreciate the raw beauty in Sylvia Plath's poem "Daddy," one similarly does not have to be a suicidal fan of a pop idol in order to at least intuitively appreciate the psychological depth that exists with a song as complex at "Stan." Yet in a more immediate sense, there may be something in "Stan" that applies directly to the lives of many youth, regardless of race. Dysfunctional parent/child relationships are quite the norm in a contemporary society with a divorce rate as high as that of America's. Parents often raise their kids (perhaps especially the wealthy kids) by remote control, relying on babysitters, nannies, boarding schools, and ultimately child peer groups to substitute for parent/child contact time that is increasingly impossible to offer in a world where an hour of adult free time is more rare than a donation of blood. Many white youth are angry, not because they are victims of neglect and abuse in an inner-city ghetto that reeks of poverty and crime, but because they perceive that there is something missing in their lives, something as valuable as it is psychological. The pain associated with this absent element cannot be resolved with physical goods, as one can make a child happy with a candy. This type of pain has deeper roots, and Eminem is speaking directly to the source of this pain.

But there is yet more to the lure of white youth to hip-hop. There is a sterility to suburban culture that is simply unpleasant for many young people. As observed by N. R. Kleinfield, hip-hop is attractive because "lots of white kids found in it a way to flee their own orderly world by discovering a sexier, more provocative one" (*The New York Times*, Thursday, 6 July 2000, p. A1[N]). This now addresses the broader issue of ghetto-centric hip-hop finding an audience among non-ghetto youth of all races. This is a phenomenon that cuts across national borders as easily as it does cultures. The African American ghetto is not the only place where pain is experienced. Wherever one goes in the world, one finds people who suffer. They suffer in their communities, and their pain is nearly always a collective one shared among those with whom they live. Hip-hop is thus much more than a form of social expression relevant to African American youth. Hip-hop is an invented means expressing individual, social, and political views in a manner in which the raw tenor of the associated emotions is not suppressed. Hip-hop has spread quickly in our world because our world needs such a means of expression. The embrace of hip-hop by suburban white youth is just one example of this more broadly-based phenomenon, and it is perhaps more suitable to recognize the common psychological needs of cultures who find an outlet in hip-hop rather than to wonder why the differences between cultures cannot stop the embrace of hip-hop as a socially and politically relevant musical form.

To outsiders, relatively well-off suburban white youth may seem like rebels without a cause, but that is not how it feels to the youth themselves. Someone's failure to understand the cause of someone else's discontent does not make the discontent any less real. Sylvia Plath had a family, sufficient income, and a home in which to live. In a physical sense, her long lost father was no longer relevant to her life. Similarly, Stan's father was no longer a factor in the physical reality of his own life either. But in each case, the psychological underpinnings of the perceived pain was more relevant than the physical realities. What is in the mind really does matter, and this is the message conveyed in a number of Eminem's songs. As one crosses from one culture to another, the issues change even if the hip-hop vehicle of expression relating to those issues does not. Sometimes the issues are as directly political and volatile as ghetto rap's portrayal of inner-city class warfare. But sometimes the issues are more subtle, and thereby more intensely psychological. Regardless of the sources of those social and political issues, their voicing through hip-hop is likely to be a phenomenon that will remain with us for the considerable future.

Primary Sources for Further Reading

Neal, Mark Anthony, and Murray Forman, Eds. 2004. *That's the Joint!: The Hip-Hop Studies Reader*. New York: Routledge.

Tate, Greg. 2003. "Hip-Hop." In the *Encyclopedia Britannica 2003 Deluxe Edition*.

West, Cornell. 1999[1982]. "On Afro-American Music: From Bebop to Rap." In *The Cornell West Reader*, New York: Basic *Civitas* Books, chapter 40.

Westbrook, Alonzo. 2002. *Hip Hoptionary: the Dictionary of Hip Hop Terminology*. New York: Harlem Moon and Broadway Books.

CHAPTER 8

Political Music and the Transformation of Civilization

The music industry has changed a great deal from the days of Beethoven. As I have argued earlier in this volume, political music emerged as a significant presence in human society when music started to be performed in theaters which ordinary people could attend by just paying for a ticket. Theaters still matter, perhaps more than ever before, as I shall explain below. But the music industry's largest period of growth overall happened with the birth of technological means of distribution, such as radio, television, vinyl records, tapes, CDs, and now the Internet. Interestingly, music has become more important to our political lives because of the growth of technology, as is evidenced by the protest music that erupted out of the social and political turbulence of the 1960s and 1970s. Recent changes in the technologically-based music and broadcast industries are likely to precipitate changes in the way political music influences the evolution of our societies.

A heuristically useful example of how changes in industrial organization can affect the dissemination of political information in our society can be found with respect to the broadcast industry generally. Since the 1980s in the United States, there has been a continual consolidation of the broadcast industry. In the United States, there previously were strict limits on the number of radio and television stations that any single person or company could own in any city, or even nationwide. But these limits are collapsing, one by one, and nearly all legal constraints against consolidation may eventually be eliminated as a result of constant broadcast industry lobbying. This consolidation has a direct impact on the way all forms of political information is disseminated in our society. For example, in a recent essay published in *The New York Times*, Princeton economist Paul

Krugman pointed out that this consolidation will have a wide-ranging impact on how television news is presented, a phenomenon he calls "the China syndrome" ("The China Syndrome," *The New York Times*, Tuesday, 13 May 2003, p. A31[N]). The name refers to the way Rupert Murdoch's media empire (which includes a large number of news outlets, including Fox news) compromised its packaging of news channels by eliminating BBC's World Service from its satellite programming in order to make the package more acceptable to the Chinese government. The authorities in China did not want the influence of BBC's wide-ranging news reports to increase in China. Apparently, other news sources were less threatening than the BBC since they could be more easily manipulated, albeit indirectly. According to Krugman, the Chinese authorities also successfully requested the cancellation of a book that was about to be published by one of Mr. Murdoch's publishing companies because the Chinese government was criticized in the book. It is worthwhile noting that Mr. Murdoch's news outlets have a reputation for putting a conservative and (American) patriotic slant on the presentation of the news. Thus, it is particularly noteworthy that such a media empire was willing to compromise such principles for the purpose of landing a profitable contract with a communist government. If consolidation in the broadcast industry can affect the dissemination of political information via traditional news outlets, will it not also affect the spread of political content through other means? Indeed, Mr. Murdock's recent acquisition of Dow Jones & Company and *The Wall Street Journal* gives this point urgent relevancy.

The implications of broadcast industry consolidation are tremendous for the future of political music. Most broadcast outlets these days rely on "play lists" that are very restrictive. The play lists for many stations contain as few as 10 to 15 songs, and these songs are repeated ad nauseam hour after hour, day after day. The purpose of airing these songs is to attract the largest number of listeners who will suffer through commercials in the hopes of hearing their "favorite song" in a few minutes. Since media ownership is consolidating, the same play lists are spreading across a larger number of stations, resulting in the same love songs being played across the dial.   There is no economic benefit for these companies to play songs that do not attract the largest numbers of listeners.   Inevitably, this means that love songs dominate the airwaves, and love songs—as nice as they are—are not political songs.

But there is more to this story. The owners of the media outlets tend to be wealthy conservatives who typically do not subscribe to the types of politics that are common fare for political songs.   Such owners have a great financial stake in the continuation of the status quo, since it is that very same status quo that supports their wealthy position. These very same owners are unlikely to endorse a political agenda that might threaten this status quo, and thus they are unlikely to encourage their own stations to play a significant selection of political songs, many of which would inevitably campaign for changes in contemporary political personnel, laws, and institutions. In short, political songs are not likely to be played frequently in the major broadcast media now, or in the foreseeable future.

The Underground

This seemingly dire situation does not at all mean that political music will fade as a significant force influencing the evolution of human societies. Political change is like life itself; it will find a way to manifest. At this point, a personal story may help illustrate what I believe will be a characteristic of the distribution of political music in the future. Back in December of 1983, I was finishing up my Peace Corps duty in Kenya and traveling with a friend through the Middle East. We ended up staying for awhile in a youth hostel in East Jerusalem. The people who worked at the hostel—and especially in the eating area (sort of a restaurant)—were Palestinians. During meals I was intrigued to hear these workers playing music on portable tape decks that was unambiguously Palestinian protest music aimed at the youth audience. Some of these songs had English lyrics that I could easily understand, and I was astonished at the explicit nature of the political messages that these songs conveyed. Moreover, I was equally astonished that such music could be played in East Jerusalem at all, given the seriousness of the Israeli military occupation. Yet the more I watched these Palestinian youths listen to their music, the more I began to realize why they listened to it so quietly, often holding the speakers quite near their ears. I was fortunate to be close enough to hear the music for extended periods from time to time, and I was quite disappointed when the youths walked too far away from me, effectively putting me out of range. The bottom line is that the Palestinian youths knew that this music could not be listened to publicly without risking their own arrest. I also noted that these youths could easily flick a switch at a moment's notice to have the player switch to the built-in radio such that it would immediately begin playing an accepted local station. The youths were clever. In difficult times, politics needs to be clever.

The underground can be an especially potent source of political content. Recall that the Ayatollah Khomeni orchestrated from his base in Paris much of the Iranian revolution that deposed the Shah in the mid-1970s. The most critical ingredient of this campaign was the use of cassette tapes that contained messages from the Ayatollah. These recorded messages (officially illegal) were eventually distributed throughout rural Iran and played in countless mosques. While it is true that the Shah's own political policies were not successful in addressing the complaints of the Iranian masses, it is equally true that a highly potent rebellion was organized right under his nose using audio recordings with prohibited content. The Shah's highly feared military police were powerless at stopping this effective political campaign.

Some regimes are better than others at stopping offending information from penetrating the public's consciousness. They try harder. For example, Kim Jong-il's regime in North Korea manages to control what its populace knows to an uncanny extent. The police have informants just about everywhere, and when radios are distributed to the masses, the tuners are soldered firmly to the single frequency used by the state. Apparently, radios are occasionally inspected as well to see if anyone has tampered with the tuners. But such regimes are the exception rather than the norm. Outside of such severe situations, the relatively uncontrolled underground can be a vibrant source of political information.

In today's world, the most significant method to distribute political music through the underground is via the Internet. File sharing is one of the most useful technologies in this regard. This phenomenon began in earnest with the creation of the short-lived but exceptionally popular Napster file-sharing system. New technologies emerged that addressed issues of making peer-to-peer file sharing possible without the need of a centralized computer system that orchestrated the swapping of files. Also, while file sharing initially focused on files encoded with the MP3 sound compression format, new technologies allow all sorts of files to be shared, including video, text, programs, and alternatively encoded sound files. It is also possible to stream music from a web site, and some sites featuring political music have favored this approach. But streaming normally does not allow a person to keep a copy of the song that is streamed, and the quality of the music is not as good as a file that has been encoded in, say, MP3PRO (which is a modern form of MP3 encoding that offers higher audio quality with much lower file sizes). It is certain that the technologies related to file sharing will continue to evolve in terms of both capability and user-friendliness. It is moreover interesting to note that the creators of political music are looking at this evolving technology with a strategic eye.

Yet the growth of file sharing does not mean that political music cannot be distributed on CDs or other physical media. Indeed, it is through the Internet underground that many politically motivated creators of music reap large fortunes through the sale of such music. Also, web sites themselves offer opportunities to promote political music, either through streaming technology, direct downloads, or the sales of CDs. One no longer needs to have access to a physical store in order to sell political music.

To illustrate how powerful the distribution of political music through the underground can be, it is useful to note a particularly disturbing situation in which the Internet underground has been used to create a huge market for various fascist and neo-fascist groups. This genre is generally known as "hate music," and some might argue that it can trace its origins to early examples of such music that were written by people such as the country singer and songwriter David Allan Coe (see "Songwriter's Racist Songs from 1980's Haunt Him," by Neil Strauss, *The New York Times*, Monday, 4 September 2000, p. 1E). These days such music comes in a variety of musical flavors, examples of which tend to arise from four dominant labels or categories that suggest both subtle and more significant differences. These four identifying labels are "White Power Rock," "National Socialist Black Metal," "Racist Country," and "Fascist Experimental," the latter of which one might think of as a fascist version of the "alternative" music category. Very few major organizations track the creators and distributors of such music. But one important group that does follow the worrisome activities of the hate music genre is "The Southern Poverty Law Center" which is based in Montgomery, Alabama. This group's primary publication is the *Intelligence Report*, one of the few publications where academics and others can obtain information on a wide range of extremist groups that are primarily centered in the United States and Europe.

Among the underground outlets that distribute hate music, one of the most important is the Resistance record label. Its web site is www.resistance.com. The web site enables the company to sell over 300 CD titles, and it also is the contact point for Resistance Radio, an Internet radio that streams hate music 24 hours daily. There is also the magazine, *Resistance*, which can be located and purchased on the web site. William Pierce, the former owner and guiding light of the Resistance label, died in 2002. He was also the author of *The Turner Diaries*, the novel about a racist revolution that was apparently a major inspiration to Timothy McVeigh with respect to his terrorist attack on the Oklahoma City Federal Building in 1995.

Another popular venue for underground hate music is Panzerfaust Records. Their web site is www.panzerfaust.com. This Minnesota-based music label offers over 250 CD titles. Its name is based on a Nazi-era anti-tank weapon. On the home page of its web site this company declares, "The experienced staff at Panzerfaust Records is committed to doing its best in providing the audio ordinance that's needed by our comrades on the front lines of today's racial Struggle" (www.panzerfaust.com, accessed July 2002). This company offers white-power CDs, t-shirts, patches, books, flags, and much more.

Although Resistance and Panzerfaust are perhaps the largest distributors of hate music, smaller labels also exist. One such label is the New Jersey-based Micetrap Distribution, whose web site is www.micetrap.net (formerly www.whitepride.com). This web site is particularly notable for its publication of reviews of hate music releases. Micetrap acts mostly as a secondary distributor of hate music created by other labels.

In general, it is impossible to overstate the strength of the blunt invective coming from these hate music outlets. Nor is there any shortage of bands to create such music. Each country has its own contributors to this genre. For example, in the United States alone, there are over 80 active groups producing hate music in the "White Power Rock" category of the hate music genre. Such groups include Angry Aryans, Angry White Youth, Bludgeon, C.I.S. (Christian Identity Skins), Das Reich, Day of the Sword, Definite Hate, Elite Terror, Fürher, Hate Crimes, Hated and Proud Infantry, Kick to Kill, Kill or Be Killed, Patriotic Front, People Haters, Vanguard, White Hope, White Terror, and many others. In the Racist Country category there are groups such as Big Reb, Otis and the 3 Bigots, Roughneck Rebel, and others. In the National Socialist Black Metal genre there are Aryan Tormentor, Infernal Hatred, Open Grave, Order from Chaos, and many others. From the Fascist Experimental category there are Blood Axis, Control Resistance, Robert X. Patriot and the White Devil Conspiracy, and others. These are only a small selection of such groups, many more of which can be found in the Fall 2001 edition of *Intelligence*

Report (Issue 103, p. 31). Many other similar groups exist in other countries as well, and one should not minimize the strength, depth, or breadth of this movement to create hate music.

Outside of the web sites for these outlets for hate music, the other primary way listeners of this type of music obtain copies of these songs is through file-sharing services on the Internet. The way they operate is usually to set-up chat rooms using some file-sharing program. People who are searching for such music are drawn to the very obvious names of these chat rooms. Once inside a chat room, users can browse the musical selections on the hard drives of others who are also in the chat room. After finding some desired selections, a user can then download the selections directly from the hard drives of the original user. As long as one has an Internet connection, the download is free. Such music can then be burned to a CD or loaded onto an MP3 player just as any other type of music for convenient listening.

People who listen to such music often begin to organize themselves. This sometimes results in conventions that draw participants from all over the world. A good example of one such convention is the Hammerfest 2000 gathering that occurred just outside of Atlanta, Georgia in October of 2000 (*Intelligence Report*, Issue 103, Fall 2001, p. 24). The local and national news outlets generally ignored the event, presumably so as to avoid giving the gathering any additional publicity. But such strategies may not work in a world in which people are connected more individually through the Internet. One need only remember that the terrorist attacks in the United States that destroyed the World Trade Center and much of the Pentagon were orchestrated by a group working in secret while staying in contact via the Internet. News coverage of Al Qaeda and other organizations would not give such groups any more publicity than they eventually obtain through their own violent activities, and it is likely that news coverage of such organizations that pre-dates terrorist incidents would likely assist law enforcement officials in obtaining leads that would help prevent future attacks. Thus, these groups often do not mind the lack of news coverage. It keeps many of their activities "under the radar," which obviously is the primary problem of such groups with respect to the remainder of society.

The Future of Political Music

At this point it is worth returning to Plato's warning that "the modes of music are never disturbed without unsettling the most fundamental political and social conventions" (Republic, Book IV: 424). Music is an especially powerful medium through which political messages can be conveyed. One day during a semester when I was teaching the class "Politics and Music" at Emory University, I presented some of the hate music composed and performed by David Allan Coe. Normally I like to let students listen to about 20 minutes of this music, which when interspersed with some comments along the way, requires a total presentation of about 30 minutes. At first many of the students chuckle when they begin to hear this music, thinking that this must be a joke of some sort. But after about 10 minutes, the students become deadly quiet, realizing that the songs are serious. During the final 10 minutes, many students become quite uncomfortable, and one can see some of them shifting nervously in their seats, worried about what more might possibly come from the classroom speakers. In this particular instance, one of the students was sufficiently disturbed by the presentation that the student discussed the matter with one of my colleagues in my department, someone with whom I talked later about the issue of presenting Coe's music in class. There was never a question as to whether or not such music should be presented in class. Such highly potent political music is certainly a valid subject for a class that specifically focuses on the political content of music. But my colleague made an observation during that discussion that I felt was particularly important. My own paraphrasing of my colleague's comments is that music is not like other forms of information transfer. It penetrates deep into the mind. It can affect one on a level that a newspaper article or even a television news presentation cannot normally match. At the end of the discussion, both my colleague and I agreed that the only way to address this is to ensure that an adequate level of class discussion is made available at some point to allow students sufficient opportunity to sort through their feelings that are the result of being exposed to such music.

But to myself, the conversation with my colleague accented another point that I find very relevant to the subject of political music broadly defined (that is, not just music in the hate genre). The political content of music is much more profoundly relevant to our society today than perhaps at any other time in the history of our species precisely because of the special potency of this form of communication.

Consider, for example, a restrictive definition of political music. The basic requirement of political music is that it must have a political or social meaning that minimally is conveyed through some combination of rhythm and/or tone. Poetry, of course, is the most elemental of such musical forms since it has both meter and rhyme, and it is worth emphasizing in this regard that rap music is spoken poetry with a musical background. Indeed, hip-hop is essentially responsible for having initiated a renaissance in public interest in poetry, or at least hip-hop's variety of it. Rap has become one of society's most important mediums of political expression across a large segment of contemporary youth precisely because of the potency of the musical medium.

Even in societies in which complex musical forms are shunned, the most powerful political messages are often conveyed through poetry. Consider, for example, some selected lines of poetry written by Dr. Abd-ar-Rahman al-Ashmawi and Sheik Osama bin Laden, "Why in our area do we see Nothing but parapets and pits? Is it because America has come Manipulating funds and media? You, father, do not crave An easy living from mankind. ... I swear by God the great That I shall fight the infidel" ("Verses From bin Laden's War: Wielding the Pen as a Sword of the Jihad," by David Rohde, *The New York Times*, Sunday, 7 April 2002, p. 16A[N]). Can anyone doubt that these and similar words delivered with Arabic rhythm hold a potent ability to bond together in common purpose many of the members of Al Qaeda? If it matters in situations such as these, can we afford to ignore the more general developments of political music if our goal is to understand the complexities of contemporary society?

In the most comprehensive of terms, political music sometimes has the potential to affect us more deeply than political content conveyed through other means. There is something deeply psychological about the musical method of delivery with regard to political thought. Strong political messages seem to be amplified in their effect on others when the messages are imbedded in some fashion with well-crafted music. This is as true of Beethoven's representative and associative masterpieces as it is of hip-hop's explicit tirades. It is worth studying political music precisely because its potential potency is so great. In those cases in which it matters a great deal, we want to be listening.

It is true that political music is not played on radio or television with a frequency that would make it competitive in a ratings war with love songs. But that does not make political music irrelevant to our lives. Indeed, the opposite is true. Political music is important to us precisely because of how it conveys its information, both deeply on a psychological level as well as less visibly from the perspective of a mass audience. This points to some of the many reasons for us to want to listen to political music even if it is not thrust in our ears each time we awaken our car radio. Indeed, in the extreme case with regard to the music of hate groups, it is precisely what we are not listening to that may come back to haunt us in the form of terrorism. As a society, can we afford deaf ears?

This volume has described a significant part of the large range of political music, from various approaches to revolutionary politics to conservative exhortations of patriotic fervor, and much in between. Political music's great variety accents the importance of this type of music to us. In truth, no one really knows how our world will continue to develop. But one thing of which we can be certain is that there will be many unexpected turns in the evolutionary path of our human societies. As we collectively mature across the decades and centuries, we will seek guidance as we struggle both to understand and to change our fates. Much of that guidance will come to us in the form of politically inspired music. Indeed, our deepest understandings of our lives may only come after we contemplate our existence in the presence of rhythm and tone.

We need to listen to this music—indeed to study it—not just because of its value as entertainment. Its composition derives from the deepest intuitive levels of human thought. When our world arrives at crucial moments in its development, when our societies seem on the verge of great change, when our lives become confused and we appear to loose our collective moorings, it is then that we need to listen to such music most closely. In the most positive of situations, here we will locate the wisdom of some of our most profound future prophets as we find guidance in our moments of greatest need. Here also will we find the inspiration to face our future bravely, grounding ourselves with needed wisdom when the times truly are changing. I can see the arrival of no intermediating factors that might possibly diminish the urgent relevancy of political music as an essential element in our collective human destiny, however mundane or sublime that may be.

References

Abraham, Gerald E. 1974. *Borodin: The Composer and His Music*. New York: AMS Press.

Abraham, Gerald E. 1975. *Rimsky-Korsakov: A Short Biography*. New York: AMS Press.

Abraham, Gerald E. 1982. *On Russian Music: Critical and Historical Studies of Glinka's Operas*. New York: Irvington Publishers.

Adorno, Theodore. 1981. *In Search of Wagner*. Translated by Rodney Livingston. New York: Schocken Books.

Arendt, Hannah. 1958. *The Human Condition*. Chicago: The University of Chicago Press.

Arnold, Ben. 1993. *Music and War: A Research and Information Guide*. New York: Garland Publishing, Inc.

Baher, Hans. 1963. "Lieder machen Geschichte." In Joseph Wulf, ed., *Musik im Dritten Reich: Eine Dokumentation*. Götersloh: Sigbert Mohn, pp. 235- 262.

Ballantine, Christopher. 1991(March). "Music and Emancipation: The Social Role of Black Jazz and Vaudeville in South Africa between the 1920s and the Early 1940s." *Journal of Southern African Studies* 17(1): 129-52.

Becker, Howard S. 1974. "Art as Collective Action." *American Sociological Review*, 39.

Berelson, Bernard R., Paul F. Lazarsfeld, and William N. McPhee. 1954. *Voting: A Study of Opinion Formation in a Presidential Campaign*. Chicago: University of Chicago Press.

Berger, William. 1998. *Wagner Without Fear*. New York: Vintage Books.

Berger, William. 2000. *Verdi with a Vengeance*. New York: Vintage Books.

Beuick, Marshall D. 1927 (January). "The Limited Social Effect of Radio Broadcastin." *American Journal of Sociology* 32(4): 615-22.

Blau. Judith R. 1988 (June). "Music as Social Circumstance." *Social Forces* 66(4): 883-902.

Bokina, John. 1997. *Opera and Politics*. New Haven, Connecticut: Yale University Press.

Brown, Courtney. 1982 (June). "The Nazi Vote: A National Ecological Study," *American Political Science Review*, 76(2): 285-302.

Brown, Courtney. 1987(February). "Mobilization and Party Competition within a Volatile Electorate," *American Sociological Review*, 52(1): 59-72.

Brown, David. 2002. *Musorgsky: His Life and Works*. Oxford: Oxford University Press.

Budden, Julian. 1992. *The Operas of Verdi: From Oberto to Rigoletto*. Oxford: Clarendon Press.

Campbell, Angus, Philip E. Converse, Warren Miller, and Donald E. Stokes. 1960. *The American Voter*. New York: Wiley.

Cerulo, Karen A. 1984 (June). "Social Disruption and Its Effects on Music: An Empirical Analysis." *Social Forces* 62(4): 885-904.

Cerulo, Karen A. 1989 (September). "Sociopolitical Control and the Structure of National Symbols: An Empirical Analysis of National Athems." *Social Forces* 68(1): 76-99.

Cooper, Martin. 1985. *Beethoven: The Last Decade 1817-1827.* Oxford: Oxford University Press.

Dennis, David B. 1996. *Beethoven in German Politics, 1870-1989.* New Haven, Conn.: Yale University Press.

Donington, Robert. 1969. *Wagner's 'Ring' and Its Symbols: The Music and the Myth.* New York: St. Martin's Press.

Donington, Robert. 1990. *Opera and Its Symbols: The Unity of Words, Music, and Staging.* New Haven, Connecticut: Yale University Press.

Downs, Anthony. 1957. *An Economic Theory of Democracy.* New York: Harper & Row.

Ford, Charles. 1991. *Cosi? Sexual Politics in Mozart's Operas.* New York: University of Manchester Press.

Fowke, Edith, and Joe Glazer. 1973. *Songs of Work and Protest.* New York: Dover.

Fowke, Edith, and Joe Glazer. 1960. *Songs of Work and Freedom.* Chicago: Roosevelt University Press.

Fox, William S. and James D. Williams. 1974(Autumn). "Political Orientation and Music Preferences Among College Students." *Public Opinion Quarterly* 38(3): 352-71.

Gutman, Robert. 1968. *Richard Wagner: The Man, His Mind, and His Music.* New York: Harcourt, Brace & World, Inc.

Heffer, Simon. 2001. Vaughan Williams. Boston: Northeastern University Press.

Hetherington, Marc J. 2001(September). "Resurgent Mass Partisanship: The Role of Elite Polarization." *American Political Science Review* 95(3): 619-31.

Huckfeldt, R. Robert and John Sprague. 1988. "Choice, Social Structure, and Political Information: The Informational Coercion of Minorities." *American Journal of Political Science* 32:467-82.

Kaiser, Charles. 1988. *1968 in America*. New York: Grove Press.

Katz, Jacob. 1986. *The Darker Side of Genius: Richard Wagner's Anti-Semitism*. Biddeford, Maine: University of New England Press.

Kaiser, Charles. 1988. *1968 In America: Music, Politics, Chaos, Counterculture, and the Shaping of a Generation*. New York: Grove Press.

Knight, Frida. 1973. *Beethoven and the Age of Revolution*. New York: International Publishers.

Lee, M. Owen. 1990. *Wagner's Ring: Turning the Sky Around*. New York: Summit Books.

Leonard, Richard Anthony. 1957. *A History of Russian Music*. New York: MacMillan.

Leppert, Richard, and Susan McClary (Eds.) 1987. *Music and Society: The Politics of Composition, Performance, and Reception*. Cambridge: Cambridge University Press.

Lukes, Timothy J. 2001 (September). "Lionizing Machiavelli." *American Political Science Review* 95(3): 561-75.

Magee, Bryan. 2000. *The Tristan Chord: Wagner and Philosophy*. New York: Metropolitan Books.

Mann, Thomas. 1985. *Pro and Contra Wagner*. Translated by Allan Blunden. London: Faber and Faber.

Martin, Peter J. 1995. *Sounds and Society: Themes in the Sociology of Music*. New York: Manchester University Press. (Distributed by St. Martin's Press.)

Mattern, Mark. 1998. *Acting In Concert: Music, Community, and Political Action*. New Brunswick, New Jersey: Rutgers University Press.

McNeil, Donald G. Jr. 2002. "Killer Songs: Simon Bikindi Stands Accused of Writing Folk Music that Fed the Rwandan Genocide," *The New York Times Magazine,* 17 March 2002, pp. 58-9

Mead, G. H. 1934. *Mind, Self, and Society*. Chicago: University of Chicago Press.

Neal, Mark Anthony, and Murray Forman, Eds. 2004. *That's the Joint!: The Hip-Hop Studies Reader*. New York: Routledge.

Newman, Ernest. 1930. *Stories of the Great Operas and Their Composers*. Garden City, New York: Garden City Publishing Co., Inc.

Peterson, Richard A., and Paul DiMaggio. 1975 (March). "From Region to Class, the Changing Locus of Country Music: A Test of the Massification Hypothesis." *Social Forces* 53(3): 497-506.

Plato. *The Republic*. In *Plato: The Collected Dialogues*. 1961. Edited by Edith Hamilton and Huntington Cairns. Princeton, New Jersey: Princeton University Press.

Pollack, Howard. 2000. *Aaron Copland: The Life and Work of an Uncommon Man*. Champaign: University of Illinois Press.

Rackwitz, Werner. 1971. "Die Bedeutung Beethovens für die sozialistische National-kulture der Deutschen Demokratischen Republik." In Heinz Alfred Brodkhaus and Konrad Neimann (Eds.), *Berickt über den Internationalen Beethoven-Kongress 10-12 Dezember 1970 in Berlin*. Berlin: Verlag Neue Musik.

Renshaw, Patrick. 1999. *The Wobblies: The Story of IWW and Syndicalism in the United States*. Chicago, Illinois: Ivan R. Dee, Inc.

Rosselli, John. 2000. *The Life of Verdi*. Cambridge: Cambridge University Press.

Rux, Carl Hancock. 2003. "Eminem: The New White Negro." In *Everything but the Burden*," Greg Tate (Ed.). New York: Broadway Books, pp. 15-38.

Schröder, Heribert. 1986. "Beethoven im Dritten Reich: Eine Materialsammlung." In Helmut Loos, ed., *Beethoven und die Nachwelt: Materialien zur Wirkungsgeschichte Beethovens*. Bonn: Beethovenhhaus, pp. 198-235.

Scott, John T. 1997(August). "Rousseau and the Melodious Language of Freedom." *The Journal of Politics* 59(3): 803-29.

Shaw, George Bernard. 1966(1898). *The Perfect Wagnerite*. New York: Dover.

Smith, Gibbs M. 1984. *Joe Hill*. Layton, Utah: Gibbs Smith Publisher.

Solomon, Maynard. 1977. *Beethoven*. New York: Shirmer.

Solomon, Maynard. 1968. "Beethoven and Napoleon." *Music Review* 29: 96-105.

Spotts, Frederic. 1994. *Bayreuth: A History of the Wagner Festival.* New Haven, Connecticut: Yale University Press.

Swafford, Jan. 1998. *Charles Ives: A Life With Music.* New York: W.W. Norton & Company.

Tate, Greg. 2003. *Everything but the Burden.* New York: Broadway Books.

Tate, Greg. 2003. "Hip-Hop." In the *Encyclopedia Britannica 2003 Deluxe Edition.*

Unger, Irwin, and Debi Under (Eds.) 1998. *The Times Were a Changin': The Sixties Reader.* New York: Three Rivers Press.

Valentin, Erich. 1938(July). "Beethovenfest der Hitlerjugend: Bad Wildbad (Schwarzwald) 20. Bis 22. Mai 1938)," *Zeitschrift für Musik 7*, p. 735.

Wagner, Cosima. 1980. *The Diaries of Cosima Wagner.* Edited by Martin Gregor-Dellin and Dietrich Mack, translated by Geoffrey Skelton. New York: Harcourt Brace Jovanovich.

Wagner, Richard. (n.d.) *Richard Wagner's Letters to August Roeckel.* Translated by Eleanor C. Sellar. Bristol, Great Britain: J.W. Arrowsmith.

Wagner, Richard. 1996(1895). *Art and Politics.* Translated by William Ashton Ellis. Lincoln, Nebraska: University of Nebraska Press.

Wattenberg, Martin P. 1984. *The Decline of American Political Parties, 1952-1980.* Cambridge, Massachusetts: Harvard

University Press.

West, Cornell. 1999[1982]. "On Afro-American Music: From Bebop to Rap." In *The Cornell West Reader*, New York: Basic *Civitas* Books, chapter 40.

West, Cornell. 2001[1991]. "Nihilism in Black America." In *Race Matters* by Cornell West. New York: Vintage Books.

Westbrook, Alonzo. 2002. *Hip Hoptionary: the Dictionary of Hip Hop Terminology*. New York: Harlem Moon and Broadway Books.

White, Timothy. 2000(1983). *Catch a Fire: The Life of Bob Marley*. New York: Henry Holt and Co.

Williams, Ursula Vaughan. 1992. *R.V.W.: A Biography of Ralph Vaughan Williams*. Oxford: Clarendon Press.

INDEX

Listing Note: When searching for a name, check both the first and last names. First names especially are useful when referencing a performer, composer, or noted personality, since first names are integral parts of formal identifiers regardless of whether or not the full names have one part (as in Madonna and Bono) or two parts (as in Africa Bamtaattaa and Dr. Dre).

Breinigsville, PA USA
26 November 2009
228156BV00002B/127/A